MW00333494

TIBETAN THANGKA PAINTING

Methods and Materials

Tibetan Thangka Painting

METHODS & MATERIALS

David P Jackson
Janice A Jackson

Illustrated by Robert Beer

Snow Lion Publications
Ithaca, New York USA

Snow Lion Publications
P.O. Box 6483
Ithaca, New York 14851
U.S.A.

© 1984 by David P. and Janice A. Jackson
Second revised edition 1988

All rights reserved. No part of this book may be reproduced
by any means, without the prior written permission from the publisher.

ISBN 1 55939 037 9

Library of Congress Cataloging-in-Publication Data

Jackson, David Paul.
   Tibetan Thangka painting: methods & materials / David P. Jackson,
Janice A. Jackson,—2nd ed.
   p. cm.
Bibliography: p.
Includes Index.
ISBN 0-937938-67-X
   1. Tankas (Tibetan scrolls)—Technique.   2. Painting, Tibetan.
3. Painting, Buddhist—China—Tibet.   I. Jackson, Janice A.
II. Title
ND1432,C584J3   1988   88-6688
75,4—dc19   CIP

Published by arrangement with Serindia Publications, London
Printed in the U.K.

CONTENTS

To the Thangka Painters of Tibet

Preface

Tibetan thangka painting is one of the great arts of Asia. It is rich not only in its iconography, religious content and stylistic development, but also in terms of the materials and skills that the painters and their patrons lavished upon it. Anyone examining even a small number of these fine old scroll paintings *(thang ka)* cannot help being impressed by the exquisite materials and consummate skill that went into their creation. Just what these materials were and how they were applied were questions that attracted our interest years ago, when as college students we first came into contact with Tibetan art. But when we tried to learn more we could not get very far because the subject had not then been studied in much detail by Westerners.[1] Therefore we decided to go closer to the source and to learn what we could from the living painters of Tibet.

In the years that followed we made five journeys to Asia, sometimes staying for a year or more. During those trips we met and learned from many thangka painters. These artists represented most of the main regions of Tibet, as well as many of the border areas in the Himalayas. While preparing this study we received the kind assistance of some twenty artists, most of whom are still living in various parts of India, Nepal and America. The names of those whose knowledge helped shape this book are presented below in alphabetical order, in grateful acknowledgement of their help.

Dorje from Amdo Rekong
Dorje Drakpa and his monk brother from
    Kham Lingtshang
Dorje Gyaltsen from Western Tsang
Gömpo from Kyirong
Jampa from Lhasa
Jamyang from Amdo
Kunzang Tobgye from Bhutan
Legdrup Gyatsho from Phenyul Nalendra
Loden from the borderlands of Amdo
Losang Khedrup from Mongolia
Pema Könchok from Kham Lingtshang
Saga from Kham Lingtshang
Thargye from Lhatse in Tsang
Tshedor from Kham Lingtshang
Tshoknyi Gyatsho from Kham Gakhok
Wangchuk from Ladakh
Wangdrak from Shekar
Wangdu from Ladakh
Wangyal from Dolpo

The particular circumstances of our travels enabled us to study for longer periods with three of these painters, who thus became our main teachers and informants. One of these was Thargye, whom we first met in Nepal in 1972. As the first thangka painter we had the privilege of meeting, Thargye-la did much to encourage us at that crucial first stage by the lively interest he took in answering our questions and by his animated sense of humor. Poor health and pressing personal affairs kept him away from Kathmandu during our last two visits to Nepal when we were finalizing many details of this study. Thus, though he contributed so much, his name does not appear below as often as it should.

Our second main teacher was Legdrup Gyatsho, a monk and artist from Phenyul Nalendra near Lhasa. We met him too for the first time in 1972, when he was in India, and later we studied with him in Nepal for some months in 1973. Afterwards in 1976 we had the good fortune to study with him again for several months. He was genuinely kind and patient — not only with us and our interminable questions, but also with the rambunctious young monks who ran to and fro along the high scaffoldings while we all worked on the Lumbini murals.

We are also especially grateful for the help and friendship of our third main teacher, Wangdrak from Shekar Dzong in Western Tsang, whom we were fortunate enough to meet in India in 1975. In many ways Wangdrak is for us the quintessential Tibetan painter: quiet, unassuming and modest, but a living treasure-trove of knowledge concerning the techniques, materials and lore of every branch of Tibetan painting.

During the preparation of this book we also had the good fortune to study with the venerable lama Dezhung Trulku Rimpoche. Although he is not a painter, he opened our eyes to many of the figures and symbols appearing in thangkas, and to the religious culture that is the basis of Tibetan art. Here we would like to express in a small way our great gratitude to him.

Several friends from the West also assisted us when we were writing this book, and we take this occasion to acknowledge their help. It is no exaggeration to say that Tibetan studies are now in the midst of a far-reaching revolution, the result of the vast work of reprinting Tibetan texts that has been under way in India for the last decade and a half. Although we are now seeing just the initial results, the continuing appearance of these texts will eventually have an impact on Western scholarship of the same order as the discovery of the Tun Huang manuscripts or the exodus of the Tibetan scholars in 1959. Needless to say the preservation of these books also renders an incalculable service to the Tibetans themselves. No one has played a greater role in making this project possible, and in coordinating it than Mr E. Gene Smith. We are indebted to him not only for his selfless labors in that great work, but also for his help in locating the most important literary sources on our topic, and for many other acts of kindness and hospitality.

Two others who took an interest in this study during its preparation were Ms Ann Shaftel and Ms Kathleen Peterson. Individually both of them read and offered valuable comments on an early draft of Chapter 2 and parts of Chapters 3 and 4. We are also grateful to Ms Shaftel for having communicated to us some of her own findings on the materials of thangka painting.

We would here like to acknowledge our gratitude to the following individuals and institutions who helped us obtain illustrations and for permission to reproduce them (numerals refer to page numbers): Mr Brian Beresford: 5, 8, 102; Dr Lokesh Chandra: 75, 78, 79, 80, 81, 82, 112, 113, 114, 115 (from 'Jam-dpal-rdo-rje *Gso byed bdud rtsi'i 'khrul med ngos 'dzin. Sata-piṭaka Series,* Vol.82); Mr Hugh Downs: 44, 68, 74, 94, 104, 107, Han-Shan Tang Ltd. 35, Dr C. Jest: 9; Professor Fosco Maraini: 90, Collection of the Newark Museum: 10, 11, 14, Mr Hugh Richardson: 4; Professor David Snellgrove: 12, Ms Zara Fleming and the Victoria and Albert Museum: 24, 29, 30, 31, 32, 33, 34, 36, 37, 76, 77, 110, 128, 132, 133, 134. Photographs not listed above are by David Jackson.

We are also happy to present in this book numerous line drawings by Mr Robert Beer, formerly a student of Lhasa Jhampa and Au Leshey, and now one of the finest Western exponents of Tibetan art. Unless otherwise stated the line drawings are all by him. We are also indebted to Mr Beer for information about pigment sources in Europe. Finally we must express our appreciation to Mr Anthony Aris for the enthusiastic interest he has taken in this study from the time of our first meeting and for his encouragement during the long years it took to complete.

What in particular have we tried to accomplish in this book? Throughout its preparation we have concentrated on recording the *traditional* colours and techniques. Many of the materials have radically changed since the artists came to India and Nepal, and therefore we have always tried to ascertain what they *traditionally* used in the old setting of Tibet and the Himalayas. With the same goal in mind, we also gathered together and examined the few presently known written sources that deal with the materials and techniques of Tibetan painting. These texts by and large confirm the accounts of the living painters, and a few brief extracts from them have also been translated and presented below.

No doubt some readers will go through this book with the idea of one day trying their hands at thangka painting. We trust that they will be encouraged by what they read. The methods involved in painting a thangka are not hopelessly difficult or complex; the main thing is always to follow an orderly step-by-step approach, as Tibetan painters themselves do. With the help of this book you can learn many of the basics without a teacher. Those who study alone should definitely begin by copying a simple example, preferably a real thangka. Do not make the mistake of choosing a design with over twenty figures for your first attempt, as we did. If you can trace the composition of a thangka onto a thin sheet of paper and then onto your canvas, the difficulties of making an original composition can be avoided. Tibetan block-prints are also good sources for compositions, although they lack the colouring that is crucial for guiding the beginner. Even if you work alone you can still enjoy the experience of grinding and mixing your own paints (on obtaining the raw pigments see Appendix B: *Resources*). Meanwhile you should continually train your visual perception by viewing real thangkas whenever possible, and by examining reproductions and illustrated books. With practice, anyone with some previous experience in painting should be able to achieve good results by following the steps outlined below.

Nevertheless, working by yourself is no real substitute for studying with a living painting teacher. For those who are fortunate enough to find a teacher, the present book may be useful as an introduction to the general materials and techniques used in one of the main painting traditions, the Menri of Central Tibet. Even if your teacher belongs to a different tradition, most of the names of the materials and tools will be similar. Our listing of Tibetan terms, both in the text and afterward in a separate glossary, may solve some of the problems of terminology for the Western student. When learning the particular details of technique, however, do not rely on this book; instead, carefully follow your own teacher, especially in the beginning. As Bo-dong Paṇ-chen recommended five centuries ago at the conclusion of his own brief description of painting methods: "Learn in more detail from one who is expert in the practice [of painting]."[2]

In this book we have concentrated mainly on the technique of thangkas, and have not dealt with murals and other branches of painting. Even within the topic of thangka painting we have limited our account for the most part to just one major tradition, that of Wangdrak and Legdrup Gyatsho: that is the Menri *(sman ris)*, a painting style that originated in the 15th century and that in recent centuries became the artistic *koiné* of Central Tibet. Here and there we have also pointed out a few differences between the tradition of our main informants and the practice of others. But anyone who studies with painters from other regions and traditions will quickly discover many more divergences in technique. These should be carefully noted. Detailed studies of such traditions as the Karma Gardri *(karma sgar bris)*, the New Menri *(sman ris gsar ma)* of Kham, and the regional styles of Amdo and Shigatse would make welcome additions to current knowledge of Tibetan painting.

When we began this study eleven years ago we thought that we were recording and preserving a dying tradition. Now, however, it seems clear that thangka painting on the whole is in no danger of becoming extinct. Although traditional art is today moribund in Tibet proper, it is flourishing in the Tibetan settlements of South Asia on a scale that nobody could have predicted two decades ago. Some of the younger painters are even showing promise of one day reaching the high levels attained by the early masters.

Perhaps the only aspect of Tibetan painting that has suffered markedly in the new environment is the use of traditional materials. Many of the painters have tried to continue to use the old pigments and dyes, but unfortunately a few crucial pigments such as azurite and malachite have become rarer than gold in recent years. (India has deposits of these minerals, but there is as yet no means of distributing them to the artists). A small number of painting teachers have even succumbed to the temptation of employing only the cheap and readily available commercial colours. As a result they have unintentionally created in their students a group of Tibetan painters who have never used the traditional colours. If we could influence any aspect of the living tradition we would encourage such young painters not to give up the traditional pigments without trying them. Ten or twenty years from now they may reach the same conclusion themselves when they see how their poster colours have faded. Meanwhile we have no doubt that the majority of Tibetan artists will continue to paint with as many of the traditional colours as they can, for these are colours with not only a glorious past but also a bright future.

Mussoorie,   David and Janice Jackson
April 1982

Notes

1. Although no detailed study of Tibetan painting methods and materials was undertaken by Western scholars in the past, interest in certain technical aspects of Tibetan art goes back to the great pioneer of Tibetan studies, Csoma de Körös. As early as 1825 he wrote that he had extracted from the *Tanjur* as a representative sample a treatise on technology, one that "enumerates what must be the proportion in feet, inches, lines of a statue representing Buddha or Shakya." See Theodore Duka, *Life and Works of Alexander Csoma de Körös* (New Delhi, 1972), p.50. Evidence of similar interest is also found in M. H. Godwin-Austen's article, "On the System Employed in Outlining the Figures of Deities and other Religious Drawings as Practiced in Ladak, Zaskar, etc.," *Journal of the Asiatic Society of Bengal*, vol.33 (1864), pp.151-154. On some of the subsequent research on Tibetan iconometry in particular see the sources cited by A. K. Gerasimova in her "Compositional Structure in Tibetan Iconography," *The Tibet Journal*, vol.3 (1978), p.40 and also below, Appendix A, note 1.

   Studies on the practice of Tibetan painting, however, did not get a good start until Rahula Sankrityayana wrote his "Technique in Tibetan Painting," *Asia*, vol.37 (1937), pp.711-715. Before that, G. N. Roerich had given a few details in his *Tibetan Paintings* (Paris, Librarie Orientaliste-Paul Geuthner, 1925), p.18f. And after Sankrityayana a few other scholars briefly touched on the topic, among whom we could mention Marco Pallis, *Peaks and Lamas* (New York, Alfred A. Knopf, 1940), pp.332-338; G. Tucci, *Tibetan Painted Scrolls* (Rome, 1949), vol.1, p.268, and D. L. Snellgrove, *Four Lamas of Dolpo* (Oxford, 1967/8), vol.1, p.58. Much of the information in the main early sources was summed up by John C. Huntington in his "The Technique of Tibetan Paintings," *Studies in Conservation*, vol.15 (1970), pp.122-133.

   New and more detailed technical information on pigments became available only with the appearance of V. R. Mehra's "Notes on the Technique and Conservation of Some Thang-ka Paintings," *Studies in Conservation*, vol.15 (1970), pp.190-214. Nearly identical information was also presented by O. P. Agrawal in "Conservation of Asian Cultural Objects: Asian Materials and Techniques; Tibetan Tankas," *Museum* (UNESCO), vol.27 (1975), pp.181-197.

   One source that regrettably was not available to us during the preparation of this book was the film by C. Jest: *Ma-gčig "la Mère", Peinture d'une thanka*, Centre National de la Recherche Scientifique, 1968.

2. Bo-dong Pan-chen Phyogs-las-rnam-rgyal, *Mkhas pa'jug pa'i [sgo] bzo rig sku gsung thugs kyi rten bzhengs tshul bshad pa, Collected Works* (New Delhi, 1969), vol.2, p.262.2: "*zhib par lag len mkhas la sbyang.*"

The Potala Palace in Lhasa during the New Year's festival with two great appliqué thangkas displayed.

One
The Artistic Wealth of Old Tibet

In the past Tibet was so inaccessible to Western travelers that its name still evokes images of supreme remoteness and impenetrability. One Western historian has even described the culture of Tibet as the living fossil of an otherwise extinct civilization, preserved mainly because of that great isolation. There is no denying that formidable barriers existed along much of the Tibetan borderland. And in some ways Tibet was indeed a great preserver of things. In its cool, dry climate manuscripts, works of art and monuments could remain for centuries without noticeable decay. The inhabitants of Tibet too, with their respect for sacred traditions and their desire to maintain them, succeeded in keeping alive religious and intellectual currents that had long ago vanished from their source of origin, India. Still, Tibet was never quite as isolated as it sometimes appeared to the Western world. Throughout its history and especially in early times Tibet maintained various contacts with neighboring countries. These contacts made possible not only the development of the traditional Buddhist culture of Tibet, but also the flourishing there of a rich tradition of arts and crafts.[1]

Even before the advent of Buddhism in Tibet, various craftsmen and artisans plied their trades there. Ancient records relate that since the time of their earliest contacts with the civilizations of China, India and Central Asia, the Tibetan people already had among them skilled artisans, especially metal workers talented in the making of weapons and the like. Moreover from an early period Tibetans were keen to receive the arts and artisans of other countries. From the 7th and 8th centuries onward, many foreign artists and craftsmen are known to have worked in Tibet, and the tradition of patronizing certain foreign artisans, such as Newar silversmiths, has continued down to the present day.

Since the formative period in its civilization Tibet has remained a fertile ground for the cultivation of many arts and crafts. In pre-1959 Tibet, as in Europe only a few centuries ago, most ordinary implements and objects had to be made by the hands and tools of skilled craftsmen. Fine workmanship was the goal, and quite often it was the result. A great many objects were also decorated and embellished, so that even commonplace utensils could be appreciated for their aesthetic qualities.

Nowhere in traditional Tibet were superior artisans and their beautiful craftsmanship held in such high regard as in the centers of religious culture, the monasteries. There the various arts reached their highest expression in the service of Buddhism. The Tibetan nobility also patronized the arts, whether directly through sponsoring their own projects, or indirectly through their support of the monasteries. Even in the lives of ordinary people the handiwork of artisans was

Spituk Monastery, Ladakh.

very important, and worthy examples of arts and crafts were found in both the town dweller's house and the nomadic herdsman's tent.

Take, for example, the tents of the nomads in Northeastern Tibet. Most of them were not, as we might first suppose, poor or sparsely furnished; on the contrary, they were actually portable and completely furnished houses. Inside could be found low tables, boxes, baskets, pots and other cooking utensils, braziers, bowls and covered tea cups, churns, mills, looms, leather storage bags and still more — all the products of one craftsman or another. The most important spot in the nomadic family's tent was the Buddhist shrine, a carefully tended wooden altar on which were arranged the family's sacred images, often contained within intricately crafted silver reliquaries *(ga'u)*. Over the altar hung sacred scroll paintings, and before the shrine silver offering bowls and flickering butter lamps were placed.

For almost everything made of wood or metal, the nomads depended on outside craftsmen, and because of the remoteness and dangers of nomadic life, they had to rely especially on those who made and repaired weapons. Without craftsmen not only would the nomad's tent have been almost empty, but his very survival would have been impossible.

Tradesmen, craftsmen and artists were likewise essential to the village farmers and townsfolk of Tibet. In the largest settlements the artisan could often remain at his place of work, and his customers would come to him. In the remote villages and nomadic regions the artisan often went to the dwellings or encampments of his patrons and customers. There he would stay for as long as his services were needed, and then move on. But in all settlements in Tibet, large and small, there was a continuous demand for the various specialized skills and crafts that supported the traditional way of life.

If we could visit a household in a town we would also notice the products of a great many arts and crafts. Merely to list them, however, would not in any way indicate the diversity of materials and complexity of methods used by the craftsman in even one. Let us take a closer look at one group of allied crafts, metalworking. Workers with these skills actually constituted a number of distinct professions, each with its own special techniques and materials, and as a group they were subdivided into a number of social classes. The higher echelons consisted of the craftsmen who worked the noble metals, primarily silver, and highest of all, gold. Lowest were the blacksmiths.

The smith's main material was iron, which he worked with tongs, bellows and hammer. He fashioned various things including swords, knives, scissors, needles, and farm implements. Some smiths also fashioned objects from iron and brass together, or from brass alone. The workers who made the metal equipment used in horse riding, for instance, often used a combination of metals. Whether the metal parts were functional or merely decorative, the Tibetan horseman's saddle, bridle, crupper, breastplate and stirrups were often examples of excellent iron and brass metalwork, the finest specimens of which were also sometimes gilded with gold.

Another type of metalworker belonged to the group that made molds and then cast objects with molten metals. Such craftsmen produced not only cast-metal ritual implements and religious statues, but also such everyday things as bells and buttons.

Yet another group of metalworkers fashioned objects from the softer metals — copper, silver and gold. They had their own special skills, such as the raising of bowls from flat sheets, cutting, welding, soldering, chasing, stamping and engraving. Much of the Tibetan silversmith's time was spent on objects for Tibetan Buddhist worship such as reliquaries and the water bowls and lamps used for making offerings before shrines. Silversmiths also made household objects for the well-to-do: teacup stands and covers, silver linings for wooden cups, silver spoons, and so forth. At the pinnacle of the metalworking profession were the goldsmiths, whose main occupation was fashioning gold ornaments for personal wear and setting them with turquoises and other precious stones.

Silver reliquary *(ga'u)*.

Such craftsmen often needed to know a large number of complex techniques for their own single vocation. The manufacture of some objects, furthermore, was complicated by the necessity for two or more craftsmen to work in cooperation. Metalworking, for instance, often combined with woodworking: smiths were often called upon to make handles, latches, hinges, decorative ornaments and locks for wooden objects such as boxes and doors. The making of riding equipment also required cooperation: in addition to metalworking, the finished piece required the technique of cloth-sewing and leather-working. Many craftsmen required several types of expertise, and at the same time depended upon other artisans for their tools. Furniture makers, for example, used hammers, chisels and saws made by the smith, and with them they built such things as tables, boxes and altars. Such wooden objects often required detailed carving, which in turn was not complete until painted. Likewise the turners, whose lathes and metal tools produced various types of wooden bowls, containers and churns, often returned their products to the metalworkers to be lined with silver or banded with brass. A thoughtful examination of even a single commonplace object such as a table or a butter-tea churn can thus reveal the complex interplay of the arts and crafts in old Tibet.

It is still possible to visit areas of traditional Tibetan culture in the Himalayas where many of these arts and crafts are still cultivated, and the complexity and richness of the artistic and technical traditions of Tibet proper can be partially reconstructed on the basis of the wonderfully crafted objects in museum collections and from the memories of older Tibetans. But in addition there exists another revealing window on Tibetan artistic and material culture, one which until now has hardly been used: the written records that survive within the literature of Tibet.

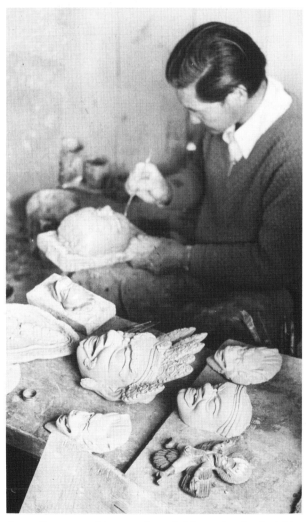

A craftsman making papier-mâché masks in Ladakh.

A number of Tibetan texts exist that deal directly with artistic theory and practice. Books that discuss the making of sacred images form the largest part of a branch of Tibetan literature called "technical treatises" *(bzo rig bstan bcos)*. The main works of this sort describe the dimensions and characteristics of sacred figures, as well as giving similar information on such other religious objects as stūpas, maṇḍalas, vajras and bells. A few of these texts also give accounts of the techniques and materials involved, for example, in the casting of metal images, the construction of clay and papier-mâché figures or the painting of thangkas and murals.

Besides such books that describe the major arts, there also exist a small number of texts specifically devoted to the methods and materials of the lesser arts and crafts. A splendid example is the *Bzo rig za ma tog* of 'Jam-mgon Mi-pham-rgya-mtsho (1846–1912).[2] Not only is this book a remarkable source for the study of many little-known crafts and techniques, but it is also a sort of compendium showing the astounding diversity of skills, methods and materials that were once cultivated by Tibetan craftsmen. Consider the following topics dealt with by Mi-pham-rgya-mtsho in 1906:

1. incense manufacture
2. ink preparation from nine different materials
3. penmanship
4. paper-making
5. stones for polishing paper, and the polishing support
6. drawing lines for guiding calligraphy
7. the penknife
8. the pen and its characteristics
9. preparation of powdered gold for lettering
10. preparation of powdered copper, brass and silver
11. imitation gold and silver inks
12. preparation of paints: grinding, mixing, etc.
13. preparation of a cloth painting support
14. imitation gold varnishes made with mica
15. varnishes used with paints
16. linseed oil and its uses
17. Chinese lacquer
18. shellac
19. dyeing silk, cotton and woollen cloth
20. felt dyeing
21. leather dyeing
22. paints for applying to iron and metals
23. various finishes
24. crystalline substances
25. fashioning objects from unmeltable precious substances
26. casting of metals
27. powdering of gold for "cold" gilding
28. "hot" gilding by the mercury-evaporation process
29. refining gold for various uses including gold leaf
30. borax soldering

31. alchemical formulas for transmuting substances into gold
32. other solders and related techniques
33. tattooing
34. ways of drawing on iron with gold and silver
35. "modeling paste" and its application in relief drawings
36. applying gold, silver or tin leaf
37. writing on stone
38. writing on bone
39. working ivory
40. working with stone
41. clay and earth technologies
42. mending broken crockery
43. woodworking, including carving and ornamentation
44. leather-working
45. cardboard, papier-mâché, and leather-like products derived from wood, cloth or paper
46. medicinal compounding
47. preparing different saline substances
48. mercury manufacture
49. flammable mixtures
50. cleaning agents for gilded and cast-metal images
51. storing meat without spoilage
52. drum making
53. units of measure for cloth
54. magical techniques and contrivances; foreign machines
55. preserving flowers and fruits

According to its author this text was "but a drop from the ocean of crafts."

Masks of the eight manifestations of Padmasambhava in a sacred dance.

People of Tarap (Dolpo) viewing thangkas during a religious gathering.

Paintings in the Religious Life of Tibet

Among all these arts and crafts painting occupied a very special position. Not only was it essential for designing, decorating and finishing many mundane objects, but it was also a highly developed and important means of religious expression. To understand the place of paintings in Tibetan culture it is thus necessary to look into the religious beliefs and practices that led to their creation.

Painting (along with sculpture) was crucial to the religious life of Tibet because it was a medium through which the highest ideals of Buddhism were evoked and brought alive. A sacred painting was for the Tibetan a "physical support" – in other words an embodiment – of enlightenment. Naturally, the faithful of Tibet delighted in creating such images, but sacred paintings were not always inspired by a joyful or pious urge to produce an object for worship. The commissioning of

thangkas was also very much tied up with sad and unavoidable events in the lives of ordinary people.

A Tibetan artist once explained to us why most of his patrons requested the painting of a thangka. The main reasons he mentioned were (1) sickness or troubles, (2) death in the family and (3) the need for an image in connection with a particular religious practice. Like any other virtuous deed the commissioning of religious art was believed to earn merit *(bsod nams)*, the only thing that in the Buddhist view could give rise to future benefits and happiness. This wholesome force could be directed to improve a troublesome situation or produce a desired good. Thus ordinary Tibetans were often advised by their religious preceptors to commission a painting for the "removal" of physical or mental "obstacles" *(bar chad sel ba)*, or to create the prerequisites for "a long and healthy life" *(zhabs brtan)*. Usually there was an important connection between the deity designated for portrayal and the desired result. Tārā, for instance, was effective in removing obstacles and granting protection, while Amitāyus bestowed long life. After the creation of the sacred image the patron was often expected to practice the recitations and prayers appropriate for that deity.

A second reason that impelled ordinary people to commission thangkas was the death of a relative or dear one. Thangkas painted for this purpose were called *skyes rtags* ("signs of [good] birth"?). They were commissioned in the name of the deceased, and were meant to create the conditions necessary for propelling the deceased to a happy rebirth. Such paintings had to be executed soon after the person's death, during the seven-week period when he or she was believed to have not yet entered into the next existence. Lamas determined the most appropriate deity for such thangkas, usually by consulting Buddhist astrological texts, but sometimes simply from their own insight into the life and character of the deceased.

Many paintings were thus inspired by the universal human desire to avoid suffering, to gain happiness and longevity, and to ensure a happy state of existence following death.

Religious teachers encouraged their lay followers in these activities because such undertakings were based upon a belief in the mechanism of moral cause and effect: good deeds lead to happy experiences. Nevertheless, from the teachers' point of view an act motivated by this belief alone was not complete. For the true Mahāyāna Buddhist the ultimate goal of every meritorious thought and action should be the attainment of Buddhahood, for the good of all living beings.

Thus, in addition to the desire for some immediate benefit, there should also be a "wish to attain enlightenment" *(byang chub kyi sems)*. This altruistic thought was believed to imbue the good act with the strongest power, so that its force would persist until the attainment of enlightenment and not become exhausted after conferring a merely temporary benefit.

At its conclusion, the commissioning of a work of sacred art also entailed the "dedication of merit" *(dge ba bsngo ba)*, which was closely linked to the desire for enlightenment. Merit dedication consisted of prayers by means of which a final seal was placed on the meritorious act, directing the merit thus accrued to its ultimate fruition in enlightenment. Together with the wish to attain enlightenment, the dedication of merit guaranteed that the deed would not be wasted in yielding some small benefit, but would bear the highest and lasting fruit. Thus, following the commissioning of paintings or statues as a part of the funeral observances *(dgongs rdzogs)* for a religious teacher or great person, a religious assembly would gather in a temple and formally dedicate the merit through the recitation of prayers.

The third main reason why people commissioned sacred paintings was to use them in connection with their own religious practice. Thangkas could be important aids for Buddhist practices and observances, and Tibetans therefore commissioned them according to their particular needs. The creation of a thangka was not only a meritorious act in itself, but it also made possible further religious activities in relation to the sacred image. An icon of the Buddha acted as a focus

Thangka in a formal photograph of the King of Derge's family.

Large appliqué thangka unrolled on a hillside at Labrang in Amdo, Eastern Tibet, c.1930.

and support for the practicing Buddhist's faith *(dad rten)* and it was also a reminder *(dran rten)* of the Buddhist's commitment to travel the path set by the Buddha. Occasionally a simple Buddha image was used as the object of focus *(dmigs rten)* during concentration meditation *(zhi gnas)*, but more commonly it functioned as a worthy object for worship and offerings, one which provided the Buddhist with the right circumstances for adding to the accumulation of merit required for spiritual advancement.

Furthermore, thangkas were sometimes used to bolster the visualizations generated during meditation. Tibetan Buddhists who were accomplishing the preparatory practices *(sngon 'gro)* of the Vajrayāna often had paintings made which depicted their teacher and his lineage in the form of a "tree of refuge." A painting of the "refuge tree" inspired and strengthened the meditator's own internal image of the vast assembly towards which such practices as going for refuge, bowing in homage, and the offering of symbolic maṇḍalas were directed. In the same vein, a monk who every day recited the Confession Sūtra might commission a painting of the thirty-five Buddhas of Confession in whose presence he envisioned himself when reciting the scripture. Similarly, meditators who applied themselves to the main practices of Vajrayāna often kept thangkas not only as objects of devotion and sources of inspiration, but also as points of reference for clarifying their visualizations. Thus those who were about to enter a special retreat would sometimes order a painting to be made of the deity who was to be intensively worshipped and propitiated.

Thangkas also had public ceremonial uses. We have seen Buddhist funeral processions in Nepal and Sikkim led by a man bearing a staff from which a thangka was hung. Srid-pa-ho thangkas were similarly used in processions of lamas, or in the procession of a bride's party. Wandering bla-ma maṇi-pa teachers commonly traveled with thangkas that they unrolled and used to illustrate their tales when reciting before an audience. Similarly, thangkas could be used by ordinary lamas to illustrate their discourses. And some monasteries possessed huge (usually appliqué) thangkas that were unrolled on certain holidays for viewing and worship.

Finally, we should not forget that in all of these activities the sacred image was not meant to be the object of simple idolatry. For knowledgeable Buddhists the image of an Enlightened One embodied the realization of potentialities that lay latent in every sentient creature. The ultimate responsibility for gaining that realization rested on the shoulders of each individual. The Buddha — to say nothing of his physical representations — could be neither pleased nor displeased by worship or the lack of it, for he was believed to be beyond all attachments and sufferings. Instead, it was the practitioner who benefited from acts of worship, advancing closer to the ultimate goal through strengthened faith, deepened insight and purer vision.

Tibetan Painters

Who were the artists who fashioned the sacred scroll paintings? In the past many people thought that thangka painters were yogis who ritually evoked the deities and then depicted them in painted form. Although such a characterization has a slight basis in fact, it does not adequately describe most painters. Tibetan thangka painters by and large were ordinary artisans, the same people who also painted wooden furniture and decorated the walls and architectural details of wealthy people's residences. The majority of them were pious laymen, and they usually came from families whose hereditary occupation was painting.

The misconception of the thangka painter as yogi no doubt mainly derives from textual sources. A number of texts, including both indigenous Tibetan treatises and translations from the Sanskrit, set forth the ritual steps and visualizations that should accompany the painting of certain images. Yet in their everyday practice few artists followed such methods. Though Tibetan painters on the whole were religiously minded, none of our teachers mentioned such practices as forming part of their standard method. Nevertheless, Tibetan Buddhism required that its painters be tantric initiates in a formal sense at least. According to Vajrayāna Buddhism any artist who depicted the deities belonging to the four classes of Tantras had to have been ritually initiated into each of these classes. Most Tibetan painters had in fact received such initiations *(dbang bskur)*.

In the history of Tibetan art a few paintings are known to have been directly inspired by yogic visions. Such visions, however, were usually experienced by those who were meditators by calling, and not by professional artists. Still, professional artists could make a contribution during the creation of these extraordinary paintings. Once, for example, the 15th-century religious master Gong-dkar-ba Kun-dga'-rnam-rgyal had a vision of Mahākāla during his meditations late at night. That same night he made a sketch of the deity as it had appeared to him. The next day, however, he entrusted the coloring and completion of the painting to the famous artist Mkhyen-brtse chen-mo. Some other great religious masters were themselves highly accomplished painters who needed no assistance. The Tenth Karma-pa Chos-dbyings-rdo-rje (1604-1674) and Si-tu Paṇ-chen Chos-kyi-'byung-gnas (1700-1774) were two such masters, and their paintings are held in special esteem. Even more revered are paintings that great religious teachers had made with exceptional materials; some used, for instance, the blood of their own nosebleeds.

On the other hand there were special occasions when even ordinary painters produced thangkas through a process of ritual and meditation. The most common instance of this was the "day-thangka" *(nyin thang)*, a painting that to be ritually efficacious had to be completed within one day. Such paintings commonly depicted the goddess White Tārā, and they were commissioned yearly for the longevity *(zhabs brtan)* of great religious leaders. The monk-artist Legdrup Gyatsho

Sherpa thangka painter at work in Solu-Khumbu in 1954 with second paintbrush behind ear.

recounted to us how he once went to Mtshur-phu with many other artists to paint a day-thangka for the longevity of the great hierarch the Karma-pa. Each artist was assigned a monk-servant to help him, and a tailor to sew a thangka frame of brocades. Every possible preparation was made in advance: all the materials and tools were accounted for and laid out. Then on the appointed day, the eighth day of the tenth lunar month, the artist awoke before dawn and prepared the canvas. He had to hold the damp primed canvas over hot coals to speed its drying, and when its preparation was complete he feverishly painted the image of the goddess, all the while performing the sādhana of the deity and reciting appropriate mantras. Following its completion the painting was consecrated by a group of eight monks. Afterwards the artist was rewarded with a festive celebration and generous offerings. It is safe to say that paintings produced in this way accounted for only a small fraction of an artist's total output.

Traditionally, Tibetan painters were handsomely recompensed for their skills. Although they were sometimes conscripted by the government to do compulsory work *(lag khral)* on restoration projects, even then they were usually well paid. And for private commissions their pay was usually even better. These commissions were not supposed to be merely cash transactions. The payment that the patron made to the artist after the completion of the work was thought of as a pious offering, a kind of religious "ransom payment" *(slu yon)* which allowed the patron then to "invite" *(gdan 'dren zhu)* the sacred image to its new home. Nevertheless, before the work began the patron and artist usually agreed on some minimum payment, as well as on the amount of gold to be used.

Skilled and famous painters could and sometimes did enrich themselves by peddling their work for the highest possible fees. Such artists provoked the satire of the 16th-century mad yogi 'Brug-pa Kun-legs, and the following is a loose rendering of his diatribe against them:

> And as for those "divinely emanated" painters of religious images — Phooey!
>
> Their crooked images possess neither correct shape nor proportions — Phooey!
>
> Without making clear the "eye-opening" of the deity by means of their colors and shading,
>
> They do shading with dark and dilute lac dye — Phooey!
>
> Not thinking of the payment offered by the patron as being a basis for gathering a stock of merit,
>
> They fix a price of one *bre* for each deity — Phooey!
>
> Without restoring the murals of old temples
>
> They sell for a profit the thangkas that they lazily paint — Phooey!
>
> I have still more gossip of various kinds about such painters.
>
> Even if I do not utter it, I would like to![3]

Although perhaps not all Tibetan painters can escape the criticisms of 'Brug-pa Kun-legs, the ones that we knew best were conscientious in their dealings with patrons and not avaricious. Being basically religious in their outlook, they took care to paint images with correct proportions, and they did not unduly inflate their fees. It is easy for someone who does not paint to overlook the tremendous amount of time and work that goes into a fine painting.

Among Tibetan painters there is still another personality type that deserves to be mentioned. There existed a small number of brilliantly talented artists who were very reticent about their work. Not only did they not appreciate the prying eyes of foreign visitors, but they were said to object even to their own relatives watching while they worked. One such artist whom we met in India was sometimes even said to be a "divinely emanated fashioner of images" *(sprul pa'i lha bzo)*. Such artists had a reputation for taking no students, and often they would die without passing on their knowledge. Secretiveness was in fact characteristic of many Tibetan artists, as well as of many doctors, astrologers and other specialists.

Our main teachers, however, were not excessively secretive, nor were they miserly in teaching students. We heard of painters who put their students through demanding apprenticeships, not revealing the secrets of the craft until many years had passed. Yet we were fortunate in finding teachers who took a pleasure in imparting their knowledge. In addition to teaching us the details of painting techniques and materials, they often described at length their former way of life as artists in old Tibet. In so doing they introduced us to many things which, though of no practical use to a novice painter, were essential if we were to understand their world. Thus in the end we came to view our teachers as remarkable not only for their knowledge and skill as artists, but also for their kindness and generosity.

'Brug-pa Kun-legs, from a modern Bhutanese thangka.

Notes to Chapter 1

1. We owe to Daniel V. Thompson, *The Materials of Medieval Painting* (London, 1936), our inspiration for this way of introducing a tradition of painting by describing the general wealth of arts and crafts in the culture to which it belongs.

2. Mi-pham-rgya-mtsho, *Bzo gnas nyer mkho za ma tog, Collected Writings* (Gangtok, 1975), vol.9, pp.71-138.

3. The Tibetan text of these lines is:

   /sprul sku lha bris pa rnams kyang e hong/
   /tshugs dang thig tshad mi ldan pa'i/
   /ya na yo na'i gzugs brnyan e hong/
   /tshon mdangs spyan 'byed mi gsal ba'i/
   /rgya tshos nag bla'i (=sla'i?) mdangs 'byed e hong/
   /dge rtsa'i yon du mi bsam par/
   /lha rer bre re'i gong rgyag e hong/
   /lha khang logs bris mi gso ba'i/
   /lag dal thang sku'i khe tshong e hong/
   /da rung kha 'chal sna tshogs yod/
   /mi lab byas na'ang lab snying 'dod/

   See John A. Ardussi, "'Brug-pa Kun-legs, the Saintly Tibetan Madman," M. A. Thesis, University of Washington, 1972, p.251. In the same text 'Brug-pa Kun-legs also gives amusing criticisms of cobblers, weavers, silversmiths and blacksmiths. See *ibid.*, pp.163-165.

The painter Tsering and his canvas in the Norbu Lingka, Lhasa 1937.

Two
The Preparation of the Painting Surface

The painters of Tibet pursued their art in an orderly and systematic way. When creating thangka scroll paintings they proceeded through six clearly defined steps. The first step was the preparation of the painting surface. Second came the establishment of a design on that surface by means of a sketch or transfer. The third step involved laying down the initial coats of paint, and that was followed by steps four and five: shading and outlining. The sixth and last step consisted of several finishing touches. This book is essentially a detailed description of just those six practical steps. In the following chapters we will describe those techniques (and the materials they entailed) in the same order that they occur during the actual painting of a thangka.

Basic Painting Techniques

Although Tibetan artists knew of more than one painting medium, when painting thangkas they applied their basic coats of colour in distemper. Distemper paints consisted of powdered pigments mixed with a binder of gelatin size (a dilute solution of hide glue).[1] Such paints were fast-drying and water-soluble, and they dried to a matte finish. Other binders were also known to Tibetan artists, including linseed oil and gluten from roasted wheat, but these did not have wide applications in either thangka or mural painting.[2] With very few exceptions, size or hide glue *(spyin; ko spyin)* was the binder.

Hide glue, moreover, could be employed in different ways. The most commonly used mixture of glue and pigment was the standard opaque distemper. The technique that used such paints was called in Tibetan *rdzogs tshon* ("complete colour") or *tshon chen* ("great colour"). There was also a contrasting technique that employed thinner, more transparent washes of paint. Called *hang tshon* ("faint colour"?) by some artists, the latter technique stood in relation to the opaque distemper as watercolour to gouache.[3] In the past the *hang tshon* technique was sometimes used as a shortcut method in mural painting, but in the painting of thangkas it was normally employed only for colouring very small figures.

Distemper paints by their nature called for a deliberate and almost businesslike procedure. To begin with, such paints worked best with a clear and well-defined design. Distemper was suited to designs that contained relatively large and distinct areas of colour, and became more difficult to handle with designs that had many small or convoluted areas of different colours.

Also, many of the paints had little covering power. This made corrections and late deviations from the design difficult to render successfully, especially if the painter wanted to paint with a light colour over dark. But generally speaking, Tibetan painters avoided these problems. The artists would finalize a clear design during the process of sketching (step two), before applying a single drop of paint. The initial coats of opaque paints could then be applied (step three) to suitably distinct areas. To complete the painting, however, something beyond opaque distemper paints was needed. For achieving the final, detailed results the painter applied the techniques of shading and outlining (steps four and five), both of which utilized colours of a different sort: dyes and lakes.

The Painting Surface: Support and Ground

Tibetan painters, like the artists of many other countries, laid down their colours on a painting surface that consisted of two main layers: a support and a ground. At the core of the painting surface there was a supporting material such as a cloth, a wooden panel or a bare wall. This underlying material held or "carried" the subsequent layers of ground and paint, and it was what is called the *support* of the painting. Although artists in Tibet painted on a variety of supports, for the depiction of religious subjects the most common supports were walls and cloth. Without additional preparation, however, neither of these materials was suitable for painting; therefore another layer, consisting of a "gesso" or a similar mixture, had to be applied over the support. Such a top layer, which completed the painting surface, was what is called the *ground* of the painting.

No matter what the support, it was very important to prepare a proper ground over it. Any defects in workmanship at this stage were apt to show up later in the overlying layer as cracking, crumbling or peeling paint. In the case of thangkas the preparation of a good ground was even more important, since thangkas were painted on a cloth support *(ras gzhi)*. They were rolled up for transportation or storage and then unrolled for display.

The preparation of a good painting surface was not very difficult. By following the procedures established within the artistic traditions even a beginner could prepare a canvas that with proper handling could last for centuries. It seems, in fact, that most of the damage done to the old thangkas that survive was not caused by defects or deficiencies in the ground, but by external causes such as water or smoke, or by the surprisingly rough treatment to which even exquisite masterpieces were sometimes subjected.[4]

Cotton Cloth

The first item required for the making of a thangka was a suitable piece of fabric, and the most common cloth used by our main informants in Tibet was a plain-weave Indian muslin. Similar cotton fabrics from China were also sometimes used, particularly in eastern parts of Tibet. In all of the cases that we observed in India and Nepal, modern artists used a light-weight Indian cotton of fine but slightly open weave. Legdrup Gyatsho, one of our main informants, stated that it was advantageous to use finely woven cloths since these were less trouble to coat with gesso. Cottons of coarser weave required thicker coats of gesso to fill in their textured surface. Nowadays the cotton fabric is available in quite wide dimensions. In Tibet, however, it was often necessary to stitch together two pieces of cloth when preparing the support for larger paintings.

Before the preparation of the cloth support, the cloth sometimes needed washing. This has become even more important in recent years for painters who use modern Indian cottons. The latter commonly contain manufacturer's size, which affects the application of the primer and ground. After the sizing had been washed out the cloth usually shrank a bit as it dried. Then, when completely dry, the painter could cut the cloth to fit the wooden stretcher frame.

In the past, scroll paintings were also executed on other materials such as silk, linen and leather or skin. In addition, one occasionally comes across paintings made on block-printed silk or paper. But in modern thangka painting these support materials are relatively rare.

The Stretcher

The painting surface of the thangka was made from a cotton cloth by stretching it in a wooden stretcher frame *(rkyang shing)* and then coating it with a layer of white paint for the ground. Many painters prepared this "canvas" *(ras gzhi)* themselves, but it was also common for them to leave this task to their assistants or students.

Tibetan painters used stretchers of various dimensions, but the most common type for a single thangka was rectangular and approximately two by three feet. To fit within this outer wooden stretcher the cloth was cut approximately thirty inches long by twenty inches wide.[5] The cloth was so much smaller than the stretcher because the fabric was not attached directly to the stretcher, but had to be tied within it by a looping string. When the cloth was fastened, the cloth and stretcher looked something like a miniature trampoline. Not surprisingly, since the wooden stretchers were one of the artist's necessities, a painter often insisted that they be made according to his precise specifications. Some of the better stretchers that we saw had been constructed by carpenters out of seasoned hardwood strips measuring approximately two inches wide by one inch thick. The four pieces were often joined by snugly fitted mortise and tenon joints. The tenons projected from both ends of the shorter pieces and fitted into mortises near the ends of the longer strips. The ends of the two longer pieces usually extended several inches past the point of junction with the shorter strips. During painting the artist commonly positioned the stretcher with one of the short sides resting on his lap, and thus the projecting ends of the longer sides prevented the stretcher from shifting. Wooden stretchers of this type did not need nailing and were renowned for their sturdiness, whereas those that were made without interlocking joints soon became loose and wobbly.

The Inner Frame

Fastening the cloth to the stretcher usually involved two main steps. First, the painter stitched a sort of inner frame, which consisted of four supple twigs or bamboo splints, to the four edges of the fabric. Second, he fastened this cloth with its light frame of twigs to the heavier outer stretcher by a series of loops of twine. The use of an inner frame helped to distribute the tension evenly around the edges of the fabric during the priming of the cloth support, and to maintain that even tension until the completion of the painting. Any bulging in the fabric that developed during the preparation of the canvas due to uneven tension became a permanent feature that could not be corrected after the coats of size and gesso had dried.

To prepare the inner frame the artist first cut four sticks of bamboo or twigs of some supple wood a few inches longer than the sides of the cotton cloth. These sticks could be about one-quarter or three-eighths of an inch in thickness — thick enough to support tension but not so thick as to be inflexible.

Before fastening the sticks to the edges of the cloth, some artists began by scoring all four edges of the cloth with a large needle, dragging the tip of the needle in a line about three-quarters of an inch within the borders. This established a crease along which the artist could then easily fold back a thin strip on each edge. He next placed the first stick outside the cloth, alongside one of the creased and folded edges, and sewed the stick to the cloth with a series of evenly spaced overhand stitches about half an inch to one inch apart, using a large needle and some strong thread.

When the artist reached the corner of the cloth (which was also near the end of the stick), he placed the next stick over the preceding one at a right angle, parallel to the next side of the cloth, and wrapped a few loops of the heavy thread around the intersection of the two sticks. After that he continued to stitch on as before, until reaching the next corner. There he repeated the procedure with the next stick, placing the third stick underneath the second. Continuing in this way, when he reached the last corner he securely tied and knotted the thread.

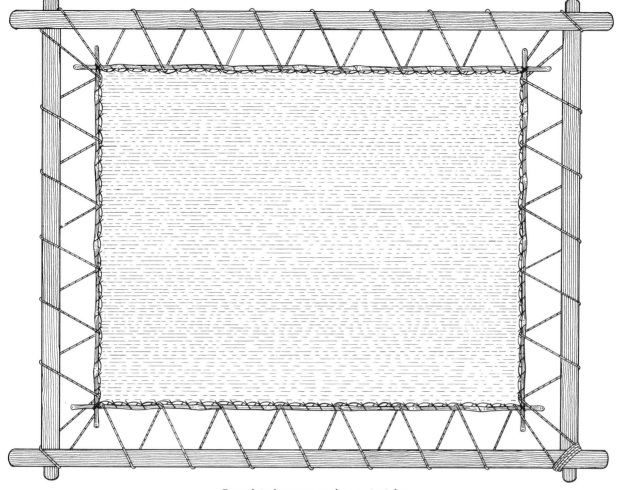

Completed canvas ready on stretcher.

Inner Frame Materials

Artists in Lhasa sometimes gathered bamboo canes for use in making inner stretcher frames from the bamboo groves of the Norbu-lingka, the Dalai Lama's summer palace. If the artists could not get the thin canes, they could prepare suitable splints by splitting and whittling down larger and thicker pieces of bamboo. In mountainous parts of Tibet where bamboo did not grow the artists used straight sticks from various trees. Newly cut sticks, being more pliant, were preferred to old wood. Larger thangkas were often too long for a single small stick to extend the full length of the cloth. In such cases the artists sometimes tied two or three small sticks together at their ends, forming a line that ran the full length of the long edges of the cloth.

Tying the Inner Frame Within the Stretcher

Once the inner frame had been completed it was placed within the outer stretcher frame and lashed to it. For this the painter took a strong and very long, non-stretching cord, and knotted one end of it to one of the projecting corners of the outer stretcher. Then he began to work his way around the stretcher, looping the cord at regular intervals around the outer stretcher and passing it through the gaps between the inner frame and the cloth. After the stretcher and inner frame were tied

together on all sides he tied the loose end to the same corner from which he had begun. Then he went around the stretcher again, pulling each loop to gather any excess slack and taking care not to let the cloth and inner frame be pulled out of alignment. When he again reached the end, he retied the cord tightly at the corner.

Detail of a corner of a stretcher.

It was important for the cloth and inner frame to be at least two inches or so smaller in length and breadth than the outer stretcher because the cloth stretched during priming, and if it was not given enough space it would stretch until it reached the outer edge. When this happened it was often impossible to tighten the cloth sufficiently and the "canvas" thus became slack and prone to warping. Nevertheless, in some cases the artist could still do something to correct this problem; we once observed an artist who inserted small wedges of wood into the joints of the stretcher. The wedges pushed apart the boards, slightly expanding the size of the stretcher and making just enough extra room for the cloth support to be drawn taut.

Alternatives to the Inner Frame of Sticks

The use of an inner frame of sticks, although a widespread custom, was not a necessity, and many painters found ways to do without it. One alternative method entailed the stitching of a heavy cord all along the scored and folded-back edge of the cloth, much as the inner frame of twigs was sewn in place. This was the method of Wangdrak, the artist from Shekar Dzong. When preparing the rope frame around the cloth, he left a special loop at each corner that could be pulled to tighten the cloth during priming. Then he attached the cloth with its rope frame to the outer wooden stretcher in the same manner as with the inner frame of wooden twigs. Wangdrak said that he had picked up this method from some painters from Amdo with whom he had worked in India. He adopted it, he said, because it saved him the trouble of having to find sticks and yet still gave good results.

An inner frame of rope was especially suitable for the painting of oversized thangkas and many painters used it for this purpose. Unlike the cloth supports with sticks for their inner frames, those with rope frames could be rolled at the top and bottom, and lashed tightly at the sides. This allowed an artist to execute very tall paintings in a room with a low ceiling, and even in rooms with high ceilings it did away with the need for scaffolding or ladders. But to begin with such large canvases had to be stretched on an oversized stretcher. Then they could be rolled as necessary on one or both ends and then tied within a smaller stretcher.

Some artists omitted the inner frame of rope or sticks entirely, and merely scored and turned back the edges of the cloth for reinforcement. Then with needle and a strong doubled string they attached the cloth within the outer stretcher by a series of regularly spaced looping stitches. As with the other methods, these artists first secured the end of the string to a corner of the stretcher before making the first stitch and once the cloth was loosely sewn in place they increased the tension of the cloth by going around the stretcher again, tightening the string loop by loop.

The advantage of using an inner frame of twigs or rope was that much larger projects could be undertaken with less risk of losing the tension on the primed surface of the thangka. The single-frame methods were quicker and simpler, but with them there was more danger that the strings (which had to be small enough to be sewn with a large needle) would break during priming or painting. However, any one of these methods would give good results if carefully applied.

Sizing the Cloth

To prepare the cloth as a suitable painting surface some of our informants from Central Tibet performed three operations: sizing the fabric, applying the gesso, and polishing the gesso. Sizing, the first step, coated and stiffened the cloth. It was quick and easy: the task mainly consisted of preparing a solution of warm hide glue and applying that to both sides of the cloth with the help of a large brush or wadded-up rag. After the cloth became saturated and any excess had been wiped away, the artist tightened the cord that connected the cloth to the stretcher, and then set the canvas aside to dry. Many artists, however, did not apply size to the cloth in a separate operation. Instead they began by applying a coat of gesso.[6]

Size (ko spyin)

In Tibet the adhesive used for sizing consisted mainly of gelatin. Tibetan artists could produce this gelatin or size by boiling clean, dry skin or leather in water. Prolonged heating at about boiling point caused the protein collagen, one of the main constituents of the skin, to change into gelatin as the skin itself slowly dissolved. When the transformation was complete, the artists strained the liquid to remove any solid residue. Then, when it had cooled and had begun to set, they poured it out into a clean pan so that it would congeal into a thin flat sheet.

Once the gelatin size had set and cooled completely, the artists often cut it into strips. Then, to speed up the drying, they either hung the strips over a rope in a warm, dry place or laid them out on a piece of cloth until the gelatin was hard and dry. In this state chunks of size could be stored indefinitely.

The painters of Tibet preferred to use the purest size available, which was usually a gelatin made from skins alone. Such size of the best quality — which was also the "glue" for mixing paints — was known as "deity-glue" (lha spyin), and it was made from skins that were free from fat, hairs and other impurities.[7] Nowadays most of the Tibetan artists living in India and Nepal do not use the traditional sizes made from yak or cow skins. Instead, they obtain their size and binder from ready-made glues that are available in the local bazaars. In Nepal one common type is said to be prepared from water buffalo skins. These glues are sometimes of low quality, and in that case have to be warmed, skimmed and filtered. It is difficult to say whether these common adhesives of India and Nepal are actually size or glue since glue, properly speaking, is partly made up of gelatin but also contains other proteins and organic materials, whereas size is a more or less pure gelatin produced from skins.

Wangdrak preparing a canvas: a) pouring the gesso, b) spreading with a gesso knife, c) tightening the rope around the wet canvas, d) dampening an area of dry canvas.

The Preparation and Application of Size

The preparation of size from the dried gelatin or hide glue simply consisted of soaking a piece of the adhesive in water and then gently warming it. The size was normally mixed in relatively small quantities – just enough to last for a day or two. When mixing it or reheating it the artist had only to take care that he did not darken it by placing it over too hot a fire. Usually he would warm it gently by placing its pot over a brazier that contained a few hot coals.

The strength of the dried size varied a little from batch to batch, but this made no difference to the painters, who always mixed their binders by "feel" and not by measure. In the absence of recipes, the artists performed simple tests to judge the strength of the size. For example, some painters would rub a little between the thumb and index finger, and then quickly press together and pull apart the finger and thumb several times. As they did so, the water evaporated from the size and the strength of the solution became apparent: the tackier the size, the more the finger and thumb stuck together. Also, when accustomed to the same type of size or glue, an artist could tell something of its strength just from its odor.

After the size had been evenly applied to both the front and back of the painting and the fabric had been tightened again, the painter set the stretcher aside and allowed the cloth to dry completely. Most artists preferred to dry it slowly, and many advised against putting the newly sized fabric into hot direct sunlight. They usually dried their sized canvases either inside or in a shady spot out of doors.

Preparing the Ground

Once the cotton support had been stretched and sized, there only remained the application of a layer of gesso and its polishing to complete the preparation of the ground. When properly applied and finished this layer of gesso united with the underlying cloth, presenting the painter with a surface that was excellent for both sketching and painting.

Gesso ('dam)

The "gesso" used by Tibetan painters was simply a mixture of the most available white earth pigment – either a chalk or a white clay (kaolin) – added to some size solution.[8] The usual Tibetan name for their white earth colour was *ka rag*, although it was also known as *sa dkar* ("white earth") or *dkar rtsi* ("whitewash"). Where whites of the best quality were scarce, any local whitish earth could be substituted, providing that it had been properly washed, ground, and filtered through a cloth.[9]

After a coat of this gesso the white cotton support became even whiter. It should also be noted that some painters, particularly those from Eastern Tibet, preferred a gesso that had a slightly ochreish hue. To achieve this they added a small amount of ochre or yellow pigment to the gesso.[10]

The Preparation and Application of Gesso

To prepare the gesso the painter began by partially filling a paint bowl with some of his finely ground dry white pigment. He next poured in a little size solution, stirring it in with a blunt-ended stirring stick *(snur skyogs)*. He then continued to add size, a little at a time, until the powder became the consistency of stiff dough. He carefully stirred and ground this mixture for some time, using the pestle-shaped end of the stirring stick to crush any lumps or pockets of dry pigment. When it had become thoroughly mixed he added a little more size, and continued to stir. Sometimes he tilted the bowl to the side and ran his stirring stick along the bottom to make sure that all of the heavy lumps had been pulverized. Finally, he added just enough size solution to bring the gesso to the consistency of buttermilk – the preferred consistency not only for gesso but also for paints in general. This mixture was then strained through a cloth to eliminate any remaining lumps or bits of solid matter.

As usual, the Tibetan painter did not use measures when preparing gesso. Nevertheless, when questioned, one artist estimated that he used approximately two parts of *ka rag* to one part of size solution. There was a certain amount of leeway in how strong the size had to be. Some artists said that for gesso the size should be almost twice the strength of the ordinary size solution. But others employed a size of about the same strength as they used for sizing the cloth and for mixing ordinary paints.

To apply the gesso to the cloth, our main informants used a wadded-up rag or a gesso knife *('dam khri)*. Some other artists also used oversized brushes. Whichever applicator was used, the gesso had to be applied in thin, even coats to both sides of the stretched cloth. Wangdrak, who used a gesso knife, applied the gesso sparingly, using the rounded tip of the knife like a spatula, and being careful to scrape off the excess gesso and leave a clean, smooth surface. The artist Legdrup Gyatsho, one of those who applied the gesso with a rag, smoothed it while it was still wet and worked it into the support by rubbing the surface with the heel of his hand. With his hand he also wiped off the excess. Afterwards, when the cloth support had become saturated with gesso, both artists again tightened the strings around the stretcher frame, making the canvas taut and flat.

Next, when the first coat of gesso on both sides of the cloth had dried, the artist had to determine whether a single coat had provided enough coverage. He would hold the canvas up to a source of light and if he could see many "pin holes" of light he knew that he had to apply another coat.

Care had to be taken in obtaining the correct proportion of pigment to size. Too much size in the mixture resulted in a hard and brittle canvas which might crack and also cause flaking of the colours applied over it, due to not enough 'grip' in the excessively sized surface. Not enough size in the mixture could also cause flaking and powdering, especially when the thangka has

Tshedor finishing a canvas; first checking for pinholes after the application of gesso, then moistening the canvas in preparation for damp polishing.

been rolled and unrolled many times. A mixture of the right 'grip' was obtained through experience.

Polishing the Ground

The final step in the preparation of the ground was to make the surface perfectly smooth and even by polishing it. Some Tibetan painters actually used two types of polishing: one called "damp polishing" *(rlon dbur)*, which was polishing over a dampened surface, and the other called "dry polishing" *(skam dbur)*, burnishing over a dried coat of gesso.

Damp Polishing

Once the earlier coats of gesso had dried and the artist was convinced that they gave enough coverage to constitute a good ground, the next step was to moisten slightly a portion of one side of the cloth in preparation for polishing. No more than a third or a fourth of a standard-size canvas needed to be moistened at a time, otherwise parts of it would begin to dry before the polishing was finished. Next, the artist had to lay the stretcher over a smooth board or some other smooth surface. Then, taking a polishing stone *(dbur rdo,* usually a smooth alluvial stone) or some similar hard object with a smooth, rounded bottom, such as a conch-shell, he rubbed the moistened part of the gesso, working back and forth along one axis of the cloth. Having completed that area, he then moistened and polished another part of the cloth, and continued until the whole of one side had been gone over once.

Both sides of the cloth required damping and polishing in this manner. However, before the artist could proceed to burnish the back, he had to wait until the cloth had completely dried, but he did not need to stop work if he was preparing a batch of several canvases simultaneously. By the time he had finished burnishing his third or fourth canvas on one side, the first canvas would be dry and ready to be done on the reverse side.

The artists we worked with usually polished each side of the cloth twice by this damp-burnishing method. If the surface had been polished along the vertical axis the first time, the artist would burnish it along the horizontal axis the second time. Others only polished the canvas once on each side. Burnishing the dampened canvas made it smooth and even, so that the texture of the underlying cloth stood out less. A smooth board beneath the cloth during polishing facilitated this process by allowing the artist to bear down a little without gouging the canvas.

Dry Polishing

Having burnished the cloth on both sides, some painters next carefully examined each side for its merits and defects. Then they turned the best side down and polished the back of the canvas one last time. This time they applied no water to the dry gesso; they simply rubbed it with the polishing stone. This was the so-called dry polishing, which left the back of the cloth with a very smooth – and sometimes even a glossy – finish. The better side of the cloth was not dry burnished. It was the side to be painted, and the final

Tshedor polishing the canvas with a smooth stone after moistening it.

damp burnishing left it a bit more textured. This was desirable since the painting side of the canvas needed more "tooth" for it to accept paint readily. But some painters, such as Wangdrak, did not dry polish at all during this stage.

Different Techniques for Preparing the Support and Ground

Painters from different regions and different artistic traditions sometimes departed from the above generalized method. One finds, for example, a record of a painter from Ladakh who when stretching his cotton cloth sewed dried barley stalks to the edges of the cloth to serve as his inner frame.[11] Another Ladakhi artist, Wangchuk, a present-day painter who was trained by a master from Gtsang, used to apply alternating damp and dry burnishings to both sides of the cloth until he had achieved the desired surface quality. And there are many other variant methods, far too many for us to list them all. But in spite of these differences it is clear that the basic methods for preparing the cloth support in thangka painting are very old and have been passed down from teacher to student over many generations. A description of a very similar method survives, for instance, in the writings of the 15th-century master Bo-dong Paṇ-chen Phyogs-las-rnam-rgyal.[12]

Characteristics of a Good Thangka Canvas

The cloth supports and gesso grounds used by living painters from the various schools and regions differ slightly in their appearance and constitution. The painter Wangdrak, for instance, described the ideal thangka canvas as resembling soft deerskin, and his canvases were quite soft and pliant by Central Tibetan standards. By comparison, the canvases used by some other informants from Dbus and Gtsang were somewhat heavier and less flexible, while those of some Eastern Tibetan artists were often even softer and finer than Wangdrak's.[13] Still, certain characteristics were valued by all Tibetan artists. The gesso ground had to be strongly fixed to the underlying cloth, and not so thick or brittle that it cracked when rolled and unrolled. It had to be smooth, so as not to impede in any way the detailed sketching and painting that were executed upon it, but not so smooth that it lost its porosity. It also had to be free from excessive glue in the ground, so that the paints readily and permanently attached themselves to it. If the major defects could be avoided and the main necessities achieved, the painter was free to follow whatever minor variations in technique suited him or his tradition.

Notes

1. Please note that the term *distemper* is used in the sense given by the *McGraw-Hill Dictionary of Art* (1969): "Aqueous painting medium composed of water, powdered colour, and size (glue) or casein." Distemper is sometimes confused with tempera, and indeed the French word *détrempe* has both meanings. Tibetan painters are not known to have used egg tempera. However, in the past other sorts of egg preparations were sometimes employed in painting. Bo-dong (1375-1451) described the use of an egg-white glair as a protective coat for paintings. See his *Mkhas pa*, vol.2, p.262.1. The later scholar Sum-pa mkhan-po Ye-shes-dpal-'byor (1704-1788) mentioned the use of an egg mixture when preparing vermilion for application with varnish *(pra rtsi)*. See his *Sku gsung thugs rten gyi thig rtsa mchan 'grel can me tog 'phreng mdzes, Collected Works* (New Delhi, 1975), vol.4, p.399.3. See also Mi-pham-rgya-mtsho, *Bzo gnas*, p.90.2, which here is based on Sum-pa mkhan-po.

   Nowadays some forgers of antique thangkas are said to be using an egg-white glair to coat the front of the paintings. A supposed test of the antiquity of a thangka is to rub some of its paint with a moistened finger to see if any colour comes off. The egg glair forms a waterproof protective coating over the paint.

2. These two binders are mentioned below in connection with gold and inks. Another adhesive used by Tibetan artists was made from the root of a plant called *dbang po'i lag pa* or *dbang lag*. In the recent *Bod ljongs rgyun spyod krung dbyi'i sman rigs* (Peking, Bod ljongs mi dmangs dpe skrun khang, 1973), illustration no.346, this plant is identified as *Gymnadenia crassinervis* Finet.

3. We have not seen the term *hang tshon* in any text. The spelling given is based on the pronunciation of Wangdrak from Shekar Dzong. Perhaps its written equivalent should be *hal tshon*. The latter occurs in the phrase *"zhal thang hal tshon ma"*, which is found in a biography of the Third Dalai Lama. See *'Phags pa 'jig rten dbang phyug gi rnam sprul rim byon gyi 'khrungs rabs deb ther nor bu'i 'phreng ba* (Dharamsala?, n.d.), vol.2, p.81, lines 1-2. Some painters differentiated rich or full-coloured paintings from light or pale-coloured ones using the terminology *snum tshon* for the former and *skya tshon* for the latter. For the pronunciation of these and other Tibetan terms see the Glossary.

4. Ms Ann Shaftel, a conservator specializing in Tibetan paintings, informed us that most of the marked horizontal cracking that is characteristic of many damaged thangkas probably resulted from improper handling during rolling and storage.

5. In the tradition of Legdrup Gyatsho, a single painting executed on a cloth of this size would measure more or less what was considered to be a standard "thangka size" *(thang tshad)*: three spans and three finger widths by two spans and two finger widths or about 25 by 16 inches. This "standard" size seems to have been what the artists in that tradition used when painting common sets of thangkas or certain standard compositions. However, it was not obligatory, nor did artists of other traditions adhere to it. A patron could specify any size of thangka that he or she wanted. Elsewhere one hears of thangkas measuring an "arrow's length" *(mda' tshad*, approximately four spans), the "height of a man" *(mi tshad*, about eight spans or about five feet) and the "height of one storey" *(thog tshad*, approximately nine or ten feet). The same measures were commonly applied also to statues.

6. According to Ms Ann Shaftel (personal communication) some recent painters of Khams did not size their canvases. However, Mi-pham-rgya-mtsho (a 19th-century scholar and artist from Khams) described the practice as standard. See his *Bzo gnas*, p.89.6. Mi-pham here followed the earlier account of another Eastern Tibetan, Sum-pa mkhan-po (vol.4, p.399).

7. L. S. Dagyab, *Tibetan Religious Art* (Weisbaden, 1977), p.45.

8. One painter from the Lhasa area used to add a little *dbang-lag*-root adhesive to the hide glue. This was thought to reduce the danger of cracking. On *dbang lag* see above, note 2.

9. Ms Ann Shaftel in a personal communication informed us that some Khams-pa painters also used slaked lime.

10. This technique was commonly used by painters working in the *Karma-sgar-bris* and the *Sman-bris gsar-ma* styles of Khams. It was particularly effective there because these techniques used thin washes and the minimal application of paint. The ground itself showed through in places and a plain white ground would have been glaring and unpleasant.

11. Pallis, p.292. The approach of the Ladakhis continues to be above all practical. Nowadays some artists there use thin bendable metal rods in their inner frames.

12. Bo-dong, *Mkhas pa*, vol.2, pp.254.4.-255.3. See also Sum-pa mkhan-po, p.399, and Mi-pham-rgya-mtsho, *Bzo gnas*, pp.89.6-90.1.

13. One can also find considerable differences among the supports and grounds of thangkas from other periods. See Huntington.

Painting of Bskal-bzang-rgya-mtsho, the Seventh Dalai Lama. Victoria and Albert Museum,
Royal Loan reproduced by Gracious Permission of Her Majesty the Queen.

24

Three
Composition

By the time the painter sat down to begin his sketch he already had in mind the main contents and design of the thangka. Usually the patron had indicated to the painter precisely which deities he wanted depicted. Sometimes the patron also furnished a diagram that showed the names and relative positions of each figure in the painting, such diagrams often having been composed by the lama of the patron. When the patron provided no diagram but knew exactly what he or she wanted, the painter carefully noted down the plan for his records, particularly if the painting was at all complicated or if he had a backlog of commissions.

With such a diagram or plan in hand, the job of establishing the composition was simplified. The artist then had only to divide up the painting surface, allocating the proper amount of space to each figure and sketching in the general outlines of the landscape. But if the patron could provide no more than the names of the figures to be painted, it was often up to the artist to design a suitable layout. For a painting with multiple images the artist would first determine from the patron which figure was to be the main one and which figures were subordinate, and he could then proceed with laying out the design. In many instances, however, no consultation or new composition was necessary. A large number of the compositions were fixed by Buddhist iconography and artistic tradition, and these the painter could simply draw from memory or according to standard examples.

In the following pages we will describe in more detail some of the ways in which the painter established his sketch, including the techniques and principles which he followed for new compositions. But it will be best to introduce these methods and principles indirectly, by first describing and classifying the main types of compositions, especially those with established forms and contents. This is the best approach since the basic principles can be seen most clearly in the established compositions.

Classification of Religious Paintings

According to Tibetan Buddhist thinking, most Buddhist art functioned as *rten* (literally "supports"), that is, as physical representations and embodiments of enlightened body, speech or mind. The majority of thangkas were *rten*, as were sacred statues, stūpas and scriptures. For a sacred object fully to function as a *rten*, it had to be ceremonially imbued with the spirit of enlightenment by means of a ritual consecration ceremony *(rab gnas)*. Religious paintings that were not *rten* also existed in Tibet, including paintings that taught or illustrated some aspect of Buddhist doctrine but did not mainly depict the form of Buddhas or deities. Paintings of the latter type could probably best be called "didactic" paintings. They include both straightforward illustrations of religious objects and monastic accessories, and symbolical representations of religious and cosmological concepts and themes. Only a small number of paintings did not fit into either the *rten* or didactic classes. Among them were, for instance, paintings that had a ritual use as surrogate offerings in relation to a main *rten* image, such as the *dmar rdzas* (depictions of sacrifices) placed before the images of wrathful guardians in the Protectors' Chapel *(mgon khang)*. There were a few other unusual types of painting, such as poetical diagrams and protective and astrological diagrams and yantras. But here we will mainly be concerned with *rten* and didactic paintings and the varieties that they included.

Paintings as *rten*

Paintings that depicted the bodily forms of enlightened beings were considered to be *sku rten* ("body supports"). Such paintings made up the vast majority of thangkas. We may also mention in passing a slightly different kind of *rten* painting in which inanimate sacred objects were depicted. When examining a large group of thangkas one occasionally comes across paintings of stūpas, as well as of important temples and monasteries. These too are *rten* paintings, because temples were thought of as varieties of "body support",[1] and stūpas were "supports" of enlightened mind.

The Presence or Absence of a Temporal Framework

Paintings of animate *sku-rten* figures can to some extent be further classified according to whether they do or do not express a definite temporal framework. Most thangkas placed their subjects in a realm beyond ordinary space and time, i.e. in a pure realm *(dag pa'i zhing khams)* or Buddha field. They depicted no particular moment or event although as *rten* they embodied a living and immediate presence. By contrast, some compositions clearly attempted to portray one or more episodes in the career of the subject, thus locating the event in the historical or legendary past. We could call such thangkas "narrative paintings."

Some narrative thangkas portray a succession of notable events in the life of an enlightened one or saint. Examples include thangkas of the twelve great deeds of the Buddha and of the important events in the life of Milarepa. Such paintings could be called "biographical". The subjects need not always be events in the life of a historical personage. A thangka showing episodes from the epic cycle of King Gesar of Ling would also constitute a biographical thangka.

Another type of narrative thangka is that which portrays events from a succession of the past lives of some great being. Outstanding events in the past lifetimes of Śākyamuni as set down in the *Jātaka* tales *(skyes rabs)* were sometimes the subject of paintings. All types of narrative paintings could be painted either as single works or as a series of compositions each of which depicted one or many events. In paintings that portrayed several episodes the episodes were separated from each other by walls or boundaries, or by empty spaces in the landscape. Some single paintings depicted only one episode from the life of a saint, such as the meeting of Milarepa with the hunter. In such paintings the main figure was commonly portrayed in a more realistic manner, placed (as far as the style permitted) within an almost three-dimensional landscape.[2] When drawing such episodes from a saint's life the artist generally had a greater amount of compositional freedom.

The remaining types of *rten* thangkas are those that portray the sacred figures in their general aspect within a pure realm, and not as actors in a particular situation. The simplest of such compositions merely consists of a single figure placed in the middle of a background. Here the only differences in composition between similar paintings derive from the varying complexity of the backgrounds. But when the composition consists of many sacred figures, another distinction has to be made. Some paintings depict figures whose identities and positions are iconographically prescribed. But distinct from those there are also many paintings in which the needs or wishes of the patron determined the selection and placement of the particular figures.

Established Groupings

Among the compositions that consisted of a fixed grouping, most possessed a main figure *(gtso bo)* and a "retinue" or group of lesser figures ('*khor)*. Some paintings, however, depicted groups with no main figure, showing each figure as an equal of the others. The eighty-four siddhas, the thirty-five Buddhas of confession, and the sixteen "arhats" could be painted in the latter way, although they could also be combined with a main figure or with some other groupings. The eighty-four Mahāsiddhas, for example, could be painted around the central and main figure of the Buddha

Vajradhara. Similarly, artists almost always painted the composition of the sixteen arhats around the central figure of the Buddha Śākyamuni. This composition would also include the two main disciples of the Buddha, Śāriputra and Maudgalyāyana, the two companions of the arhats, Hwa-shang and Dharmatala, and the four Lokapālas, the great guardian kings of the four directions.

Other examples of a fixed grouping with a main figure and retinue are found in paintings involving Padmasambhava. He is sometimes depicted as one of three figures: the Dharmakāya Samantabhadra *(chos-sku kun-tu-bzang-po)*, the Sambhogakāya Vajrasattva *(longs-sku rdo-rje-sems-dpa')*, and the Nirmāṇakāya Padmasambhava *(sprul-sku padma-'byung-gnas)*. The great master Padmasambhava is also shown together with a retinue of his twenty-six main disciples. Another grouping depicted him in eight famous manifestations. Furthermore there existed a famous set of block-prints depicting all twenty-six disciples in combination with the eight manifestations.

Maṇḍalas

The example *par excellence* of the fixed composition involving a main figure with retinue was the maṇḍala. The symbolism of a maṇḍala is complex, but essentially the form depicts a coherent group of deities seated symmetrically around a main central figure within the ground-plan of a divine mansion. The maṇḍala represents the citadel of enlightenment, portraying it as a dynamic integration of complementary aspects and energies. Maṇḍala paintings on cloth supports were sometimes made up into thangkas and framed in brocades in the usual way, but in Vajrayāna consecration rituals and in certain other rituals and meditational practices they were more commonly used unframed.

A Main Figure in its Pure Realm

Another type of composition consisting of a chief figure with a retinue showed the main figure in his or her special pure realm. In general, the idealized backgrounds of most thangkas and murals were meant to portray the physical surroundings of a Buddha field or pure realm *(dag pa'i zhing khams)*. However, in some compositions the artist made a special effort to depict a specific realm. Amitābha and Avalokiteśvara were commonly painted as if in the realm of Sukhāvatī. Padmasambhava often appears on his famous copper-coloured mountain *(zangs mdog dpal gyi ri)*, and the kings of Śambhala are also portrayed in their own special domain.

Repetitive Depictions

One of the most straightforward types of composition also involved a large number of figures. These compositions consisted of a central main figure surrounded by many smaller identical figures, although sometimes the surrounding figures would be another aspect or manifestation of the same central deity. The lesser figures were arranged in vertical and horizontal columns and usually were painted only in outline. The number of these smaller figures was often between one and two hundred and their size would be anywhere from half to one fifth of the size of the main deity. Such thangkas did not contain a background landscape but were usually painted with either a red or black background and with the smaller figures painted in gold outline. Occasionally the background was painted in gold and the figures in this case would be outlined in red. The main figure was usually painted in full colour, although sometimes this would also be an outline painting with only certain parts of the deity rendered in colour. Such compositions were commissioned because there was felt to be greater merit in numbers; by multiplying the number of figures the patron also multiplied the force of his merit or the force of the deity to counteract a threatening obstacle or problem.

Compositions That Depict Lineages

Another type of group composition that involved a main figure with a retinue portrayed the complete transmission lineage of a particular religious teaching. Nowadays the two most common varieties are the so-called "refuge trees" and the "assembly fields" (tshogs zhing). For the religious practitioner these paintings embodied the whole lineage through which the tradition descended, from its ultimate origin down to the practitioner's own teacher. Such paintings could be used by a meditator in the tradition as a support for his or her visualizations.

Refuge Trees

The "refuge tree" depicts the objects or beings in which the practitioner takes refuge (skyabs su 'gro ba'i yul), that is to say it represents the beings and things in which the Buddhist places his trust as preparation for and as an actual part of religious practice.[3] The common "refuges" of Buddhism are the Three Jewels: the Buddha, Dharma and Saṅga. In Vajrayāna Buddhism bestowers of refuge also include the gurus (both one's immediate teacher and the earlier teachers of the lineage), yi-dam deities, ḍākas and ḍākinīs, and the protectors of the Dharma.

Usually the givers of refuge were envisioned as dwelling in a great "wish-fulfilling tree" (dpag bsam gyi shing). In the center was one's teacher in the form of the main figure, whose identity depended on the particular tradition being practiced. Then on branches of the tree, which radiated out to the four cardinal points, were seated four of the other "refuges". In practices stemming from new-translation-era Tantras one might find yi-dam deities on the front branch, Buddhas on the branch to the main figure's right (i.e. to the left with relation to the viewer), the Dharma in the form of a stack of sacred scriptures to the rear, and the Ārya Saṅgha in the form of a group of monks and bodhisattvas on the branch to the main figure's left. Above the

tree in the sky (or sometimes seated around the main figure in a circle) was depicted the line of teachers through whom the lineage had been transmitted to one's immediate teacher. In the sky below the main branches of the tree there dwelled a host of protectors and guardians.

Assembly Fields

Thangkas or murals called "assembly fields" also served as a help for the meditator in some traditions to visualize the totality of his lineage. Here again a great many figures were pictured, but not with the same spatial orientation as in the refuge tree. The assembly field was a group of exalted beings who were worshipped and to whom offerings were made. The group constituted a special "field" (zhing) in relation to which the meditator could greatly increase his "assembly" (tshogs) of merit. The Dge-lugs-pa tradition produced most of the thangkas of this type, including those of the Graduated Path (lam rim) and Guru Worship (bla ma mchod pa) practices.[4]

Assembly-field paintings contained a characteristic placement of their figures. The main, central figure occupied the central pinnacle of a lotus seat, and he was surrounded by descending concentric rows of exalted beings. Each row or group of rows below the main figure consisted of figures belonging to one of eight classes of beings. In their descending order these were:

1. Gurus
2. Yi-dams
3. Buddhas
4. Bodhisattvas
5. Pratyekabuddhas
6. Śrāvakas/Sthaviras
7. Ḍākas
8. Dharmapālas

In the sky above the main figure there were three separate assemblies of teachers. The teaching lineage of the tantric empowerments and practices constituted the central group. On the main figure's right there was the "Lineage of the Vast Conduct" (rgya chen spyod brgyud), the lineage of the Yogacāra Mahāyāna descending from Maitreyanātha and Asaṅga. On the other side was the "Lineage of the Profound View" (zab mo lta brgyud), the Madhyamaka tradition coming down through Mañjuśrī and Nāgārjuna.

At the bottom of the composition, beneath the great lotus seat, there existed lesser deities who were not refuges, such as the four great guardian kings, the great worldly gods Brahma and Indra, and a number of goddesses making offerings. Finally, to indicate the relationship of a practitioner to this vast assembly, a monk was often depicted in a lower corner making a symbolical offering of the universe and its contents in the form of a maṇḍala.

Tibetan astrological diagram.

Vajrasattva maṇḍala. Victoria and Albert Museum.

One of several narrative paintings in a series depicting episodes in the life of Buddha
Śākyamuni. Victoria and Albert Museum.

Amitābha in Sukhāvatī, with a retinue of eight boddhisattvas and other deities. Victoria and Albert Museum.

Padmasambhava in his pure realm. Victoria and Albert Museum.

The King of Śambhala. The foreground shows the overthrow of the 'Barbarians' *(Kla Klo)*
and their asura protectors, as predicted in the *Kālacakra Tantra*. The land of Śambhala is
depicted in the upper left. Victoria and Albert Museum Royal Loan reproduced by
Gracious Permission of Her Majesty the Queen.

33

Repetitive design with Amitāyus as the repeated theme. Victoria and Albert Museum.

Gelugpa assembly field. Han-Shan Tang Ltd.

A composition with asymmetrical balance. Subhūti, one of the Buddha's greatest
disciples, is shown subduing the nāgas. Victoria and Albert Museum.

36

Thangka illustrating the placement of the main figure (Cittaviśrāmaṇa Avalokiteśvara) in the centre with other figures (the eight boddhisattvas) arranged around him in symmetrical balance. Victoria and Albert Museum, Royal Loan reproduced by Gracious Permission of Her Majesty the Queen.

Blockprint of the universe in the form of a maṇḍala. At the centre is Sumeru, the king of mountains. Our world Jambudvīpa is the main continent to the right.

The Wheel of Existence *(srid pa'i 'khor lo)*

Principles of Composition in Individually Designed Thangkas

In some of the established groupings that consisted of a main figure with a retinue, such as maṇḍalas and assembly fields, not only were the identities of the figures determined but their placement within the composition also was rigidly controlled by textual prescription or traditional usage. In certain other fixed-grouping paintings, however, the artist himself could determine the placement of some of the figures, and to some extent he could add to or improvise with the layout. Yet even where such compositional leeway existed, the artist's sketch was still guided by certain general principles of composition. Such principles were almost universal within Tibetan religious art, and they are the very principles that we must spell out when describing how a painter could sketch a grouping of deities that he had never seen before.

Many of the thangkas that we have seen painted were begun merely on the basis of a list of the deities that the patron desired to be portrayed (such chosen deities were called 'dod lha).[5] The artist's first task was to arrange those figures on the painting surface. What principles guided his work at this time?

To begin with, most rten thangkas contained one main figure and a number of lesser ones. To indicate the relationship between the figures the artist employed both size and placement. The most important figure was the largest and was painted in a central position, usually exactly upon the central vertical axis of the composition.

The next prominent principle of layout had to do with the lesser figures; they were usually placed in symmetrical balance around the main figure, commonly above, below and on both sides of it, depending on the number of figures involved. Certain compositions called for asymmetrical balance, with the main figure drawn in a superior size but positioned to the right or left of the central axis, with the face in partial profile. However, most Central Tibetan painters used this sort of composition only when executing those for which established models such as famous block-prints existed.

Another important principle of composition in Tibetan painting was that of hierarchical arrangement. This principle was not evident in every rten thangka, but it was very important for the painter when he designed a new composition. In a painting that depicted a number of smaller figures in the background, such as gurus, yi-dam deities, Buddhas and protectors, these figures were not only arranged in a symmetrical pattern around the central figure, but were generally grouped according to class — each class occupying a relatively higher or lower position within the composition.

In a multiple-figure composition whose "retinue" included depictions of gurus from the transmission lineage (brgyud pa'i bla ma), these figures traditionally occupied the highest elevations in the painting. Often at the top center there was depicted the ultimate and primordial teacher: Vajradhara in the new-translation-era (gsar ma pa) tantric cycles, and Samantabhadra in the old (rnying ma pa). Similarly, the lord of the Tathāgata family (rigs bdag) of the main figure occupied this position in some compositions, as when Amitābha was placed above the main figure of Avalokiteśvara. When a painter depicted many gurus or all of the teachers in the lineage, he would usually place these figures in a descending chronological sequence. He would begin first at the top center of the painting, arranging the figures in two series sloping down and away from the top center and then down both sides of the painting. The temporal sequence of the figures at the top was center, its right, its left, second right, second left, and so on. In an elaborate composition with many figures of different classes, the next stratum below the gurus could be occupied by yi-dams and by Buddhas who were not conceived of as gurus of that particular lineage. (As mentioned above, a Buddha could also be depicted at the top as the originator of the lineage). Finally, the major and minor protectors of the lineage were placed on the bottom levels.

The system of hierarchical stratification only operated in a relative way, that is, only among the figures actually present within the composition, excluding the main figure. If no gurus were depicted, for instance, the next appropriate class could occupy the highest stratum. If no class but protectors was depicted, even they could be painted in the highest positions.

Although a few established compositional types did not follow the above principle, such stratification was typical of complex thangkas of "desired deities" ('dod lha) that the painter had to design for a patron. At the very least the painter almost invariably placed gurus above, and protectors below, other types of figures.

This sort of hierarchical stratification was reflected in the composition of the "assembly fields" described above. It also appeared in certain visualizations codified by ritual texts, and it was followed in other spheres of Tibetan Buddhist religious activity as well. The Venerable Dezhung Rinpoche pointed out to us that the ordering of the lesser figures in the background of a thangka (i.e. the figures apart from the main, central figure) corresponded to the order in which the same classes of deities were addressed with benedictions (bkra shis) in the chanting of religious assemblies. The traditional sequence was as follows:

1) Gurus
2) Yi-dams
3) Buddhas
4) Bodhisattvas
5) Ḍāka and Ḍākinī
6) Dharmapāla
7) Yakṣa (gnod sbyin)
8) Gods of wealth (nor lha)
9) Lesser deities (Mahānāga, gter-bdag, etc.)

A learned lama was quick to notice when the deities were placed out of order, whether in the liturgy chanted in the temples or in a thangka. We once heard a Sa-skya-pa scholar criticize the composition of a recent painting where the artist had wrongly placed the yi-dam Hevajra above some of the gurus of the Sa-skya-pa lineage. As he reminded us, the preeminence of the guru over the yi-dam is an important point that one also finds in biographical literature, for example in the life of Marpa the Translator (1012-1099) when the great Indian siddha Naropa projected the form of the yi-dam and asked Marpa to whom he would bow, to the yi-dam or to the guru himself. A similar episode also occurred in a dream that Rje-btsun Grags-pa-rgyal-mtshan (1147-1216) had of his father Sa-chen Kun-dga'-snying-po (1092-1158).[6]

It bears repeating that the principle of hierarchy did not govern all compositions. In thangkas depicting teachers or great yogic adepts (mahāsiddhas), yi-dams were sometimes placed above and before them in the sky, as if appearing there in a vision. (But here the yi-dam was usually painted on a smaller scale.) Also, for aesthetic reasons such as balance and equal distribution some artists placed members of different classes on the same level of the painting (although the relative status of the deities could still be shown by putting one deity outside and a little below the other). Furthermore, a few painters were ignorant of these precise hierarchical conventions. Nevertheless most knew in general that they should put such figures as Buddhas and teachers above, and wrathful figures below.

Didactic Paintings

Didactic paintings express through a pictorial medium some aspects of Buddhist doctrine. In a sense even a didactic painting was a *rten*, being a receptacle or embodiment of religious truth. Typical examples include those that illustrate the arrangement of the physical universe as taught in the *Abhidharma*, the layout of the animate universe in the form of the Wheel of Existence *(srid pa'i 'khor lo)*, illustrations of monastic garb, implements and practices as taught in the *Vinaya*, and illustrations of meditative postures and states. We could even include some medical and astrological paintings within this class of religious art because they too often grew out of scriptures held by tradition to be the word of the Buddha.

Another related group of paintings represented Buddhist teachings or themes through the more indirect means of symbols. The eight-spoked wheel of Dharma and other such symbols were the earliest manifestations of Buddhist art in India. When Buddhism spread to Tibet many centuries later, such symbolical representations were also introduced. The depictions of certain auspicious symbols still common in Tibetan wall paintings are a continuation of this tradition.

A more complex symbolical composition is the "Mongol Leading the Tiger" *(sog po stag 'khrid)* which represented the three great Mahāyāna bodhisattvas Avalokiteśvara, Mañjuśrī and Vajrapāṇi in the form of the Mongol, the tiger and the chain connecting them. Some versions symbolize the suppression of the four

Emblem of Manjusrī.

'Mongol leading the Tiger', drawing by Wangdrak.

Māras by two rabbits placed beneath the paws of the tiger and two small men being trodden down by the Mongol. Another famous symbolic painting was the "Emblem of Mañjuśri" *(jam dpal phyag mtshan ri mo*, sometimes also referred to as *Sdom brtson dam pa)*, originally painted on one of the walls of the Samye complex by Sa-skya Pandita (1182-1251/2). The detailed symbolism of this painting included the representation of the great king Khri-srong-lde'u-btsan by a flaming sword, Padmasambhava by a lotus, the two great Indian masters Kamalaśila and Śāntarakṣita by the two-headed yellow water fowl, and the great translators Ska-ba Dpal-brtsegs and Cog-ro Klu'i-rgyal-mtshan by a two-headed green parrot.[7] The lake beneath the lotus was said to have been meant as an antidote to the danger of fire that plagued Samye. Although symbolic representations seldom constituted the main content of a thangka, they could be important elements in them. Within the painting of the 'Wheel of Existence' for example, the three primary emotional poisons (confusion, desire and hatred) were represented by a black pig, red rooster and a green snake. Impermanence was symbolized by the Lord of Death, Yama, clutching the wheel in his clawed hands, feet and teeth, and the twelve links of interdependent origination were pictorially represented in the outer rim of the wheel by various people and animals in different poses.

Individual Artistic Expression

Within the general framework of compositional types and principles of design, the painter depicted most of the particular elements in his paintings in ways that were governed either by canonical authority or by strong artistic tradition. Indeed, there was very little place in the painting for individual, original creation. When a master painter began a given painting he had very probably painted many similar works in the past. Even if some of the figures were new to him, he had almost certainly executed similar compositions scores of times. For most painters layout and composition were basically a matter of inserting the specific elements of a new commission into one of their familiar compositional formulas.

Originality of conception was thus not required. For most artists it was enough to adhere to the paradigms and practices that they had learned from their own teacher. The main chance for an artist to express his own sensibilities was in the decorative parts of the painting, such as the landscape and the details of ornamentation. Even there, however, his treatment often became stereotyped. Sometimes he continued to reproduce these details in the very way that he had originally learned them as a novice. In extreme cases the art of painting was reduced to faithful copying, "composition" consisting of nothing more than the exact reproduction of someone else's original by tracing or pouncing, and every step of the painting from start to finish being just a mechanical repetition of motions expended on innumerable paintings before. Although some Westerners find this aspect of Tibetan painting strange and even a little repugnant, such close adherence by the artist to his tradition guaranteed the continuity and religious authenticity of Tibetan art.

Yet even with the prevailing limitations on individual expression a few master artists were more than mere copiers and craftsmen, and in their work one gets glimpses of the creativity and imagination possible within the tradition. Painters could express a creative bent most obviously in the types of composition that gave them more room to improvise, such as certain biographical or narrative paintings. And even within the set formal compositions there existed chances for an artist to display his particular gifts, for example in the treatment of landscapes and miniature details. Any artist who had the basic skills and knowledge and in addition possessed a flair for fine depictions of facial features and other details could easily attract a surplus of commissions. The most skilled of such artists, those who could transform an ordinary composition into something vibrant and extraordinary, were always in demand. As their fame spread far and wide such gifted painters sometimes even acquired the reputation of being "divinely emanated artisans" *(sprul pa'i lha bzo)*.

Notes

1. One authority who classified temples as *sku rten* was Bo-dong Paṇ-chen. See his *Rten gsum bzhengs tshul bstan bcos lugs bshad pa, Collected Works*, vol.2, p.332.5.

2. See also Gerasimova, "Compositional Structure", p.48.

3. The classifications "refuge tree" and "assembly field" are not mutually exclusive. Here they have been distinguished merely on formal grounds. Refuge trees can function as assembly fields, and *vice versa.* Refuge trees for instance are "assembly fields to which one goes for refuge" *(skyabs su 'gro ba'i tshogs zhing).*

4. We have seen a photograph of a rare Sa-skya-pa *tshogs zhing*, painted by the father of Legdrup Gyatsho at 'Phen-po Nalendra. The central figure was Sa-skya Paṇḍita. Refuge-tree paintings were also relatively uncommon among the Sa-skya-pa in Tibet, although the visualization itself was standard.

5. The term *'dod lha* ("desired deity" or "chosen deity") for deities placed in a thangka according to individual preference is also attested in Tibetan literature. See for example Zhu-chen Tshul-khrims-rin-chen, *Chos smra ba'i bande tshul khrims rin chen du bod pa'i skye ba phal pa'i rkang 'thung dge sdig 'dres ma'i las kyi yal ga phan tshun du 'dzings par bde sdug gi lo 'dab dus kyi rgyal mos res mos su bsgyur ba. The Autobiography of Tshul-khrims-rin-chen of Sde-dge and Other of His Selected Writings* (New Delhi, 1971), pp.331.4.; 546.2.

6. An early thangka that was not in exact agreement with the hierarchical ordering outlined above is described in a biographical sketch of Nag-tsho lo-tsā-ba Tshul-khrims-rgyal-ba (fl. 11th century). See Khetsun Sangpo, *Biographical Dictionary of Tibet* (Dharamsala, 1973-), vol.5, p.9. The story is related of how Nag-tsho lo-tsā-ba commissioned an Indian master painter named Kṛṣṇa to paint a large thangka with Jo-bo-rje Atiśa as its main figure. According to this account, at the top of the thangka the yi-dams of Atiśa were portrayed, and beneath them were painted Atiśa's twelve main gurus. The image of Atiśa himself was in the center, with an attendant depicted both to his right and to his left. On the outer right and left edges the painter portrayed the main events in Atiśa's life. Beneath the great master were painted the major Tibetan disciples of Atiśa, including Khu, 'Brom and Rngog, all shown as if studying in a religious school. Finally, beneath all of them, Nag-tsho lo-tsā-ba himself was pictured in a pose of reverent supplication.

7. The description of this design given in our English caption in Chogay Trichen, Thubten Legshay Gyatsho, *Gateway to the Temple* (Kathmandu, 1979) p.53, contained some mistakes, here corrected.

Au Leshey using compass.

Four
Sketching and the Theory of Iconometry

Returning now to the artist at work, let us see how he actually imparted his design to the prepared thangka ground. This job involved several steps, the first of which was to lay down the main lines of orientation. Most important was the central vertical axis, for this would be the exact center of the painting around which the artist would plan the rest of the composition. As already mentioned, the vertical axis usually marked the center of the main figure, and it was in relation to this line that all the other figures were also positioned. The correct establishment of the vertical and horizontal axes was also important from a religious point of view. Thangkas being an expression of religious ideals through art, their figures — the ideal bodily forms of enlightened beings — had to be perfectly oriented in relation to the central axis. Indeed, correctness at this point was crucial since a mistake here would affect the accuracy, and hence the religious value, of the subsequent work.[1]

The Eight Major Lines of Orientation

Thus before beginning the sketch the immediate task was to determine a true vertical axis. This was followed by the establishment of a horizontal line perpendicular to it, and four outer lines for defining the edges of the rectangular painting area. Hence at this stage the artist drew a total of eight major lines: two diagonals, the vertical, the horizontal and the four outer borders.

To preserve their clean, freshly prepared ground a few artists established these lines on the back of the canvas. Later, when they began to sketch figures on the front, they could hold the canvas up to a source of light and the main horizontal and vertical lines would show through.

Diagonals

The first two of the eight "major lines" were the diagonals — lines drawn from one corner of the canvas to its diagonal opposite. These two lines enabled the establishment of the vertical and horizontal, and thus had to precede them. To lay down these lines the artist only needed a chalk line or "marking string" *(thig rkud)*. A simple and serviceable chalk line could be devised by rubbing a length of string with a little pigment powder between the palms of the hands. The chalk line of most artists, however, was a string that passed through a

powder bag *(thig rkyal)*. This bag was commonly made of leather but was sometimes sewn from cloth; the marking powder it contained was usually ochre or a mixture of ochre and charcoal. Moving the bag up and down the string loaded the string with the coloured powder. By positioning and snapping the loaded string the artist could establish a line wherever he wished. Lines thus established with dry powder and string were called "dry lines" *(skam thig)*, as opposed to "wet lines" *(rlon thig)* that were laid down with a wet marking string. Wet lines were used mainly in the painting of murals, and they had no application in thangka painting.

The marking line of Legdrup Gyatsho possessed not only a powder bag but also a pencil-sized stick that was tied to the end of the string. When using a chalk line with a stick an artist needed only two hands to hold the string in place and snap it. (Otherwise he needed the help of an assistant, or simply plucked the string with his lips. Wangdrak and others did the latter when working alone.[2]) The string had to be fastened securely to the very end of the stick, so the artist carved a notch in the end of the stick and also a groove around the circumference of the stick near its end. To fasten the string to the stick he pulled the string through the notched end, and then wrapped and tied it around the shaft within the groove that had been carved to receive it.

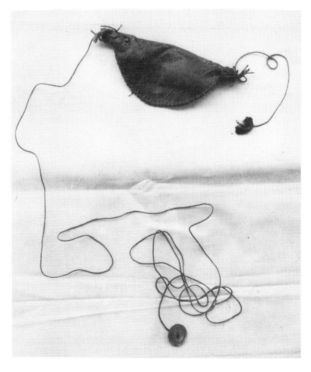

Chalk line and leather powder bag.

45

To mark the first diagonal line on the canvas using this type of marking string, Legdrup Gyatsho first placed the stick end of the string in one corner of the prepared cloth. With his right hand he held the stick with its notched end down, positioning the end of the string (and the end of the stick) in the exact corner. Next, with his left hand he stretched the string across the cloth to the diagonally opposed corner, and held it there by pressing down on it with his thumb. Then — still holding the end of the stick in place, by clasping the shaft in the palm of his right hand — he carefully lowered the top end of the stick until he could reach and pluck the string with the index finger of the same hand. The resulting snap of the string against the canvas released an imprint of coloured powder in a line along the entire length of the taut string. The artist marked the second diagonal in the same way, and in so doing he established the central point of the painting area, the intersection of the two lines.

Wangdrak using a marking line.

Vertical and Horizontal Axes

Next the artist determined the vertical and horizontal axes. As above, he used a marking line, but he could also use a compass *(skor thig)*. Two main types of compass were used in Tibetan art. The first, which was used for drawing small circles, was similar to the simple metal compass common in the West: two wooden or metal

pieces connected by a hinge, with one leg sharply pointed and the other having some provision for holding a charcoal crayon. The second common type of compass described by our informants was the "board compass" *(skor pang)*. This was used by artists from many parts of Tibet for drawing large circles. The board compass was made from two pieces of wood: one long slat and a smaller, pointed block. The pointed piece had a hole in it through which the slat was passed. The point on the small block determined the center of the circle or arc, while the drawing was done with a charcoal pencil fixed in the end of the long thin slat. The charcoal was stationary; different radii were achieved by moving the small pointed block up and down the stick. Once in place, the block was secured by inserting a thin wooden wedge into the hole between the block and the long slat.

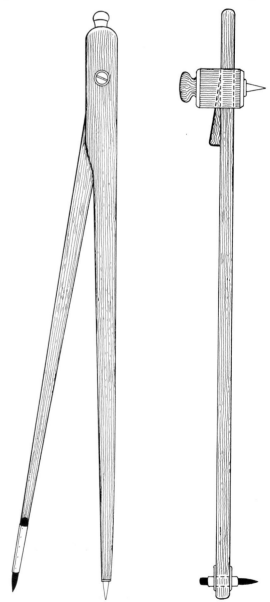

Two forms of compass.

To establish the vertical axis *(tshangs thig)*, the artist began by determining four points on the diagonal lines that were equidistant from the intersection of the lines. This was done with either a ruler or compass.

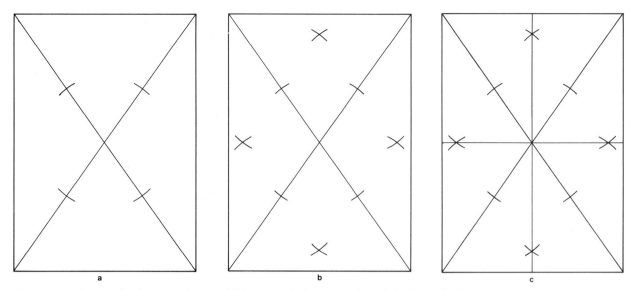

Sequence of steps leading to the establishment of the vertical and horizontal axes.
a) Lay down diagonals, then find points equidistant from the intersection, b) Draw eight
arcs, two in each of the four areas created by the diagonals, using the four points established above as the centres, c) Connect the intersection of the arcs with the intersection
of the diagonals.

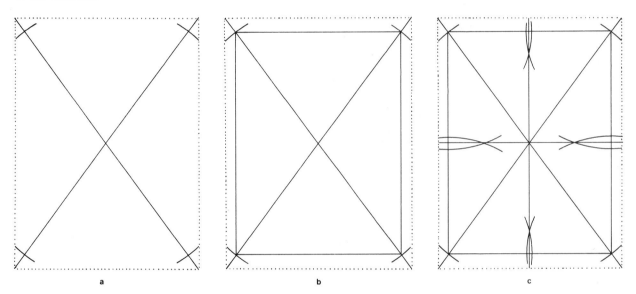

Alternative methods for establishing the outer borders and vertical axis: a) Lay down the
diagonals and find points equidistant from the intersection of the diagonals, b) Connect
those four points, c) To establish the vertical axis, find points halfway on both bottom
and top borders, then connect these through the intersection of the diagonal lines.

Next — and here a compass was helpful — the artist
drew eight arcs of the same radius in the empty quad-
rants between the diagonals, using each of the four
equidistant points as the focus of two arcs. Each pair of
arcs drawn in the same quadrant had to intersect. Then,
by connecting these points of intersection with the
center point of the canvas using a chalk line, the artist
established the horizontal and vertical axes.[3]

The Four Borders

The last four of the eight major lines, the outside
borders, were easy to establish. The painter first determined points on the diagonals near the corners of the
cloth which were equidistant from the intersection of

the diagonals, leaving enough cloth on the edge for the
later mounting of the painting within a brocade frame.
Then he connected these points with the chalk line to
form lines running parallel to the vertical and horizontal.
Although some artists first established the diagonals,
verticals and horizontals on the back of the canvas,
there was no reason not to draw the four borders on
the front, since these established the actual area to be
painted. If two compositions were to be executed on the
same canvas, the artist had to establish the borders of
each composition as well as the vertical axis within each
composition. Again he had to set aside enough of an
edge on all sides of each composition so that a brocade
frame could be easily stitched to it after its completion.

The Sketch

Once the painting surface had been determined and its central axis established, the painter began the actual work of sketching. When the painting was a simple and commonplace composition, such as a single Buddha or Tārā or the three deities of longevity *(tshe lha rnam gsum)*, an artist might already possess a completed drawing. In that case no sketch *(skya ris)* as such would be needed since he could transfer the design to the canvas by other means. But when he had no ready-made drawing or block-print of the required subject he had to sketch a new composition. At this point, if the patron had not been specific about the placement of the main figures, the artist had to decide this himself, either relying on his own knowledge or in consultation with a more learned person. On the other hand, if the configuration of the deities had been exactly dictated to him, he could proceed to sketch a new composition within those limits.

define its area the artist needed merely to draw the figure so that it filled most of the foreground. Thangkas with more than one figure generally required, as we have seen, the allocation of greater or smaller areas to the various figures depending on the hierarchy of importance within that particular composition.

The artist Wangdrak first divided up his painting surface by drawing larger or smaller egg-shaped ovals where the deities were to be located. By describing a large oval in the center astride the vertical axis he established the area of the main figure, including its seat and nimbus or surrounding flames. Then, to fill in the rest of the area to the best advantage, he drew smaller ovals for the lesser figures surrounding the main deity. He almost invariably arranged the deities of the "retinue" in a symmetrical design centered on the main image. Finally, after the places of all the deities had been established, he indicated the horizon and the general layout of the landscape with a few brief lines.

Completed drawing of Vajrasattva by Legdrup Gyatsho for use by his students.

Preliminary Division of Space

In a complex thangka the artist began the composition following principles that are by now familiar. He first determined the area that the main figure, together with its body nimbus and seat, would occupy in the foreground. This figure was usually placed in the middle of the painting area, exactly centered on the vertical axis. The exact position of the central figure relative to the horizontal axis, however, was not fixed. It could be placed higher or lower depending on the other elements in the overall composition. In the case of the simplest thangkas the central figure was the only figure, and to

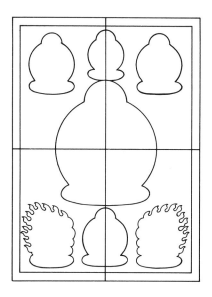

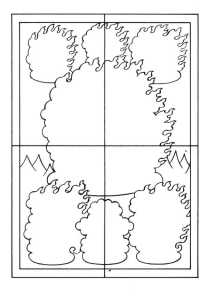

Examples of the preliminary division of space. Three scales of measurement are used here for the figures. Note how the flames are shaped to fill out empty spaces.

These and the subsequent steps of sketching will be described below in more detail, following an account of the other tools and techniques involved.

Charcoal *(sol ba)*

For his preliminary sketches a Tibetan painter traditionally used charcoal crayons. A sketch made in charcoal *(sol ris)* was easy to rub off, and this was both an asset and a drawback; mistakes could be easily erased by rubbing the sketch lightly, but any accidental brushing against the canvas with the hand or sleeve would inadvertently erase part of the finished sketch. To compensate for this, an artist when sketching generally worked from top to bottom, after first sketching the central figure. Some painters when sketching wore a small leather sheath over the little finger of their drawing hand. In addition to protecting the finger when sketching on rough surfaces, this leather sheath acted as an eraser; the artist could brush off any mistakes in the sketch with a few quick flicks of his little finger.

Many Tibetan painters used to make their own charcoal crayons. They mainly used willow *(lcang ma)* wood, often splitting and whittling down large pieces of it. In areas where willow was scarce, tamarisk *(spen ma)* twigs were used in its place. Larger sizes were prepared for sketching murals, while thin sticks were best for thangka painting and other detailed applications.

To make the raw sticks into charcoal the artist roasted them in a hot bed of coals in the absence of air. For this some artists first packed the sticks tightly into an almost airtight metal tube (tight packing eliminated much of the potential warping). The tube, its ends sometimes sealed with clay, was then put into a bed of coals and heated for two hours or more, depending on the heat of the fire. After the correct amount of heating the wood became transformed into light-weight charcoal sticks that made a "ting" sound when dropped onto a solid surface. These could be sharpened and used immediately.

Other artists used even simpler techniques for making charcoal crayons. Some merely packed a bundle of willow twigs in clay, and when the clay had dried they placed the mass into a bed of coals. This method is still used in parts of the Nepal Himalayas. Wangdrak (like several others) used to begin by wrapping a bundle of willow sticks in paper and string. Then he prepared his hot bed of coals, digging a trough in its center and packing down the edges. Next he laid the bundle of sticks in the trough, and then covered it with coals which he firmly tamped down. Smoke seeping out was a warning that air was reaching the twigs and thus allowing their oxidation and destruction. To prevent this he would pour a little fine dirt into the hole from which the smoke was emerging, until no more was visible. Then after about two or three hours he carefully dug out the bundle and deposited it in a soft bed of earth he had prepared nearby. After covering the blackened bundle with a layer of light earth he allowed it to cool.

Such charcoal was an ideal medium for sketching most parts of the thangka. Nowadays, however, many painters have abandoned home-made charcoal crayons, and use Western-style graphite pencils exclusively.

Sketching Individual Figures

To sketch the figures in a thangka the painter needed an exact knowledge of the measurements and proportions *(thig tshad)* of each deity as established by Buddhist iconometry and artistic practice. The pantheon of Tibetan Buddhism has literally hundreds of different deities, and no master painter could know all their proportions, configurations and characteristics. Still, he had to be familiar with the main iconometric classes into which the pantheon was divided, and he had to be able to apply this knowledge correctly to the individual deities that he painted.

An important part of every novice's training was the time spent under the guidance of a teacher, repeatedly copying examples of Buddhas and bodhisattvas. When doing so, the student was required first to construct a grid of exactly positioned lines *(thig khang)*, and then to draw within it the sacred figure. Through the endless repetition of these actions, the proportions and shapes of each major figure became firmly impressed upon his mind so that later he could construct perfectly proportioned figures with only a minimum of guidelines and measures. After the painter had mastered the basic proportions he could apply this knowledge by analogy to unfamiliar deities, once he had determined their iconometric class.

Pencil sketch of Padmasambhava by Wangdrak.

Iconometric Theory

Tibetan authorities on sacred art generally divided the deities of the pantheon into less than a dozen iconometric classes. There was, however, no agreement as to the exact number of these. Bu-ston Rin-chen-grub (1290-1364) and the Eighth Karma-pa Mi-bskyod-rdo-rje (1507-1554) are said to have propounded systems containing eleven main classes.[4] 'Phreng-kha-ba (16th century) and the more recent Mi-pham-rgya-mtsho (1846-1912) reduced the number of basic classes in their systems to five,[5] while Klong-rdol-bla-ma (b.1719) kept the number to a bare minimum of four.[6] In the following pages we will describe the basic system of iconometry that our main informants accepted. This system is said to derive from the practice of the great 15th-century artist Sman-thang-pa Sman-bla-don-grub, and it consists of six main classes of proportions, five for deities and one for humans.

Units of Measurement

The study of iconometry presupposes, to begin with, a knowledge of the terms for units of measure. The same specialized terminology was used by all Tibetan writers on iconometry. In brief, there were two main units of measure: small units *(cha chung)* and large units *(cha chen)*. Except in one special proportional class there were always twelve small units to every large unit. The relationship between the two was thus the same as inches to feet, but it is important to realize that unlike inches and feet the large and small units had no absolute values. They were merely used to indicate the proportional relationships *within* each sacred image, be that image one hundred feet tall or the size of a grain of rice.

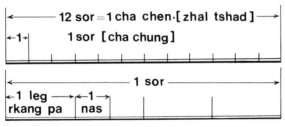

Scale of the units of measurement.

The terminology for measures was a little complicated because many synonyms existed for the two main units of measure. Most of the terms are anthropometric in origin. The larger unit *(cha chen)* was also called "face measure" *(zhal tshad)* or "face" *(zhal; gdong)*, "span" *(mtho*, meaning the distance from the end of the extended thumb to the tip of the middle finger), and "palm" *(thal mo; mthil*, the length of the palm and fingers of the hand). The smaller unit *(cha chung* or *cha phran)* was more commonly referred to as a "finger-width" *(sor mo*, or if abbreviated, *sor)*. One-fourth of a *sor mo* was called a "leg" *(rkang pa)*, and a half of that was termed a "grain" *(nas)*. In addition, Buddhist

iconometry sometimes also made use of the cubit *(gru mo)* as a unit of measure or proportion, and this was the distance from the elbow to the knuckles of a closed fist (equal to two large units).

The Main Proportional Classes

Probably the most influential treatise written on proportions by a Tibetan was the *Sku gzugs kyi cha tshad kyi rab tu byed pa yid bzhin nor bu* of Sman-thang-pa Sman-bla-don-grub (fl. 15th century).[7] Although the work itself has not been accessible in recent years, it was one of the main sources for two short passages on iconometry by the 18th-century scholar and painter Zhu-chen Tshul-khrims-rin-chen. In these passages we find a description of what appears to have been the six major proportional classes *(thig chen)* of Sman-thang-pa.[8]

1) Buddhas, 125 *sor* (= 10 *thal mo* of 12½ *sor* each).
2) Peaceful bodhisattvas, 120 *sor* (= 10 *thal mo* of 12 *sor* each).
3) Goddesses, 108 *sor* (= 9 *thal mo*).
4) Tall wrathful figures, such as the bodhisattva Vajrapāṇi, 96 *sor* (= 8 *thal mo*).
5) Short wrathful figures, 72 *sor* (= 6 *thal mo*, although some texts specify 5 *thal mo*).
6) Humans, including some Śrāvakas (disciples of the Buddha) and Pratyekabuddhas, 96 *sor* tall (= 4 cubits, although the canonical texts specify a height of 3½ cubits).

In the first three classes the height of the figure equals the arm span, and the measure of the upper half of the body equals that of the lower half. But in the case of the wrathful figures and humans such balanced proportions are not present to the same extent.

Some other iconographical systems had more "major classes," due to the subdividing of the above classes and the addition of a few rare types. However, except for a few minor additions or differences, the iconometric system of our Central Tibetan informants was as outlined above. It may be useful to describe here these six classes in more detail according to a parallel iconometric tradition that was followed by Legdrup Gyatsho of Phen-yul Nalendra. The following description of the proportions is drawn mainly from the *Gateway to the Temple* by the Venerable Chogay Trichen and represents a modern tradition descending from Sman-thang-pa.[9]

1) Buddhas

This first major class included the basic proportions of Buddhas, whether manifest in the world as "emanation-bodies" (nirmāṇakāya) such as Śākyamuni, or in the pure realms as "enjoyment-bodies" (sambhoga-kāya) such as Vairocana and the other Tathāgatas of the maṇḍala. Sometimes the ultimate realization or "Dharma-body" (dharmakāya) of the Buddha was also said to be represented in paintings, for instance in the form of Samantabhadra in some Rnying-ma-pa cycles. The usual representation of the dharmakāya, however, was the stūpa.[10] As mentioned before, the latter was considered to be the "mind-support" or "mind-receptacle" *(thugs rten)* of the Buddhas, as opposed to the "speech-support" *(gsung rten,* the scriptures containing the enlightened word) and the "body-support" *(sku rten,* mainly physical depictions of enlightened beings in painted or sculpted form).

The Standing Buddha

The proportions of the standing Buddha are as follows:

Vertical measures

head protuberance *(uṣṇiṣa)*	4
top of skull to hair line	4½
hair line to ūrṇā	4
ūrṇā to tip of nose	4
tip of nose to chin	4½
neck	4
chest	12½
stomach	12½
lower abdomen	12½
hips	4
thighs	25
knees	4
calves	25
feet	4½

Horizontal measures (one side of the body, including extended arm)

spine to armpit	12½
armpit to elbow	20
elbow joint	1
forearm	16
wrist	1
hand	12
one side	62½
full arm span:	125 *sor*

The Seated Buddha: Grid Construction

The above measures also establish most of the lines in the iconometric grid that novice artists used as the basis for their sketches. Because some additional lines were needed in the grid, certain iconometric manuals also specified the exact number of lines and the intervals between each pair of lines in the grid. The following is from the grid of a seated Buddha as drawn by Legdrup Gyatsho:[11]

Intervals between horizontal lines:

crest jewel *(nor tog)*	2
head protuberance *(uṣṇiṣa)*	4
top of skull to hair line	4½
face	12½
neck	4
chest	12½
stomach	12½
side of hip	4½
thigh to pubic zone	8
junction of crossed legs	4
lower extension of knees	4
lunar-disc seat	6
lotus seat	12

There were thus a total of twelve horizontal lines for the body grid, and two additional lines for the lunar disc and lotus seat below.

Intervals between vertical lines:

A total of nine vertical lines were laid down, and from right to left these appeared at the following intervals: 8 *sor,* 2 *sor,* 4 *sor,* 12½ *sor,* 12½ *sor,* 4 *sor,* 2 *sor* and 8 *sor.* The distance from the central vertical axis to the first lines on either side is the breadth of the chest, i.e. from the spine to the armpit. The interval between the next two lines (a total of 6 *sor*) brings one to the outer edge of the shoulder. Finally, the outer lines indicate the edge of the knees.

Differences between Nirmāṇakāya and Sambhogakāya depictions.

Buddhas in the Nirmāṇakāya form were painted with the above proportions, and they were depicted in the garb of a fully ordained monk (bhikṣu). The Sambhogakāya manifestations, on the other hand, wore the clothing and ornaments of the Universal Emperor (cakravartin), and had slightly different measures because of their different style of hair. The uṣṇiṣa head protuberance of the Tathāgatas of the maṇḍala and of certain yi-dam deities was bound up within a large top-knot of hair. Therefore the uṣṇiṣa itself was not counted as having a separate measure. Some systems assigned to the top-knot a measure of one large unit (12½ *sor*) or even 15 *sor.* In the tradition of Legdrup Gyatsho, however, these were considered too long, and instead the top-knot was given a length of 8 *sor,* the crest jewel above it 3 *sor,* and the jewel diadem in front of the top-knot 6 *sor.*[12]

Many of the great male yi-dam deities of a slightly wrathful aspect such as Kālacakra, Cakrasaṃvara and Hevajra also belonged to this same basic class since they are considered to be Sambhogakāya manifestations of Buddhahood. Finally, tantric gurus were also drawn with the same proportions as a Buddha, according to a widespread tradition that was thought to have originated with 'Bri-gung skyob-pa 'Jig-rten-mgon-po.[13]

2) Peaceful Bodhisattvas

The main members of the second class were bodhisattvas who possessed peaceful appearances, such as Mañjuśrī and Avalokiteśvara. The porportions of this class were exactly the same as those of the Nirmāṇakāya Buddhas, except that ½ sor was subtracted from each large unit of measure. The total height and arm span of such figures was thus 10 large measures of 12 sor each, or 120 sor.

Vertical measures:

head protuberance	4
top of skull to hair line	4
face	12
neck	4
chest	12
stomach	12
lower abdomen	12
hips	4
thighs	24
knees	4
calves	24
feet	4
	120 sor

Horizontal measures (half of the arm span):[14]

chest	12
upper arm	20
forearm	16
hand	12
	60
Full arm span:	120 sor

More detailed proportions had to be specified for bodhisattvas with complicated forms, such as the thousand-armed Avalokiteśvara.

3) Goddesses

Within the third main class were included the famous peaceful goddesses such as Tārā, Prajñāpāramitā and Sarasvatī, as well as semi-wrathful yoginīs such as Vajravārāhī, Na-ro mkha'-spyod-ma, and the consorts of various male yi-dams. According to some sources, peaceful male gods of the mundane sphere such as Indra and Viṣṇu also belong to this class. The proportions of these goddesses and gods are similar to those found in the first two classes, but with a few important subtractions that bring the total body length to 9 large units of 12 sor each, or 108 sor total.

Vertical measures:

top of skull to hair line	3
face	12
neck	3
chest	12
stomach	12
lower abdomen	12
hips	4

thighs	22
knees	3
calves	22
feet	3
	108 sor

Horizontal measures (half of the arm span):[15]

chest	10
upper arm	18
forearm	14
hand	12
	54
full arm span:	108 sor

The tantric goddesses such as Vajravārāhī, when depicted in a standing posture, had an actual height of less than 108 sor from the soles of the feet to the hairline. This was because some height was lost due to the bent knees, tilted head and bent torso of the figure in contrapposto ('gying).

4) Tall Wrathful Beings

This fourth main class includes the wrathful bodhisattva Vajrapāṇi, and other figures belonging to the angry Yakṣa *(gnod sbyin)* or Yama class. The class measures 8 spans in height and arm span, although due to their proud, aggressive posture the length of the vertical axis from the feet to the hairline is only 6 spans:

Vertical measures:

hair	12
face	12
neck	4
torso	36
knees	4
calves	12
feet	4
seat	12
	96 sor

Theoretically, however, if the figure stood erect it would measure 8 spans from the hairline to the feet:

face	12
neck	4
torso	36
thighs	18
knees	4
calves	18
feet	4
	96 sor

In actual practice the thighs occupy the same vertical area as the lower abdomen (here covered by a distended belly), and the vertical length of the calves is shortened by their slanted position.

Horizontal measures (half of the arm span):

chest	12

upper arm	12
forearm	12
hand	12
	48
full arm span:	96 sor

5) Short Wrathful Figures

This class actually consists of two slightly different sub-classes. The first of these sub-classes can have a height of either 5 or 6 spans, depending on whether one includes or excludes such areas as the lower abdomen and hair. The first sub-class is composed of short protectors such as Pañcaranātha (Gur-gyi-mgon-po).

Vertical measures:

hair	12
face	12
neck	4
chest	12
stomach	12
thighs	8
calves	8
feet	4
	72 sor

An alternative measure is given for figures such as Gaṇapati *(tshogs bdag)* (although in Zhu-chen Tshul-khrims-rin-chen's account the following proportions also hold good for Pañcaranātha and the like):[16]

cranium above hairline	3
face	12
neck	3
chest	12
upper abdomen	12
thighs	12
knees	3
calves	12
feet	3
	72 sor

In the above proportions no separate measure is given for the lower abdomen, which occupies the same segment of the vertical axis as the thighs. The arm span of this fifth class is given by Zhu-chen as follows (here for only one side of the body):[17]

chest	12
upper arm	6
forearm	12
hand	12
	42
full arm span:	84 sor

6) Humans

This class is made up of Śrāvakas (the early human disciples of the Buddha Śākyamuni and the followers of the Śrāvakayāna), Pratyekabuddhas, and ordinary human beings. A tantric commentary proclaims that ordinary humans should measure 3½ cubits in height and

4 cubits in arm span (= 8 spans, 96 *sor*).[18] The actual practice of many artists, however, was to portray humans as being a full 4 cubits in height, and this was the tradition of Legdrup Gyatsho as recorded in *Gateway to the Temple:*[19]

cranium above hairline	4
face	12
neck	4 (or 2)
chest	12
stomach	12
lower abdomen	12
thighs	18
knees	3
calves	18
feet	3
	98 sor

(or 96 if the neck measures 2 *sor*)

The proportions given by Zhu-chen in this case specify a neck length of only 2 *sor*, and do not mention the alternate possibility of 4 *sor*.

It is interesting to note that in at least one other artistic tradition humans were portrayed according to their canonical description, i.e. with bodies having a height of 3½ cubits (7 spans, 84 *sor*) and an arm span of 4 cubits. The following proportions are given by Mi-pham-rgya-mtsho:[20]

Vertical measures:

face	12
neck	3
torso	27
hip	4
thighs	15
knees	4
calves	15
feet	4
	84 sor

Horizontal measures (half of the arm span):

chest	10
upper arm	14
forearm	12
hand	12
	48
full arm span:	96 sor

Thus there was a certain diversity of proportions within this class. In addition Pratyekabuddhas were said to require slightly more than the normal human height because of their small uṣṇīṣa (head protuberance).[21] Śrāvakas too were sometimes given different proportions. Zhu-chen Tshul-khrims-rin-chen mentioned that such figures are found in some authoritative paintings to have the proportions of peaceful bodhisattvas, i.e. a height of 10 spans or 120 *sor*. He also said that some texts on iconometry state that this practice is permissible.[22]

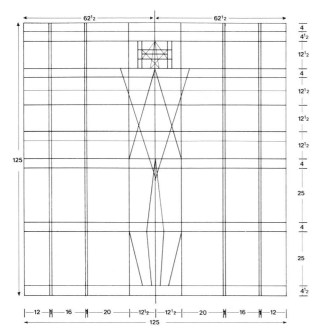

Class 1: Standing Buddha.

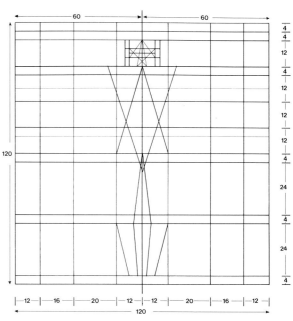

Class 2: Standing Bodhisattva.

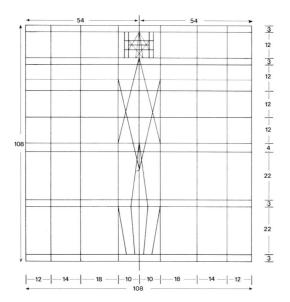

Class 3: Standing goddess.

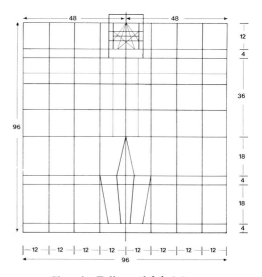

Class 4: Tall wrathful deity.

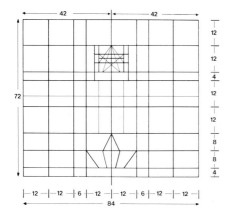

Class 5: Short wrathful deity.

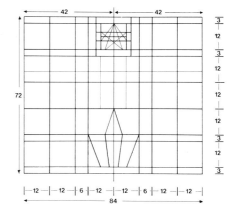

Class 5: Short wrathful deity.

54

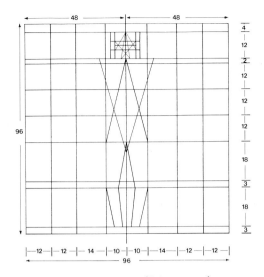

Class 6: Humans (96 measure).

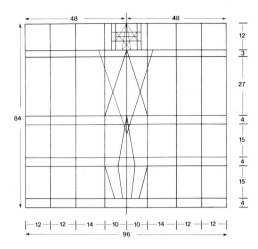

Class 6: Humans (84 measure).

Grids drawn to illustrate the theoretical proportions (heights and armspans) of the main classes of sacred figures. Different grids are used in actual practice.

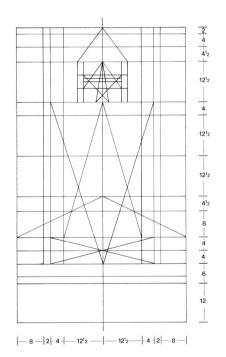

Class 1: Seated Buddha.

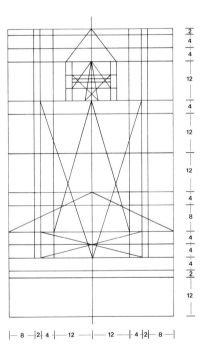

Class 2: Seated Bodhisattva.

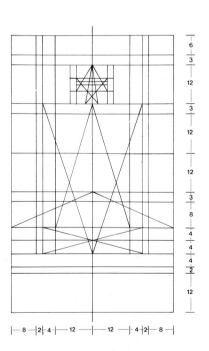

Class 3: Seated goddess.

55

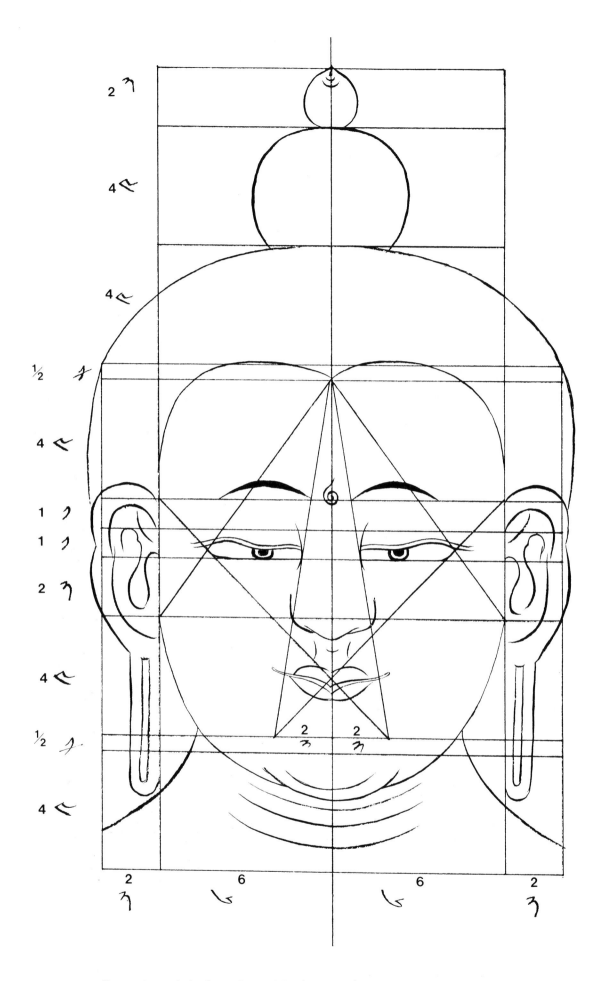

Proportions of the face of a Buddha (Wangdrak). Note that in this artist's tradition the faces are slightly larger.

Class 1: Buddhas. The Buddha Śākyamuni (Wangdrak). Note that the outer vertical lines of the body grid are drawn differently from the description in the text, though the proportions remain the same.

Class 2: Peaceful Boddhisattvas. Here Amitāyus is drawn with Boddhisattva (120-*sor*) proportions. (Wangdrak).

58

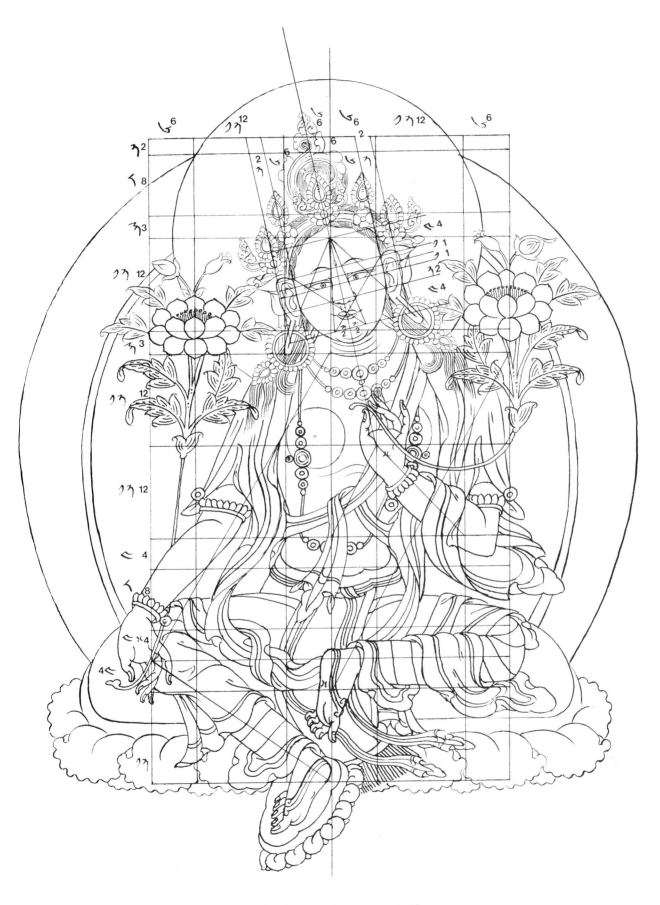

Class 3: Goddess. Tārā. (Wangdrak).

Class 4: Tall wrathful deities. Vaiśravaṇa, the god of wealth. (Wangdrak).

Class 5: Short wrathful deities. This Vajrapāni is drawn with a total height of 6 spans or 72 *sor*. It is 3 *sor* shorter than when drawn according to the proportions of Class 4 (compare the neck, knees and feet). (Wangdrak).

Class 6: Humans. A disciple of the Buddha (Śrāvaka). In this tradition these figures are depicted with basically the proportions of Class 2, peaceful Bodhisattvas. The main difference here is that there is no head protuberance and thus the total height of the standing figure would be only 116 *sor*. (Wangdrak).

Padmasambhava. (Robert Beer)

Vajravārāhī. (Robert Beer)

Vajrakīlāya. (Robert Beer)

Thousand-armed Avalokiteśvara. (Robert Beer)

Notes

1. The indigenous handbooks on art list many misfortunes that will befall the careless artist, and they describe the importance of correct orientation and proportions.

2. See also Romi Khosla, *Buddhist Monasteries in the Western Himalaya* (Kathmandu, 1979), p.130.

3. Wooden or metal compasses were not absolutely necessary since the marking line itself could be made to function as a compass. The artist Wangdrak, for example, used only his marking line to establish all of the major lines. First he established the diagonals. Then, pressing one point of the string at the intersection of the diagonals, he rubbed another point of the string beneath his thumbnail making short arcs in each corner. The equidistant points thus established were then connected with the marking string to create the four borders. Finally he established the central vertical axis by finding the half-way points of both the top and bottom borders and connecting them.

4. Dagyab, p.30. Apparently neither author's text has survived. Bu-ston's system is described in Rong-tha Blo-bzang-dam-chos-rgya-mtsho, *Thig gi lag len du ma gsal bar bshad pa bzo rig mdzes pa'i kha rgyan* (New Delhi, Byams-pa-chos-rgyal, n.d.), p.134.

5. ·Phreng-kha-ba, *Bzo rig pa'i bstan bcos mdo rgyud gsal ba'i me long* (Dharamsala, 1978), p.9.1; Mi-pham-rgya-mtsho, *Sku gzugs kyi thig rtsa rab gsal nyi ma, Collected Writings* (Gangtok, 1975), vol.9 p.3.1.

6. Klong-rdol-bla-ma Ngag-dbang-blo-bzang, *Gsung 'bum* (Mussoorie, Dalama, 1963), p.415f. Cf. Tucci, vol.1, p.299.

7. See Sman-thang-pa Sman-bla-don-grub, *Bde bar gshegs pa'i sku gzugs kyi tshad kyi rab tu byed pa yid bzhin nor bu* (Gangtok, Bla-ma Zla-ba and Sherab Gyaltsen, 1983). We are much indebted to Mr. E. G. Smith for having shown us this edition of Sman-thang-pa's treatise when the present book was in the press.

   Tucci, vol.1, p.293f. mentioned a fragment of a treatise by Sman-thang-pa: *Rdzogs pa'i sangs rgyas mchog gi sprul pa'i sku'i phyag tshad sman thang pas mdzad pa*. This is only "a part, from the seventh to tenth chapters". Tucci also mentioned there a work entitled *Bde bar gshegs pa'i sku gzugs kyi tshad kyi rab tu byed pa'i* (sic) *yid bzhin gyi nor bu* (pp.34), which we know was the title of Sman-thang-pa's great treatise. He states that the text was printed at Dga'-ldan-phun-tshogs-gling, and that the author was Dpal-blo-bzang-po. The latter name, however, is that of 'Phreng-kha-ba.

8. Zhu-chen Tshul-khrims-rin-chen, *Gtsug lag khang chos 'byung bkra shis sgo mangs rten dang brten pa ji ltar bskrun pa las brtsams pa'i gleng ba bdud rtsi'i rlabs phreng, Collected Writings* (New Delhi, 1973), Vol.7, pp.150.3-158.1. By dividing class one, the Buddhas, into two (Buddhas and yi-dams) one gets the "seven categories" of Gerasimova, "Compositional Structure", p.43f. Tucci, vol.1, pp.297-299, arrived at nine types by discerning three types of Buddhas (nirmāṇakāya, sambhogakāya and yi-dam) and two types of tall wrathful figures (his classes VI and VII).

   But in Sman-thang-pa's treatise, p.8, there are listed only *five* major proportional classes. Omitted from the list was the sixth class, humans. Later in part seven of his treatise (p.66ff.) he gave a more detailed discussion of ten topics *(don tshan)*, of which nine were the following proportions:

   1. The Buddha as Great Teacher, e.g., Śākyamuni Buddha.
   2. Sambhogakāya manifestations, such as Vairocana, and some Nirmānakāyas.
   3. Yi-dams, such as Samvara.
   4. Peaceful Bodhisattvas and Ḍākas.
   5. Goddesses, such as Vajravārahī.
   6. Great guardian deities of the worldly sphere such as Brahma and Indra.
   7. Wrathful figures such as Yakṣas and demons.
   8. Deities of dwarfed proportions such as Gaṇapati.
   9. Humans such as Śrāvakas and Pratyekabuddhas.

   The tenth topic was the sitting postures, ornaments and hand-held emblems found among the various classes of deities.

   Topics 1 through 3 belong to the first major proportional class, topic 4 equals the second major class, topic 5 equals the third major class, topics 6 and 7 equal the fourth major class, and topic 8 equals the fifth major class.

9. Chogay Trichen, pp.63-70.

10. Sde-srid Sangs-rgyas-rgya-mtsho, *Bstan bcos bai dūra dkar po las dris lan 'khrul snang g.ya' sel don gyi bzhin ras ston byed,* (Dehra Dun, 1976), vol.1, p.585.2. This is a reprint of the Derge printed edition. The same work is also available in a two-volume reprinted edition by T. Tsepal Taikhang (New Delhi: 1971), based on Lhasa Zhol prints.

11. Chogay Trichen, p.64.

12. Chogay Trichen, p.66.

13. Mi-pham-rgya-mtsho, *Sku gzugs*, p.52. The tradition seems also to have been upheld by Bu-ston, whose first class included both gurus and Buddhas. See Rong-tha, p.134.3.

14. The horizontal measures have been reconstructed from the measures for class three found in Mi-pham-rgya-mtsho, *Sku gzugs*, p.39.

15. *Ibid.*

16. Zhu-chen, *Gtsug lag*, p.157.1.

17. *Ibid.*, line 2.

18. Zhu-chen, *ibid.*, line 3, quotes from the *Vimala-prabhā* commentary on the *Kālacakra Tantra*.

19. Chogay Trichen, p.70.

20. Mi-pham-rgya-mtsho, *Sku gzugs*, p.50f.

21. Chogay Trichen, p.70.

22. Zhu-chen, *Gtsug lag*, p.157.4: *de'ang nyan thos rnams ni byang chub sems dpa'i tshad ltar skabs rer bshad pa yang yod cing lag len la'ang bris thang tshad ma rnams su de ltar byas pa mthong zhing/*. This was in fact the practice of the painter Wangdrak and some others.

Young Sherpa artist copying the drawings of his teacher.

Five
Iconometric Practice and Further Techniques of Sketching

The six main proportional classes, and especially the first four — Buddhas, peaceful bodhisattvas, goddesses, and tall, wrathful beings — were standard fare for every Tibetan student painter. When learning to draw these proportions a student often began with the first class, that of the Buddhas, and then slowly descended the iconometric scale. As a preliminary, some neophytes were made to draw such things as the sacred symbols, and also heads, hands and feet, separately. These gave them a basic familiarity with parts that later contributed to making up the whole.

When the student attempted to draw a complete figure for the first time, he had to begin by establishing a grid of correctly spaced lines within which he could construct the figure itself. He might already have learned this general procedure through drawing the sacred symbols or the head of a Buddha within a grid of guidelines. As always, the vertical axis was the starting point and main reference. But here the horizontal axis was also important, for the horizontal lines of the grid had to be drawn parallel to it. Within the rectangular grid there were also a number of diagonal reference lines that

provided additional guidance in the figure sketching to come.

When the student had completed the grid he next drew the main outlines of the naked figure. He worked with an example by his teacher before him, constantly referring back to it to check the accuracy of his copy. Finally, after the completion of the figure in an unclothed state, he drew in whatever robes and ornaments were required.

When he had reached a high level of competence the artist could dispense with the full rectangular grid and work instead from a simpler skeleton of reference lines. This technique of using abbreviated measurement lines was called *sdom tshad* (as opposed to the above *thig khang* grid of lines, sometimes also called *thig chen*). While it guaranteed a properly proportioned figure, the abbreviated method also helped the painter avoid needless tedium. Similarly, the advanced painter could quickly sketch the clothing of a figure, and did not need to waste time on a detailed preliminary sketch of the complete unclothed figure.

Sketches of hands by Wangdrak.

69

The Order of Sketching

The sequence of sketching in an ordinary thangka painting may be summarized as follows. The first step was the division of the painting surface, and here, as already described, one of our informants used ovals to indicate the places of the main figures. Next the artist established the lengths of the units of measure to be used when drawing those particular figures. For a Buddha or bodhisattva in a sitting posture the length of one large unit *(cha chen)* or span worked out at about one-eighth of the preliminary oval. For a standing Buddha or bodhisattva the large unit would equal about one-twelfth of the length of the oval.

When drawing designs that included a main figure and a surrounding group of lesser figures, a painter had to establish two scales of measures. From the beginning he assigned a larger central oval to the main figure and gave the lesser figures correspondingly smaller ovals, usually from one-half to one-fourth of the length of the main figure. The artist determined the exact relationship between these scales of measure according to the particular exigencies of each composition.

Sometimes the design entailed three or even more scales of measures: that of a main figure, that of a main retinue, that of a lesser retinue above or below, and so on. In paintings where the deities had been individually chosen by the patron or his preceptor, the different scales of measures usually did not express *a priori* hieratic distinctions, but only the main focus and descending priorities of the particular composition as determined by the patron or by the lama who originally advised him to commission the thangka.

In order to establish the values of the main measures during sketching, the artist usually marked the actual length of the span *(mtho* or *cha chen)* of the main figure on a splint of wood or bamboo. Often a painter would further subdivide this homemade "ruler" *(thig shing)* into units of six, four, three, two and one *sor mo*, since these lengths were needed in constructing the linear grids or *sdom-tshad* skeleton lines. The painter also required separate "rulers" for the lesser scales of measurement in the design.

The preparation for sketching the main figure began with the construction of a linear grid – in full or abbreviated form – to conform with the bodily dimensions of that deity or guru. For deities with bent forms, such as goddesses and wrathful figures, the artist had to fix the angles of the chest and head at an early stage. Then he could delineate the area of the head with a rectangle, followed by the drawing of the oval of the face. Next came the abdomen, followed by the arms and legs. The sketching of the robes, together with other garments and ornaments, concluded the initial sketch of the first figure. After sketching the main figure the artist proceeded to draw the other figures following the same basic procedure. Some artists, however, preferred to sketch all of the measurement grids first, before drawing any figure. Finally, after sketching the figures, the artist drew in the required halo, body nimbus (or back curtain or flames) and seat for each figure.

When this much of the sketch had been completed it was common for an artist to go back and check the main proportions of each figure. For rapid double-checking some artists compared certain key measures of height and breadth of each figure. Lastly, the artist surrounded the divine figures with sketches of pleasant landscapes or other appropriate surroundings and ornamentations. The main features of the standard landscapes were clouds, mountains, greenery, lakes and waterfalls. The artist drew these working in general from the top to the bottom of the sketch, and at this time he often added some prominent details such as flowers, offerings, auspicious jewels and animals.

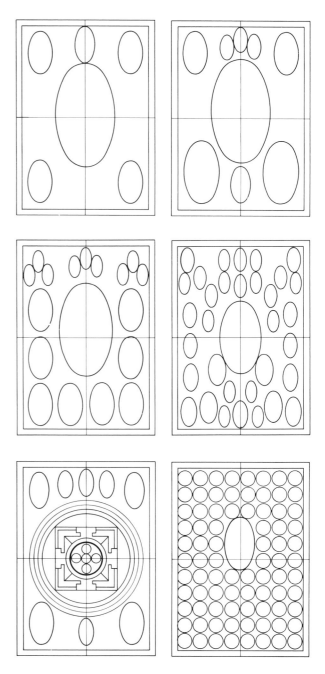

Preliminary compositions established through the use of egg-shaped ovals.

Reinforcement of the Sketch:
Redrawing with Brush and Ink

Up until this point it was easy for the artist to make minor changes and corrections in the sketch by merely brushing off the charcoal drawings with his hand or with a piece of cloth, and then redrawing. But when he was satisfied with the accuracy and beauty of his preliminary sketch he needed to convert it into something more permanent — something that would remain on the canvas as a guide throughout the subsequent stages of painting. He therefore reinforced the charcoal sketch with a brush and black ink *(snag tsha).*[1]

To avoid smearing the charcoal sketch, some artists redrew it by applying the ink from bottom to top, reversing the order of the original sketch. They took great care in this ink drawing, for it determined the permanent design of the painting except for the minor details. Here every effort was made to correct and improve upon the charcoal sketch. To steady their drawing hand some artists rested the edge of their hand on the canvas when inking in the sketch. Others worked with their drawing hand supported above the canvas on a thin wooden support, a technique that will be described below in more detail. When inking the sketch some painters held the brush as one might hold a pencil, but very near the tip. (We observed one painter who constantly rotated the brush as he worked by flicking it with his middle finger. Each flick turned the brush a little and encouraged a continuous flow of ink.) As the painter came to each figure in the design, he commonly delineated the head first, and then the other exposed portions of the body. Then came the robes and the flowing ornamental scarves. For textiles in particular the artist used continuous sweeping motions of the brush to achieve outlines that curved gracefully.

On small figures, minor details such as facial features and ornaments could be omitted from both the charcoal and ink sketches. On the main figures, however, the artists commonly sketched and inked such features even when they were sure to be overlaid by the following coats of paint.

Finally, when the whole sketch was completed and the ink dry, the artist dusted off the canvas to remove any charcoal dust that remained.

Few painters still use all the sketching methods described above. For instance we observed one who inked the sketch from top to bottom, following the usual order for charcoal sketching. This artist, however, had used graphite lead pencils for his original sketch instead of charcoal crayons. Consequently there was little danger of his erasing the underlying sketch while working above it. Some other artists who sketched with graphite pencils omitted the inking altogether.[2]

The Transfer of Designs

For the beginner, the above methods of laying out proportional grids and drawing each figure were

Wangdrak inking his sketch.

formidably complex. Fortunately he was not expected to learn all of these things within a short period. The neophyte usually spent years familiarizing himself with the main proportional classes and with the frequently recurring designs and motifs, meanwhile mastering the basic techniques of paint application and shading. As might be expected, in any project of consequence the actual designing of the layout was left to the skill and judgment of a seasoned artist.

Still, a young painter was able to work on his own quite early in his training, because he could practice copying and painting already finished designs without having to execute an original composition himself. Not only did the novice sometimes paint over drawings made by his teacher, but he also quickly learned short-cut techniques for transferring other artists' designs onto the surface of his own canvas. Master artists too made use of such techniques for transferring designs, and rightly so, since such methods saved a great deal of time.

Pouncing

The first requirement for any transfer was, of course, to obtain a good original. Often the design to be copied was a famous composition that had been carved on large xylograph blocks at such great printing centers as Derge or Narthang. The student could also use as his original an ink drawing made by his own teacher or by some other accomplished artist. However, it would disfigure the xylograph print or original drawing to use it directly as a stencil, and therefore many artists made their stencils by first tracing the print or line drawing onto another sheet of paper.

To convert the original design or some copy of it into a stencil *(gtsag par)* was easy. The artist simply perforated each line of the design with a needle, creating a series of pin pricks. Sometimes several stencils were made at the same time by placing a number of thin sheets beneath the paper bearing the drawing.

To align the stencil correctly in relation to the vertical and horizontal axes of the canvas it was necessary to mark the position of the vertical axis at the top and bottom of the stencil itself. Then, to use the stencil, the artist only needed to position it over the painting surface and dust its surface with a porous bag of powder.

As their pouncing dust the Tibetan artists often used a mixture of charcoal and ochre (the same as they used for the chalk line), or, according to one informant, sometimes a mixture of charcoal and azurite dust. The addition of an earth colour or mineral pigment to the charcoal dust gave it more weight and stability. For pouncing over dark surfaces the painters used a white dust. Modern chemical pigments are by and large unsuitable as pouncing dusts because many of them tend to stain the painting surface. However, one of our informants produced good pounces using a dust composed of white pigment mixed with a very small amount of commercial blue.

After a painter had dusted the whole surface of the stencil with the powder bag, he gently removed the stencil. Then he connected the dots of powder left behind by brush and ink, and so established his design.

Not only did artists use the technique of pouncing to transfer whole compositions, but they also applied it widely to reproduce major (and sometimes even minor) elements of a design. In an elaborate composition in which several deities of the same class were to be drawn in similar postures and to the same scale, the artist could use a single stencil to transfer the basic dimensions of all the figures to the painting surface. When he was redrawing the figures in ink, he would depart from the stencilled image when necessary, for instance to depict the exact mūdra or hand gesture *(phyag rgya)* and hand-held emblems *(phyag mtshan)* required by the specific deity.

We saw, for instance, a series of the lineal gurus of the 'Brug-pa order being transferred to a thangka and then drawn in this way. All of the figures were to the same scale. Furthermore all had the typical 'Brug-pa hat and their robes and feet were identical. The differences lay only in their mūdras and implements, so only these features needed individual treatment in the later ink drawing. Obviously, reproduction by stencil was also ideally suited to paintings where a whole field of identical Buddhas or bodhisattvas was to be painted.

Another application of pouncing was in the replication of landscape elements. The painters with whom we worked (mainly artists from traditions originating in Dbus) usually drew symmetrically balanced landscapes. In the sky, for example, they

Stencil of the Buddha. The diamond-shaped holes allow for proper alignment along the vertical axis.

Use of stencil by Wangdu.

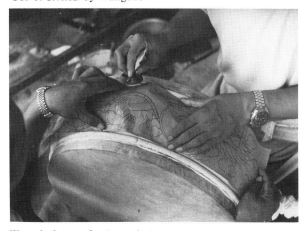

Wangdrak transferring a design onto a drum.

Pounces of lotuses.

Long stencil of repeating lotus petals.

commonly placed clusters or linear series of idealized clouds, evenly balanced to both right and left. Such a design could easily be imparted to the painting surface by a stencil. The artist drew the cloud formation on a piece of paper and perforated it. The design could then be pounced on one side of the sky and then turned over and pounced on the corresponding spot on the other side of the sky. Similarly the clouds of one side could be sketched directly on the canvas, and then traced onto paper for making the stencil. Pouncing in this way enabled the painter to produce exact mirror images, and the technique had a wide application in all types of painting.

As great time savers and as a convenient means for reproducing design elements, the artists also found stencils particularly useful in the painting of walls, furniture, and architectural features such as pillars and capitals. When painting large areas, the artist added yet another variation of stenciling which entailed the making of a long stencil in which the same design alternated or repeated a number of times. First he folded a long strip of paper back and forth at regular intervals eight or nine times, creating a fan-like or accordion-like stack of connected pages. Next he drew on the top page of the stack one unit of the design to be repeated, taking care to center it exactly. After that he punctured the lines of the design with a needle so that each page was pierced. This done, he unfolded the paper to reveal a stencil that repeated or alternated the same design element eight or nine times.

One motif especially well suited to this last type of

stenciling was the lotus petal. Such a stencil could create a running border of lotuses on a beam, an altar, or wherever the artist desired. During the actual pouncing the larger stencils had to be held in place by an assistant while the artist dusted them with the powder bag. After applying the stencil to several places he would return to redraw the designs with brush and ink while they were still fresh and clearly visible.

Tracing

Since the prepared canvas was quite translucent, an original design could be attached to the back and held up to a window for tracing. As with pouncing it was essential for the painter to align the original correctly with reference to the vertical axis of the painting. Originals for tracing were sometimes made from finished paintings by laying thin, nearly transparent paper over them and carefully tracing the main composition.

Notes

1. On the composition of this ink see below, Chapter 6.

2. The use of graphite pencils can lead to new problems. The painter has to be particularly careful to erase any mistakes or extraneous lines, for these will otherwise remain visible under light-coloured paints. Here the impermanence of the lines and sketches made by the traditional means is a recommendation.

Sherpa ink maker.

Six
Pigments

The application of colour to the thangka canvas involved two main steps: first, filling in the areas of different base colours, and second, the subsequent shading and outlining of those areas. To these steps there corresponded the two essentially different types of paint in the Tibetan palette, (1) mineral pigments *(rdo tshon* and *sa tshon)* and (2) the organic dyes or lakes *(tshos).*

The mineral pigments had to be mixed with a binder before being applied as paints. The chief binder for these pigments was size or hide glue, the same gelatinous solution that was used in preparing the "gesso" for the ground. Paints prepared in this way were used for the initial coat of colours. For the subsequent shading and outlining, however, the artists for the most part used dyes and lakes. These needed little or no binder to unite them with the underlying layers of paint, and they could modify the hues and sharpen the borders of the painted areas without adding appreciably to the thickness of the paint layer.

The Classification of Thangkas by Colour

The use of colour could vary tremendously from one thangka to another. The number and types of colours used were in fact one set of criteria by which Tibetans traditionally classified thangkas.[1] Painted thangkas can be divided in the first place according to whether all colours were used or whether just one colour prevailed. Most thangkas fell into the first group, the "full-colour" paintings in which the full palette was employed. The second group consisted of paintings in which one colour predominated and a few other colours were used in restricted roles. Paintings that employed limited palettes could be further divided into three main sub-classes according to the predominating colour: black thangkas *(nag thang* or *thang nag),* gold thangkas *(gser thang)* and vermilion thangkas *(mtshal thang).*[2] The black thangkas were more common, being used especially for depicting fierce deities, whereas the gold and vermilion paintings were much rarer, and nowadays one almost never sees these types being painted.

The palette used by Tibetan artists when painting full-colour thangkas was quite rich. It included pigments that in an unmixed state yielded all of the primary and secondary colours except purple. Also included were black and white. In the following pages we will describe

each of these pigments, following the order of their usual application in a full-colour thangka.

Mineral Colours

The first two colours used by Tibetan artists in an ordinary full-palette thangka were the mineral blues and greens. The choice of these pigments as the first to be applied, and the fact that they were initially used to paint the sky and landscape, were determined by principles of efficiency in painting technique, and not by religious or other considerations.

Azurite Blue *(mthing; mdo mthing)*

The pigment used for sky, water and other blue areas was azurite, the blue basic carbonate of copper, $2CuCo_3.Cu(OH)_2$. Azurite occurs in nature as beautiful monoclinic crystals as well as in massive and earthy forms. The main source of this mineral in Tibet was Snye-mo-thang in Gtsang, north of the Gtsang-po near the border of Dbus.[3] Because of its importance in painting, the Lhasa government strictly controlled the mining and primary distribution of the pigment, so that artists usually got it directly or indirectly from a government office.

Besides being mentioned in some Tibetan sources on painting materials, azurite is discussed in Tibetan pharmacopeias, for it was used as a medicine in the Tibetan Ayurvedic system of medical practice. For instance, 'Jam-dpal-rdo-rje (fl. early 19th century?), the author of a Tibeto-Mongolian *materia medica*, classified azurite as one of the non-melting mineral medicines *(mi bzhu ba'i rdo sman).*[4] This author also quoted another well-known work, the *Shel 'phreng* of Dil-dmar dge-bshes, to the effect that azurite occurs with malachite in the same deposits of copper ore.[5]

Black thangka of *Rnam-'jom*.

Gold thaṅка of the 35 Buddhas of Confession.

Malachite Green *(spang ma; mdo spang)*[6]

After azurite blue, the next pigment to be applied was the green derived from the closely related mineral malachite, the basic carbonate of copper, $CuCO_3.Cu(OH)_2$.
As noted above malachite and azurite generally occur together; in Tibet both minerals were in fact extracted from the same deposits in Snye-mo-thang. Malachite is also mentioned in the pharmacopeias of Tibet, where it had the additional names *spang tshon* and *tshon ljang*.[7]

The azurite and malachite from Snye-mo-thang came in a crushed, sandy form, wrapped in small leather bags. One painter informed us that up to three different colours were available from this source; in addition to the usual azurite blue and malachite green, he could sometimes also get a deep blue-green colour called *g.yu kha*.

Before they could use these colours as paints the artists had to clean and grind the crude pigments, and then separate several values of colour from each basic mineral. As a rule they had to begin by cleaning the minerals by repeated scrubbing and rinsing. To start with, an artist (or an assistant in charge of preparing colours) poured the material into a container of warm water and stirred it briskly. After allowing the mixture to settle for a few moments, he poured off the surface foam together with the dirty water bearing undesirable dust and earthy impurities in suspension. He then added a little glue, and proceeded to knead and rub the earthy mixture between his hands. Next, he again added warm water, and having stirred it up he allowed it to settle and then poured off the dirty water as before. He would repeat this process until the water poured off was clean, at which time he could transfer the mineral to the mortar for grinding.

The mortar *(gtun khung)* and pestle *(gtun)* were usually simple implements made from stone, the mortar being a shallow stone dish large enough to accommodate quantities of mineral pigment, and the pestle a hard elongated stone with smooth rounded surfaces. If large amounts of mineral pigments had to be ground, for instance while painting the murals of a large temple, the workers sometimes suspended a stone pestle just above the surface of the mortar by ropes. Due to the elasticity of the ropes the pestle could be brought to bear on the surface of the mortar by lightly pressing down on it, and in this way the workers could grind pigments for long periods of time with a minimum of exertion.

Azurite and malachite, unlike some other pigments, were subjected to "wet grinding" *(rlon rdul)*, and for this the painter would add some water to the already damp, earthy mass in the mortar before he began grinding.[8] In their crude state the mineral pigments were dull and unattractive, but after cleaning and just a little grinding the deep rich colours appeared.

The actual grinding of the pigments proceeded in a steady, smooth way. It was not necessary to grind azurite or malachite to an extremely fine powder. In fact, it was better to grind them too little than too much. Unlike lapis lazuli (another mineral yielding a deep blue that was used outside Tibet), azurite and malachite become progressively whiter and paler the more finely they are ground. If ground as finely as most pigments are, they lose their original deep colours almost completely.

This special property of the copper carbonate minerals was a reason for caution during grinding, but it also made possible a simple method for deriving several shades of colour from each mineral. Grinding reduced the original crude pigment into particles ranging in size from fine sand to very fine dust. Because different values of colour corresponded to the different sizes of particles, several lighter and darker values of green and blue could be extracted through progressive sedimentation. First the artist stirred up the ground mineral in water. When most of the heavier, darker particles had settled to the bottom, the artist poured the water and the lighter particles still in suspension into a separate dish.[9] The process could be repeated with both the lighter shades and the darker, heavier remains so that from one mineral at least four distinct shades could be derived, each known by its own name. The first, lightest suspension of azurite was known as *sngo si*; the next, sky-blue suspension as *sngo sang*; the third, medium blue as *mthing shul*; and the deep azure coarsest suspension as *mthing 'bru*. Similarly, the four gradations of malachite were, from lightest to darkest, *spang si, spang skya, spang* and *spang smug*.

In Tibet these two minerals were not extremely expensive per unit of weight. But because they were used in great quantities over large areas of sky, meadows and other parts of the paintings and since they had to be applied in relatively thick coats to produce the deeper colours, they accounted for a large part of the painter's expenses. Among the various shades of the two pigments, the bright green malachite was said to be the most expensive. And in general, nearly twice as much malachite as azurite was used.

Lapis Lazuli *(mu men)* and Ultramarine

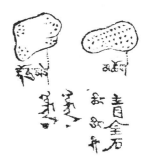

In the past some Western writers have asserted that lapis lazuli, the deep blue semi-precious stone, was the source of the blue pigment commonly used by Tibetan artists.[10] Lapis, being a colour similar to azurite, has frequently been confused with azurite in other times and places. The dark blue constituent of lapis lazuli is the mineral lazurite (sodium aluminum silicate, with sulfur), whose very name reveals a common etymological origin with azurite. Lazurite, however, is much rarer than azurite. Only a few major deposits are known in the world, the largest of which is in Badakhshan in Northeast Afghanistan. Therefore, even though lazurite was sometimes used as a pigment it was usually far more costly than azurite. In medieval Europe, for example, the precious pigment ultramarine (powdered lazurite) was weight for weight as costly as gold, and in those days ultramarine was commonly adulterated with the cheaper azurite.

Tibetans certainly knew of lapis lazuli. Although it was not normally used as a pigment, it was a well known semi-precious stone, and the Ayurvedic doctors of Tibet considered it a medicinal substance. 'Jam-dpal-rdo-rje in his Tibeto-Mongolian *materia medica* classified lapis lazuli *(mu men)* as a non-melting precious substance *(mi bzhu ba'i rin po che)*, stating that it was a mineral found in rocky mountains.[11] In medicine, at least, the variety with gold specks (pyrite) was considered best, while the plain dark blue type with no specks was less desirable.

Lapis and azurite in their mineral forms could be easily differentiated. In addition to the characteristic golden specks, lapis also commonly had veins and specks of related white sodalite minerals. Azurite, on the other hand, usually contained at least traces of the green malachite, and in a larger lump or rock the two minerals often merged imperceptibly into each other. Modern Tibetan painters were well aware of the difference between the two blue minerals, and when questioned they unanimously declared that they had never seen lapis lazuli used as a pigment.

Artificial Ultramarine

In Europe the pigment made from lapis lazuli has always been costly since only a small percentage of the lapis ore — itself a valuable commodity — could be converted into a usable pigment of the best quality. However, for years European alkali makers had noticed the occasional formation in their ovens of blue masses resembling ultramarine. From this clue, and spurred on by a sizable monetary prize, a French chemist in the late 1820s finally discovered the process for synthesizing ultramarine from such common materials as china clay, sulfur and charcoal. By the 1830s French and German factories were producing the pigment in large quantities.[12] Having both a low price and the desirable qualities of the precious natural lazurite, the artificial ultramarine soon became for European painters the deep-blue pigment *par excellence*, and in Europe it

effectively put an end to the use of both lapis and azurite.

This new technology was of significance for Tibetan painting because pigments were highly prized commodities among Tibetans. Pigments and dyes had been common articles of trade for centuries, and at times some were even used to pay taxes or tribute.[13] By the present century, and perhaps as early as the mid-19th century, synthetic pigments were finding their way into Tibet via British India, and synthetic ultramarine may have been among these. Microscopic analyses of pigments used in a sampling of eight thangkas have indicated the presence of ultramarine in two paintings that also contained azurite and malachite.[14] V. R. Mehra, the author of that study, described one of the paintings containing ultramarine as "Lhasa style" and the other as belonging to the "sNar-thang school." Presumably on the basis of style, these thangkas had been dated to the 18th or early 19th century and to the early 17th century respectively. Without inscriptions or similar evidence one cannot date such thangkas except in a very approximate way, but the finding of ultramarine in the paintings (if indeed it was synthetic ultramarine) is a sure indication that they date back to no earlier than about 1830. Unfortunately, Mehra did not indicate whether the "ultramarine" was natural or man-made, although under a microscope it is easy to differentiate between the two.[15] If the presence of synthetic ultramarine can indeed be verified by both visual and chemical tests, the art historian will be supplied with a valuable bit of evidence for the scientific dating of works containing it.

Other Synthetic Green and Blue Pigments

Curiously, Mehra's analyses also indicated the presence of an "emerald green" on two thangkas, one being the "Lhasa-style" painting of the "18th or early 19th century," and the other being described as "Indian style, early 19th century."[16] Emerald green is copper aceto-arsenite, an artificial pigment first synthesized in 1814.[17] It is not commonly identified in European paintings, and thus it is surprising to find it in these thangkas. In addition to emerald green, Mehra also identified on the "Indian-style" painting the synthetic pigment Scheele's green (copper hydro-arsenite), a similar pigment first prepared in 1788 that was widely used in Europe for only a brief period during the late 18th and early 19th centuries.[18] Here again, the presence of such artificial pigments allows the art historian to establish a *terminus a quo* in dating them. These works, for instance, could not have been painted much earlier than 1820 if these analyses are correct.

Perhaps further investigations of Tibetan pigments will uncover the presence of even more synthetic pigments in thangkas painted in the 19th and 20th centuries, particularly in works from Gtsang. The painter Wangdrak informed us that in the artistic traditions *(lag rgyun)* of Shigatse and its cultural satellites such as Lhatse, Gyangtse and Ngamring the colours imported from India through Darjeeling and Kalimpong actually predominated among artists for a time. Although these colours began to lose some popularity in the 1930s, merchants who specialized in selling imported pigments continued to do business at the seasonal trade fairs and in the main towns of Gtsang.

Finally, some synthetic blue and green pigments from China also found their way into Tibet, especially in the eastern districts, Khams and A-mdo. Sum-pa mkhan-po, writing on methods and materials of art, mentioned a Chinese green (*rgya ljang* = verdigris?), and to this Mi-pham-rgya-mtsho added a mention of a Chinese blue *(rgya mthing)*. Unlike the Tibetan blue and green *(bod mthing, bod ljang)*, i.e. azurite and malachite, which were ground in plain water, the artificial Chinese pigments were said to need grinding with size solution *(spyin chu)*.[19]

Cinnabar *(cog la ma)* and Vermilion *(mtshal)*

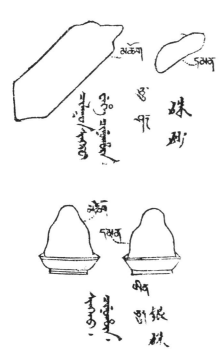

For their brightest reds Tibetan artists used both native mercury sulfide – the mineral cinnabar – and the same pigment synthetically produced. The mineral is known as *cog-la-ma* (cinnabar) or *mtshal-rgod* ("native vermilion") in Tibetan, and it is said to occur in some parts of Tibet, for instance in the Southeastern region Lho-brag.[20] Most of the cinnabar or vermilion used in Tibet, however, came from China and India, and for this reason it was also called *rgya-mtshal* ("Chinese or Indian vermilion").[21] At Chen-chou in Hunan Province in China, for instance, cinnabar was mined in particularly abundant quantities,[22] indeed, these mines were probably the ultimate source of much of the cinnabar used by Tibetan artists. When ground into a fine powder suitable for painting, cinnabar was known to the Tibetans simply as vermilion: *mtshal*.

Cinnabar is the principal ore from which mercury is produced. Once the mercury has been separated from the sulfur content of cinnabar by heating, it is still possible to recombine it with sulfur. Ordinarily, the combination of mercury with sulfur yields the black mercuric sulfide. But by carefully controlled heating and cooling, mercury and sulfur can be combined to produce the silver and red metallic crystals of artificial cinnabar.

As early as the 2nd century AD this transmutation of liquid mercury to crystalline cinnabar and back again was discovered and studied by Chinese alchemists, who considered these chemical reactions to be of fundamental importance since they so vividly displayed the transmutation of the elements, and above all since the changes were reversible.[23] The process of synthesis was also known in ancient India, and both India and China became exporters of synthetic cinnabar and vermilion to Tibet. Subsequently the technology also spread to Tibet. Authors of later Tibetan pharmacopeias, for instance, describe the technique. In Tibetan medicine cinnabar or native vermilion was classified as a "meltable mineral medicine" *(bzhu ba'i rdo sman)*, while the synthetic cinnabar, called *da chu*, was classified as a "manufactured salt" *(bzo tshwa)*.[24] Another name for the synthetic cinnabar was "white vermilion" *(mtshal dkar)*, perhaps because of the silver glint of the man-made crystals.[25]

To make paint from crystalline cinnabar, it was first crushed, and then some of its impurities were removed by repeated rinsing with clean water. In China one traditional way of clarifying cinnabar for pigments involved mixing the finely crushed cinnabar with water, and then removing the water and any material floating on it after three days. The remaining sediment contained the best quality pigment.[26] One finds a similar technique among the Tibetans as described by Mi-pham-rgya-mtsho:

> Grind the vermilion in a smooth, white mortar. Crush it finely *(phram = phra mor)*. Then pour in some *a-ru-ra (Terminalia chebula)* water, so that it just covers the vermilion. Leave it for one day, and then throw out the yellowish surface layer of water. After that, grind it with the pestle using circular motions. This is a key point of technique that will yield [a paint] that is easily ground, of excellent colour, and easy to apply. Then completely pulverize it, grinding gently and for a long time in a porcelain cup or in some other paint container *(tshon gong = tshon kong)*.[27]

Tibetan painters, however, did not always resort to special procedures for the preliminary crushing and washing of cinnabar. Although cinnabar is technically classified as a metallic substance, it is one of the softest of all the Tibetan pigments, and painters often crushed and ground it into a powder in any sort of mortar or bowl. But when it came to the fine grinding of the vermilion, many artists prescribed exacting procedures.

The pigment was believed to have the peculiar property of becoming a lighter red if ground with circular movements, or a darker red if ground with strong up-and-down pounding motions. According to one painter, to get the pure, intense scarlet, both the up-and-down and the circular motions had to be employed equally. The pigment was ground in that way slowly and gently, mixed with a little water. The Chinese vermilion makers by contrast typically ground their cinnabar without any pounding or circular grinding at all: traditionally they pulverized the vermilion in a large boat-shaped receptacle by means of an iron roller.[28]

In Tibetan painting the highest quality vermilion was a brilliant scarlet. Some grades of vermilion, although chemically pure, became a muted maroonish red when mixed with size and applied to the canvas, and so were not valued as highly. Vermilion was sometimes adulterated with cheaper red colouring matter, which could often be detected by mixing a little pigment with water in the palm of the hand and then rinsing with water. Dyeing impurities left a red mark on the palm. In such cases rinsing the pigment in water would improve the colour. In Tibetan medicine too the brighter shades were considered best, and texts on medicine likewise recommended repeated washings to improve the "dark vermilions" *(mtshal nag).*[29] The Chinese in particular were masters at producing the most highly prized, intensely brilliant shades of vermilion.

Minium Orange *(li khri)*

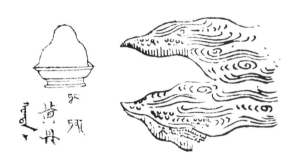

For their main orange pigment, Tibetan painters used minium, the synthetic tetraoxide of lead, Pb_3O_4. This pigment is also known as "red lead," but the varieties used by Tibetan painters were actually intense orange, and not red or scarlet. Tibet did not produce its own minium, but imported it from Nepal and China. Minium was also produced in India; the author of one Tibetan *materia medica* mentioned varieties of Indian minium that were produced from earth, stone and plants.[30] But the writers of such texts were also aware that the miniums of China and Nepal were made from lead, in spite of the fact that they classified these as "naturally occurring earth medicines" *(rang 'byung ba'i sa sman).*[31] For painting in particular, our main informants considered the synthetic miniums of Nepal to be the best.

Several techniques exist for the production of minium. A recent process used in the West involves heating lead in contact with air. The molten lead first becomes oxidized into litharge (lead monoxide, PbO), and then if heated continuously at 480°C it converts to minium.[32] Similarly, colour makers in India prepared minium by roasting white lead, the basic carbonate of lead, in the open air. First it became massicot, a lead monoxide similar to litharge, and finally it converted to the orange tetraoxide, minium.[33] In China, on the other hand, a somewhat different technique was used. According to an old Chinese *materia medica* minium was produced by adding vinegar, niter and sulfur to molten lead. Another method mentioned in this Chinese text entailed the roasting of the residue left behind from white lead manufacture together with some niter and alum.[34] These Chinese processes produced not only minium, but also impurities such as sulfates of potassium, lead and aluminum.

In Sanskrit the pigment minium is usually called sindhura. Consequently, one finds that Tibetan authorities such as Mkhyen-brtse lo-tsā-ba give the term "sindhura" as a synonym of *li-khri* (the ordinary Tibetan term for minium).[35] But other Tibetan writers, such as the influential Dil-dmar dge-bshes, state emphatically that *li-khri* and sindhura are distinct substances. According to the latter group of writers, real sindhura was like minium except that it was a little bit darker and browner, and it was also said to occur on lake shores and in rock cavities in special locales.[36] Perhaps the term sindhura was used by the latter writers to mean native litharge (yellow lead monoxide), or mixed litharge and native minium deposits, which sometimes occur on weathered lead-bearing ores.

Tibetan painters judged the purity of their minium by its weight, colour and texture. The best, purest qualities were extremely heavy, intensely orange, and not sandy but smooth to the touch. The pure powder squeaked when rubbed between the fingers. These characteristics could not be duplicated by any other pigment, but the purity of minium might be tampered with. When an artist had to work with qualities other than the best he could usually wash out most of the impurities by repeated rinsings. Minium seldom required any grinding; if it was pure, only the addition of hide glue was needed to prepare it as a paint.

Orpiment Yellow *(ba bla)* **and Realgar** *(ldong ros)*

The chief yellow pigment of Tibetan painters was orpiment, a natural yellow trisulfide of arsenic, As_2S_3. Deposits of orpiment occur near the surface of the earth, especially near hot springs or in the vicinity of silver deposits. In Tibet the most famous deposits were found in East Tibet, near Chamdo. Large quantities of orpiment are also said to have been mined at Shih-haung-Ch'ang in Yunnan Province in China.[37]

The mineral orpiment is easily identifiable by its yellow metallic lustre and its strong sulfur-like smell. It is also very soft (1.5 − 2 on Moh's scale). There are a variety of qualities; in Tibetan painting as in Tibetan medicine the pure, intensely yellow orpiments were best, while the greenish and reddish varieties were inferior.[38] Due to its eye-catching appearance and its chemical properties (like vermilion it could be artificially produced by sublimation), in early times orpiment was the object of alchemical speculations in China and elsewhere.

Orpiment always occurs in nature together with realgar, the closely related red sulfide of arsenic. Both orpiment and realgar were formerly used in European painting, but being highly poisonous their use has actually been outlawed in many places. However, in Tibet where European synthetic yellows do not seem to have penetrated in appreciable quantities, orpiment and realgar continued to have a wide application down to recent times. Realgar, it should be added, was not commonly used in thangka painting by our Central Tibetan (dbus pa) informants. For them, its widest application was in the painting of walls and wooden surfaces.

Orpiment and realgar had certain medicinal uses in the Ayurvedic medicine of Tibet, but most painters also knew the pigments to be harmful if ingested in any quantity. Therefore, although many painters licked their brush tips while applying other pigments, most were careful not to get any of these arsenic compounds into their mouths.

When preparing orpiment for use as a pigment, the artists ground it in the dry state. It could be ground vigorously,[39] but when ground extremely finely the richness of its yellow was slightly diminished.

Yellow Ochre (ngang pa)

Yellow ochre is a fine-grained earthy variety of the mineral limonite, a hydrated ferric oxide. Although ochres have been popular among Western artists for some centuries, Tibetan thangka painters seldom used them as pigments in their own right, preferring the more intense yellow of orpiment. Nevertheless, yellow ochre was widely used as the main undercoat for gold.

In Central Tibet the most highly prized yellow ochre (ngang pa or ngang sang) came from the Zhwa-lu district of Gtsang; hence the name, zhwa lu ngang pa. Because it had a very soft and earthy consistency, this pigment did not require much grinding. In fact, one painter stated that instead of grinding it in a mortar, he used to soak it in water and then use his fingers to rub off the smooth, clay-like outer layers that had become saturated and soft.

The related earth colour red ochre (btsag) was also well known in Tibet. Chemically, red ochre is identical to yellow ochre, except that the red lacks the hydrous content of the yellow. It was a cheap pigment that was often employed like whitewash for painting the outside of large buildings. Red ochre too was not widely used in thangka paintings in recent times. Investigations of older paintings, however, have indicated its presence; in the study by Mehra red ochre showed up in five of the eight museum thangkas chosen for examination.[40]

Earth White (ka rag)

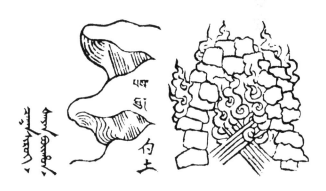

The main white pigments in Tibet were calcium compounds. The most common white was a mineral called ka rag, which seems to have been a high-grade white chalk. Like limestone and marble, chalk is basically calcium carbonate, but chalk is not to be confused with lime (rdo zho or rdo thal), the white oxide of calcium that is made by heating limestone in a kiln.[41]

In Tibet, the best known and for painting the most valuable ka rag came from Rinpung (Rin-spungs), a place roughly half way between Lhasa and Shigatse that in the 16th century was the seat of the rulers of Tibet. In parts of Tibet the fine grade of ka rag from Rinpung was quite costly; in the town of Shekar Dzong (shel-dkar rdzong) in Western Gtsang, for instance, the pigment was said to cost weight for weight as much as butter. Therefore for purposes that required a lot of white, such as the preparation of the ground, painters commonly substituted less expensive grades of white.

According to the artists there were two main varieties of the ka rag mineral: "masculine" (pho) and "feminine" (mo). The masculine type (pho rag or pho dkar) was harder and coarser, while the feminine (mo rag or mo dkar) was relatively soft and fine. However, when the masculine was left out to weather in a stream bed or in some wet place it would convert to the feminine, becoming lighter and softer. If the artist wished to effect this change even faster, he would first soak the pho rag in water for a few days, At first the pho rag made the water turn yellow, and when this happened the discoloured water had to be poured out

Monks grinding white mineral on a stone mortar.

and replaced with fresh water. When the water stopped yellowing the mineral could be ground, and again soaked in water. The need for preliminary soaking, combined with its greater hardness while grinding, made the masculine type more work to prepare, but when finally rendered into a usable pigment it could not be distinguished from the feminine variety.

Ka rag was ground dry, and then after that even the feminine *mo rag* had to be soaked in water to leach out yellowing impurities. When the pigment had been well ground, the artist might test it, by putting a small drop on his tongue and then feeling for any undesirable granularity by rubbing it with his tongue against the roof of his mouth. After final grinding and soaking, ordinary earth whites as well as cheaper earth pigments were commonly transferred to earthenware pots, which through absorption and evaporation speeded up the extraction of water from the wet pigments. By contrast, Tibetan painters always stored their expensive pigments in non-porous containers.

In addition to *ka rag*, painters in some regions of Tibet occasionally used other calcium compounds for their white. Eastern Tibetan artists, for instance, described a white pigment that they used to make by calcining animal bones. This too was a calcium white since the main constituent of bone ash is calcium phosphate. Similar bone-ash whites were used in medieval European painting. Finally, the analysis of the pigments of one "Nepalo-Tibetan, late 15th or 16th-century" thangka revealed the presence of a white pigment made

up of chalk plus gypsum.[42] Gypsum is a mineral form of calcium sulfate that has been used to make white paints in many parts of the world since very early times.

The use of synthetic whites such as lead white and zinc white in Tibetan thangkas was not mentioned by our informants. Nevertheless, by the beginning of the present century small quantities of lead white in particular must have been coming into Tibet from India or China.[43]

Carbon Black *(snag tsha)*

The blacks used as paints in Tibet were made from carbonaceous materials, and the sources — soot and black ash — were common almost everywhere in one form or another. Since carbon is chemically very inert, it was the basis for permanent, excellent pigments.

Soots and black ash were produced by heating a substance such as wood or oil without causing its complete combustion. The most common way of making soot for pigment use was to burn the chosen material slowly and imperfectly; such a fire produced smoke that consisted of millions of minute black particles of ash. These tiny particles needed only to be retrieved to form the basis for a black ink or paint.

Tibetans knew the age-old process for making ink *(snag tsha)* from soot and glue. Mi-pham-rgya-mtsho, for instance, gave the following description of ink manufacture:

The main material is soot, which is made by burning the wood of a larch tree *(larix potaninii* Batal.: *thang ma sgron shing)*, birch bark, or other materials and by causing the flames to burn into a vessel with a net covering (?) *(khog ma dra ba can)*. Alternatively, one may also use the soot of a butter lamp or from a torch. Also the soot from a roasting pan [may be used], but this is the worst; and [one may even use ashes of] puffballs that have been covered with mud and burned.

[To prepare ink] one adds to the above soot a boiled solution of size that has cooled and congealed to the point that it can no longer be pierced with the tongue. [The mixture] is stirred and churned again and again in a *thang-rkyal* container. If it dries out one should moisten it, and it should be ground by repeatedly bringing it to a paste-like consistency.

Regarding this, some people traditionally begin by grinding mica *(lhang tsher)* in a *thang-rkyal* container. Using this as their basic material, they then mix it with soot or other materials.

During or after the grinding of the ink, if one soaks [the soot paste] in a decoction of *Piper longum* and cardamom (?) *(kakkola)* [the resultant ink] will not solidify in the winter. And if one soaks it in an infusion of camphor, *Peucedanum sp. (tang ku)* and white sandalwood, [the ink] will not spoil in summer. If prepared with an infusion of musk and solidified bovine bile *(gi wang)*, it will be very runny and its flow will not be interrupted.

If one adds sugar (?) *(rgyal mo ka ra)* and lac dye, [there results] a rich colour. If one adds infusions of cloves, *Inula helenium* (?) *(ru rta)*, camphor, *Melilotus suaveolens* Ldb. *(rgya spos)*, *Nardostachys jatamansi* DC *(spang spos)*, *shu mo za* and *ar nag* it will have a good smell. If one pours in some decoction of black-roasted wheat and a solution of "calf blood" (?) *(be khrag)*, it will shine with a silver glint. A decoction of *Saussurea sp. (spyi bzhur)* gives a dark blue hue. If one adds a clear solution made from barberry bark *(skyer shun)*, it gives a golden colour. [The addition of] lac dye decoction yields a copper colour. Therefore mix [the above ingredients with the ground soot] according to one's desires.

If the ink does not flow freely due to its being too viscous, add a little bit of calcined alum *(dar mtshur)* or borax *(tsha la)*. If it is too thin, the addition of a kernel of grain or a bean will be sufficient to make it thicker by absorbing water.

[short passage on substitute binders omitted]

The way for preparing ink from soot. Lampblack gives "extensiveness" (?) [good coverage?], but it is a little difficult to pulverize. The soot of

Gentiana tibetica King *(kyi lce)* is excellent for ease of grinding, but it is not lustrous (or, instead of *'od che*, read *bong che* "extensive, of good coverage"?). Wood soot is excellent for grinding and it is also of "great extension". The soot of *dmar chen rtse ba* has good colour and is "extensive" and easily ground, yet it is a cause for spoilage [in warm weather]. Therefore, in winter the soot of *dmar chen rtse ba* is best. Otherwise, for good colour, ease of grinding and "extensiveness" one should mix lampblack in equal proportions with *Gentiana tibetica (kyi lce)* soot.

If one desires a dark blue [ink] one should add the black surface layer of some indigo dye solution and some decoction of the *Saussurea sp. (spyi bzhur)* plant. If one wants a light blue, add only the *Saussurea sp.* decoction. [Ink of a] silvery colour can be made by adding a lot of white rice decoction and *ma nu ru rta* (an *Inula* species?) decoction in equal measure, and this mixture must be ground a long time in the sun. If one wants ink of a reddish colour and lustre, it can be made by adding a little solution containing "antelope blood" (?) after the ink has been completely ground, and then grinding the mixture further in the sun without heating it over a fire. If one wants ink that is extremely black and shiny, it can be made by adding a little shellac *(la chu)* [to the ink]. One should only use this ink in a warm state, and should never add any cold water to it.

Whichever kind of ink one makes, for a smooth and - - ? - - *(rme ba)* ink, it is important to add some decoction of *ma nu ru rta*.

As a replacement for the size binder, the use of rice decoction by itself will yield an ink that is easy to apply, quick in drying, and not apt to spoil in warm weather. Adding a little *sug-pa* root solution and size will make the ink shinier.

In general, it is important to grind [the ink] for a long time, and while grinding to grind in all directions and both clockwise and counterclockwise, for this will produce an ink that will not clot up during application, and that will be easy to apply, moderately black (?) *(snying nyung)* and shiny.[44]

Although a few details of the above passages are obscure, it is clear that the Tibetans had developed their ink-making technique to a high degree.

In addition, a considerable amount of good ink was also imported into Tibet from China, and among Tibetan painters such Chinese ink *(rgya snag)* still remains a highly favored pigment. Like Tibetan ink, the inks of China were usually made from lampblack or from soot produced by burning the wood of a coniferous tree. According to Chinese manuals the manufacture of ink in China involved a process of mixing and grinding that was a little more involved than the method described by Mi-pham-rgya-mtsho. First of all the soot, glue solution and medicinal decoctions were combined in a porcelain basin, and they were stirred to make a thick paste-like mixture. This was then kneaded by hand and formed into balls, which were next wrapped in cotton cloth and steamed. After steaming the material was pounded in a stone mortar with a wooden pestle. It was then alternately steamed and pounded for some time. When it had become flexible and homogeneous it was rolled into long strips, which were then cut into small pieces weighing about one and one-half ounces each. These small pieces were then moistened and hammered, one at a time, on a piece of iron. Finally, following the addition of musk and camphor, the smooth material was rounded, shaped, and pressed into wooden molds. These molded ink sticks only required final drying, after which they could be wrapped and then stored for later use.[45]

In addition to the Tibetan or Chinese inks made from soot, the analysis of Tibetan painting materials by Mehra also indicated the presence of some other blacks, namely bitumen (asphaltum), "carbon black" and bone black. The latter pigment, now popularly also called "ivory black," is made by charring the bones of animals. Its presence was indicated in two thangkas, one described as "Lhasa style, 18th or early 19th century", and the other as "sNar-thang school, early 17th century."[46] None of our informants used these.

Gold *(gser)*

Gold, a substance recognized almost universally as a symbol of wealth and beauty, was highly prized as a pigment by both artists and patrons in Tibet. Pure gold not only possesses its own inimitable colour and lustre, but also it does not tarnish and it is extremely workable. It can be drawn into very fine wires, or it can be beaten so thin that light can pass through it. Such qualities lend themselves very well to the purposes of an artisan, for even when applied in very thin layers the reflective metal imparts to any surface the lustre and beauty of solid gold.

Tibetans used various forms of gold for artistic purposes, including gold powder *(gser rdul)*, gold leaf *(gser shog)* and mercury-gold amalgam. In thangka painting, however, the artists used only a paint of finely powdered gold. Gold applied in the form of a paint was known as "cold gilt" *(grang gser)*, as opposed to "hot gilt" *(tsha gser)* — gold applied by the process of mercury gilding in which the gilded object had to be heated to evaporate the mercury.

Tibetan painters prepared cold gilt paint in a number of ways, depending on which form of gold was available to them. Often they obtained it in a finely powdered state that needed only the addition of some binder to ready it for use. In Central Tibet the painters usually obtained their gold from Newar merchants in Lhasa, who nearly monopolized the sale of powdered

gold there. The names of some of their establishments, such as the Blue Doors East and West *(sgo sngon shar nub)*, were known to most of the painters in the Lhasa area.

The Newar gold workers kept their technique a secret. Nevertheless it is probable that their method for powdering gold had a lot in common with the technique used by Tibetans when preparing gold for the "hot" mercury gilding.[47] In the latter process a small piece of solid pure gold was beaten into gold leaf, which in turn was cut into very thin strips. The thin strips were then snipped with scissors, producing tiny rectangular specks. These specks, however, were still too coarse to be used in paint, and they had to be pulverized still further by some grinding process. It was this last and crucial step in the technique that was one of the main secrets of the Newar gold workers.

Because of its plastic qualities gold cannot be ground directly like other pigments; hence the difficulties at this stage.[48] Some intermediate substance, such as stone or a special liquid medium, had to be used to keep the particles of gold from adhering to each other and to the mortar and pestle. The need for such an effective grinding medium was painfully realized not many years ago by some Tibetan artists painting temple murals in Bodhnath near Kathmandu. They tried for a long time to grind a quantity of gold to the desired consistency, but only succeeded in producing a dull, dark mixture that was totally unsuitable for painting. After thus blackening about five ounces of gold, they finally went to the Newar proprietors of one of the "Blue Doors" who are still doing business in Kathmandu, and bought from them the required amount of powdered gold. (Another problem may have been that the gold was not sufficiently pure to begin with. The Newars were also experts at purifying gold).

When Tibetans did prepare their own "cold gold", they commonly used small pieces of crushed stone as their grinding intermediate. L. S. Dagyab described the basic process as follows:

> Small ribbon-like strips [of gold] . . . are in turn mixed with some powdered bits of stone or glass. This mixture is ground with a rounded stone and a little water is added now and then till the mixture acquires a liquid consistency like moist clay. The bits of stone and glass can then be washed out leaving the gold liquid.[49]

Artists in Eastern Tibet had developed a slightly more involved technique. Mi-pham-rgya-mtsho[50] described the process:

> [Pound] the gold into leaf that is so thin that it can be cut with the fingernails. Then, thoroughly grind it in a stone [mortar] together with *mkhar gong* [a siliceous mineral?].[51] Next, encase the ground gold in bovine dung, and when it has dried, burn it. Gently stir the ashes in some water, and the stone powder and gold will separate.

When the gold powder is very fine [but the gold ink made from it] is too runny, mix it with some nearly congealed roasted-wheat glue or grain glue[52] or animal-hide glue.

Pure gold neither tarnishes nor reacts with other pigments under normal conditions. The gold used by Tibetan artisans, however, often contained darkening impurities. These could be detected by rubbing some gold powder between two clean sheets of paper. Discolouration of the paper signified oxidation or adulterants. To obtain the brightest gold sheen the powder had to be washed before use. The artist first added a little size solution to the gold powder in a cup, and then rubbed the mixture with the thumb or fingers until it became thick and nearly congealed. Then he added a bit more size solution and repeated the stirring. After doing this two or three times the artist allowed the gold dust to settle to the bottom of the cup, and he then poured off the dirty liquid. Finally he added clear water and stirred the gold again, repeating the rinsing until the run-off water was quite clean.

Similarly, gold paints prepared previously often darkened and needed washing before use. As Mi-pham-rgya-mtsho wrote:

> If you leave this gold-powder [paint] to sit for a day, it will become [darkened] as if covered with a black film. Consequently, pour some water into [its] colour pot and thoroughly mix [the gold paint and water] with a stirring stick (shing bu), repeatedly throwing out the water which has drawn the dark contaminants into solution. Then add the correct amount of size solution . . . .[53]

Once the gold had been ground it could be stored as a dry powder or in the form of small discs or drops. Tibetans made "gold drops" (gser gyi thigs po) by first mixing the cleaned gold powder with some binder. Then they poured the mixture one drop at a time onto a smooth surface and allowed it to dry. If quicker drying was required, the drops could be poured onto a smooth board of unfinished wood, where they would solidify quicker since the water would both evaporate into the air and be absorbed into the wood. Gold paint in drop form was convenient for artists and was also popular among pilgrims and Buddhist devotees. In this form a pious person could conveniently offer a certain amount of gold to the face of a holy image or to some famous shrine, in much the same way that gold leaf is still offered by Buddhists in Southeast Asia.

Another way that Tibetan artists prepared gold paint (especially in more recent times in India and Nepal) was directly from gold leaf. It will be remembered that gold leaf was an intermediate stage in the preparation of gold powder from solid gold. However, modern commercially prepared gold leaf is actually so fine that an artist can convert it into paint without having to grind it with mortar and pestle.

Gold leaf could be made into gold paint by mixing the leaf in a cup with a little honey, and then rubbing the mixture against the side of the cup with the thumb. This technique, although easier than grinding specks of gold, nevertheless required a special touch because the natural tendency of the gold leaf was to clump up and not to dissipate into fine particles. To facilitate the mixing some artists said that it was best to stir the gold leaf continuously in one direction only.

Imitation Gold and Other Powdered Metals

Tibetans used several other powdered metals besides gold for art and related purposes. Powdered silver (dngul rdul), for example, was regularly used (as was gold) in preparing metallic "ink" for the copying of sacred books on dark, indigo-dyed paper (mthing shog). Silver was of course much cheaper than gold. One of the problems with silver was that it was more prone to tarnish and darken than gold. Silver was not widely used in thangka painting; the only time we saw silver applied to thangkas was in the paintings of the Khams-pa painter Dorje Drakpa. He employed silver in the body nimbuses of White Tārās. In the eyes of Tibetan artists and patrons, silver could never be a real rival to gold.

Other metals were also powdered and used as pigments by Tibetan artisans, but only seldom were they applied to thangkas in Tibet. Mi-pham-rgya-mtsho, for instance, gave directions for the powdering of brass

White Tārā with silver body nimbus.

and copper to make metallic paints.[54] If these powdered metals were used in thangkas it was only as imitation golds. One or two of our teachers mentioned the use of imitation golds by thangka painters in Tibet, and in recent times the use of these has increased among the painters now living in India and Nepal. The main reason for this increase is the exorbitant price of gold. Nowadays it is impractical to use gold lavishly in a thangka unless it is specifically requested by the patron, and a few painters are even willing to do paintings that incorporate no real gold at all. They use powdered brass alone for even the minimal "golden" outlines and finishing details. Nevertheless, every painter whom we knew seemed to prefer using real gold, and they were happy if the patron set aside a certain sum just to cover its cost.

Special Binders for Gold

Even though gold in thangka painting was almost invariably applied in a size medium, for painting other objects Tibetan artists also used special binders for gold. Peeling and cracking were common problems when gold was applied as "cold gilt" (i.e. in a size medium) to the faces of metal statues. Therefore for these and other metal objects, many painters employed a glutinous extract from flax seeds as an initial coating to the metal and as a binder for gold. This extract was made by merely soaking the flax seeds in a little hot water — a simple procedure compared with the extraction of another special binder, linseed oil, from the same seeds.

Linseed oil *(zar khu'i snum rtsi)* was a drying oil initially produced by pressing oil from flax seeds *(zar ma'i 'bru).*[55] A traditional method for preparing linseed oil was described by Bo-dong Paṇ-chen in the 15th century, and the same method continued to be used down to the present century.[56] Here we may summarize the traditional preparation of linseed oil by paraphrasing Bo-dong Paṇ-chen's account.

The production of linseed oil, he says, began with the cooking of the flax seeds and then kneading them into a dough-like mass. This was left to dry, and then it was thoroughly pounded. When the husks of the flax seeds had reached the consistency of *'ba' cha* (a fodder commonly made in Tibet from pressed seeds or grains), the worker put the beaten seeds into a wooden basin and moistened them with water that was as hot as the hands could bear. Then he extracted the crude oil *(mar khu)* by squeezing the warm paste with his hands. The oil was next allowed to clarify, and then it had to be refined by heating over a low fire for three days.

Sesame oil too was prepared by crushing, heating and squeezing the seeds. Then it had to be refined over a low fire. First the partially clarified oil was poured into an iron, copper or bronze pot. The worker then set this pot on a round stove that was made from clay, with holes for the addition of fuel and the removal of ashes. During heating the flames could not be allowed to burn so high that they reached out of either the front or back openings of the stove. Also, it was good to keep [the

pot?] encased in mud [to reduce the chances of an accidental fire?]. Dried and winnowed dung pellets of sheep or goats made a good fuel because their fire burned low and without much smoke. During heating the flames of the fire should just barely touch the pot.

After heating the oil for one day it was best to add a small amount of *spos-smug* resin and borax *(tsha la)*. Finally, when the oil had been heated over a low fire for the full three days, it was filtered through a clean cotton cloth and then stored in some container with a cap or lid. This concludes Bo-dong Paṇ-chen's account.

Western artists would call oil refined in the above way "boiled oil." It is also a "drying oil," which means that when it is applied in thin coats and left to dry it forms a clear, hard solid through oxidation and polymerization. The addition of certain metallic or chemical substances to boiled linseed oil greatly shortens its drying period, and this was probably the reason for the addition of borax as described by Bo-dong Paṇ-chen.[57] Some Tibetan artisans added the lead mineral *thel-gdan*, which would definitely act as a catalyst in drying.[58] In addition to its use as a medium in painting, refined oil can be applied alone as a waterproof coating like varnish, and if resin is added in substantial amounts to boiled linseed oil, a true varnish is the result.

Another special binder used for gold was a glutinous solution made from roasted wheat *(gro tshig)*. This binder was not used in thangka painting, but it was employed for instance by scribes doing gold lettering and as a binder for other inks. L. S. Dagyab described this binder as having been prepared from "fried" (i.e. roasted) grains of wheat. Once the grains had been roasted to a black colour they were "poured into a container of hot water but not boiled any further."[59]

Some painters applied "cold gilt" to the faces of statues using ordinary size as the binder, but in this case it was essential to prepare the surface in a special way. The painter Wangdrak for instance began by peeling a small white radish, which he first used to rub the area of metal that was to receive the gold paint. Next he chopped the radish into a pulp, and squeezed out its juice through a rag. To this juice he added small amounts of sugar and hide glue, and then applied one coat of this mixture to the metal. The next step was to apply a coat of "gold-base" — a paint made by mixing yellow ochre (or nowadays white with a little yellow) with size solution in the normal proportions for paint. Finally the powdered gold itself was applied. But even though here ordinary size was the binder, it was to be used in a very dilute solution containing just enough size to hold the gold in place. (Wangdrak believed that the binder in the ochre undercoat helped to hold the gold.) This technique was considered equal to the use of flax-seed binder for producing a strong gold paint over metal.

Notes

1. Here we are concerned only with painted thangkas *(bris thang)*. The term *thang ka* itself is much wider, as it includes any Tibetan work of religious art made up into scroll form. Dagyab, vol.1, p.40, lists the following types of non-painted thangkas:

   1. *tshem drub ma*: embroidered
   2. *lhan drub ma* or *dras drub ma*: appliqué
   3. *lhan thabs ma*: glued appliqué
   4. *'thag drub ma*: woven
   5. *dpar ma*: block-printed on cloth

2. In some black thangkas, however, only the backgrounds were done in *nag-thang* style, and the figures themselves were painted in full colour.

3. The deposits at Snye-mo had been worked since at least the 15th century, when the saint Thang-stong-rgyal-po is said to have obtained azurite pigment *(mthing zhun)* from there. See Lo-chen 'Gyur-med-bde-chen (b. 1540), *Dpal grub pa'i dbang phyug brtson 'grus bzang po'i rnam par thar pa kun gsal nor bu'i me long* (Bir, 1976), p.125a. This passage was brought to our attention by Mr Cyrus Stearns.

   Tucci, vol.1, p.278, also mentioned that in the 17th century when Tāranātha flourished, merchants coming to Tibet from India brought *spang-mthing*. These were probably green and blue copper pigments, and not indigo *(rams)*.

4. 'Jam-dpal-rdo-rje, *Gso byed bdud rtsi'i 'khrul med ngos 'dzin gso rig me long du rnam par shar pa mdzes mtshar mig rgyan* (New Delhi, 1971), p.55. 'Jam-dpal-rdo-rje gives *mthing zhun* as another name for azurite.

5. *Ibid: spang mthing dang zangs rdo phan tshun rgyud gcig par mthong.* See also Dil-dmar dge-bshes Bstan-'dzin-phun-tshogs, *Bdud rtsi sman gyi rnam dbye ngo bo nus ming rgyas par bshad pa dri med shel phreng* (Leh, 1970), p.136.4.

6. 'Jam-dpal-rdo-rje, p.55.

7. Mgon-po-skyabs, *Sman sna tshog gi per chad* [sic], trilingual xylograph, British Museum, f.8.

8. Mi-pham-rgya-mtsho, *Bzo gnas,* p.86.2.

9. These characteristics of ground azurite and malachite were taken advantage of in a different way by traditional Chinese painters, who allowed the darker and lighter shades to settle as separate layers in the same paint bowl. See Chieh Tzŭ Yüan Chuan (1679-1701), *The Mustard Seed Garden Manual of Painting*, translated and edited by Mai-Mai Sze (Princeton, Princeton University Press, 1977), pp.37f., 579f.

10. Tucci, vol.1, p.269. See also Chögyam Trungpa, *Visual Dharma* (Berkeley, 1975), p.17.

11. 'Jam-dpal-rdo-rje, p.37.

12. R. J. Gettens and G. L. Stout, *Painting Materials, A Short Encyclopaedia* (New York, Dover, 1966), p.163.

13. In the mid-13th century Sa-skya Paṇḍita (1182-1251/2), the Tibetan representative to the Mongols, advised the Tibetans that among other things vermilion *(mtshal)* and madder *(btsod)* would be acceptable as tribute to the Mongols. See Sa-skya Paṇḍita Kun-dga'-rgyal-mtshan, *Bu slob rnams la spring ba, Sa skya bka' 'bum* (Tokyo, 1968), vol.5, p.402.4.1.

    Also in the biography of Chag lo-tsā-ba Chos-rje-dpal (1197-1264) one finds what appears to be a reference to the dye trade. When Chag lo-tsā-ba went to Gnyal Lte'u-ra he brought so many *mdzo*-loads of books with him that some doubted that he could have so many scriptures. They said he must have a lot of raw sugar *(bu ram)* and dyes (if one reads *tshos* instead of *chos*). See Chos-dpal-dar-dpyan, *The Biography of Chag lo-tsā-ba Chos rje dpal (Dharmasvāmin)*, edited by Champa Thubten Zongtse (New Delhi, 1981), p.189.5. Here Zongtse Rinpoche has retained the spelling *chos*, although *tshos* seems demanded by the context. See also G. Roerich (transl.), *Biography of Dharmasvāmin (Chag lo-tsā-ba Chos-rje-dpal)* (Patna, 1959), p.104. Here the translation was probably meant to read "dyes" instead of "dried" for the Tibetan equivalent cited in a note is *tshos*. See also the Tibetan text, *ibid.*, p.39, line 13.

    Tucci, vol.1, p.278, also mentioned that merchants in the time of Tāranātha (fl. 17th century) when coming from India to Tibet used to bring *spang-mthing* (not indigo, but green and blue pigments) and *li-khri* (not carmine, but minium) "which would seem to have been required as part of the taxes to be paid as passage fees to the custom officials *(sgo dpon)*."

14. Mehra, p.208.

15. Gettens and Stout, p.166.

16. Mehra, p.208. These were thangkas nos.306 and 308.

17. Gettens and Stout, p.113.

18. Gettens and Stout, p.154f.

19. Sum-pa mkhan-po, p.398.6; Mi-pham-rgya-mtsho, *Bzo gnas,* p.86.3. We might add that some verdigris may have reached Tibet via Nepal. B. H. Hodgson, writing in 1831, estimated that about one-eighth of the verdigris exported from India to Nepal was re-exported to Tibet. See his *Essays on the Languages, Literature and Religion of Nepal and Tibet, Together with Further Papers on the Geography, Ethnology and Commerce of Those Countries* (New Delhi, 1972), p.109.

20. Traditional sources relate, for instance, that a deposit of vermilion was discovered in Lho-brag at a time that coincided with the birth of Sman-thang-pa Sman-bla-don-grub in the early 15th century. See for instance Dagyab, p.37.

21. 'Jam-dpal-rdo-rje, p.59: *rgya gar nag las byung ba'i phyir rgya mtshal yang zer*. But Hodgson, p.109, estimated that in 1830-31 no India vermilion was exported to Tibet by way of Nepal. However, he thought that about one-fourth of the mercury that reached Nepal from India was re-exported to Tibet.

22. Li Ch'iao-p'ing, *The Chemical Arts of Old China* (Easton, Pa., 1948), p.133.

23. Joseph Needham, *Science and Civilisation in China* (Cambridge, 1954-1959), vol.5, part 3, pp.74, 126.

24. 'Jam-dpal-rdo-rje, p.71.

25. *Ibid.* A third name for synthetic cinnabar was "vermilion salt" *(mtshal tshwa)*. Mtshal-dkar is mentioned as a pigment in Bo-dong, *Mkhas pa*, vol.2, p.256.6. Dil-dmar dge-bshes seems to have used the term *mtshal dkar* also to indicate just a brighter quality of vermilion. See his *Bdud rtsi sman*, p.118. Compare also the use of the term *mtshal nag* by 'Jam-dpal-rdo-rje, p.59.

26. Li Ch'iao-p'ing, p.134.

27. Mi-pham-rgya-mtsho, *Bzo gnas*, p.86.

28. Li Ch'iao-p'ing, p.134.

29. 'Jam-dpal-rdo-rje, p.59.

30. 'Jam-dpal-rdo-rje, p.61. See also the reference by Tucci, vol.1, p.278, to the importation of this pigment from India in the 17th century. Here *li-khri* should have been translated as "minium" not as "carmine". Strangely, Hodgson, p.109, thought that no "China red lead" or "country red lead" that reached Nepal from India in 1830-1831 was exported again to Tibet. But on white lead see below, note 43.

31. 'Jam-dpal-rdo-rje, p.61.

32. Gettens and Stout, p.129.

33. Moti Chandra, *The Technique of Mughal Painting* (Lucknow, 1949), p.21.

34. Li Ch'iao-p'ing, p.136.

35. 'Jam-dpal-rdo-rje, p.60.

36. *Ibid.*

37. Gettens and Stout, p.135.

38. 'Jam-dpal-rdo-rje, p.50.

39. Mi-pham-rgya-mtsho, *Bzo gnas*, p.86.

40. Mehra, p.208. The paintings with "iron oxide" reds were numbers 245, 246, 307 and 311.

41. The process for making lime is briefly described in 'Jam-dpal-rdo-rje, p.53.

42. Mehra, p.209.

43. Ms Ann Shaftel informed us that some analyses of thangka pigments done for her have indicated the presence of white lead. Hodgson, p.109, estimated that one-fourth of the white lead imported from India to Nepal in 1830-31 was re-exported to Tibet.

44. Mi-pham-rgya-mtsho, *Bzo gnas*, p.75f. The text seems corrupt in places, and it contains a number of unattested terms. Most of the botanical equivalents in the translation are from *Bod ljongs rgyun spyod krung dbyi'i sman rigs* (Peking, 1973).

45. See Li Ch'iao-p'ing, pp.119-132.

46. Mehra, p.209.

47. Dagyab, p.48.

48. Gettens and Stout, p.116.

49. Dagyab, p.45.

50. Mi-pham-rgya-mtsho, *Bzo gnas*, p.84.3.

51. On this mineral see 'Jam-dpal-rdo-rje, p.54. One of the characteristics of the mineral was that it did not quickly dissolve into a yogurt-like liquid when ground, unlike minerals such as limestone.

52. For other references to these wheat or grain glues see Mi-pham-rgya-mtsho, *Bzo gnas*, pp.75.6, 89.1; Dagyab, p.45.

53. Mi-pham rgya-mtsho, *Bzo gnas*, p.84.5.

54. Mi-pham-rgya-mtsho, *Bzo gnas*, p.84f.

55. The term *zar khu'i snum rtsi* is used by Mi-pham-rgya-mtsho, *Bzo gnas*, p.89.3.

56. Bo-dong, *Mkhas pa*, vol.2, p.262f. Sum-pa mkhan-po, p.399.2, also gives a brief description of the process, although the text available to us is impossible to read in places. For a more recent account see Dagyab, p.45.

57. Bo-dong, *Mkhas pa*, vol.2, p.262.

58. See Dagyab, p.45.

59. *Ibid.*

Applying colour to a Wheel of Life.

Seven
Colour

The thangka painter's palette consisted mainly of paints derived from the mineral pigments described in the previous chapter. Tibetan artists also made some of their paints by mixing the pigments with organic dyes and lakes such as indigo and lac dye. Important mixtures of this type included the blending of each of these two dyes with white. But since the dyes and lakes were mainly used during the shading and outlining stages that followed the initial application of colours, a detailed description of them and their uses will have to wait until Chapters 10 and 11.

Basic Pigment Colours

The painter Legdrup Gyatsho specifically mentioned sixteen basic pigment colours from which he derived his main range of painting colours and mixtures:

4 blues (deep, medium, light and very light)
4 greens (deep, medium, light and very light)
2 reds (one deeper, the other lighter and more intense)
2 oranges (one deeper, the other lighter)
1 yellow
1 yellow ochre
1 white
1 black

This artist made many of his paints simply by mixing the above pigments with the size binder. However, like all Tibetan painters he also made a number of important shades by mixing these main colours with white and with each other. He had learned how to prepare these mixtures from his teacher and from his own practical experience.

Although most of the pigments were compatible with each other, a few could not be mixed with good results. For instance, Sum-pa mkhan-po and Mi-pham-rgya-mtsho mentioned that orpiment and green should not be mixed or come into contact with one another. They also stated that a little vermilion can darken and spoil the orange colour of minium.[1]

Colour Theories

The mixing of colours *(tshon; tshos gzhi; tshon mdog)* also had a theoretical side, and Tibetan writers on art gave different accounts of the basic and derivative colours. Among the several colour theories current among Tibetan painters during the long history of Tibetan art, one was the system described by the 15th-century scholar Bo-dong Paṇ-chen.[2] In this system there were only five basic colours *(rtsa ba'i mdog)*. All other colours were said to derive from these:

1) white *(dkar)*
2) red *(dmar)*
3) blue *(sngo)*
4) yellow *(ser)*
5) black *(nag)*

Another system, which is known to us through the much later writings of Sum-pa mkhan-po, Rong-tha and Mi-pham-rgya-mtsho, held that there were eight main colours: seven father colours *(pha bdun)* and one mother colour *(ma)*.[3] The "seven fathers" were:

1) deep blue *(mthing)*
2) green *(ljang)*
3) vermilion *(mtshal)*
4) minium orange *(li = li khri)*
5) lac-dye maroon *(skag)*
6) orpiment yellow *(ba bla)*
7) indigo *(rams)*

The "mother" colour was white *(ka rag)*.

Obviously this system was tied to artistic practice since all but one or two of the eight "colours" mentioned were actually the names of certain pigments or dyes, and were not colours *per se*. Here the colours corresponding to the six pigments were blue, green, red, orange, yellow, white, and the two dye colours were maroon and dark blue. The various colours resulting from the mixture of a "father" and a "mother" could be called their "sons" *(bu)*. For example, the "father" blue *(mthing)* when mixed with the "mother" white produced the "son" light blue *(sngo skya)*. If white was added in greater proportions a "son" of even lighter blue *(sngo se)* was produced. In his text Sum-pa mkhan-po (and following him, Mi-pham-rgya-mtsho) went on to describe a total of fourteen "sons":[4]

"sons of green" *(ljang gi bu)*:
   light green *(ljang skya)*
   whitish green *(ljang se)*[5]
"sons of minium orange" *(li yi bu)*:
   whitish orange *(li skya)* = white + minium orange

yellowish orange *(li ser)* = orpiment yellow + minium orange

"sons of vermilion" *(mtshal gyi bu)*:

pink *(dmar skya)* = white + vermilion in equal amounts

flesh colour *(mi sha)* = vermilion + a larger amount of white

"sons of orpiment yellow" *(bla'i bu):*[6]

creamy saffron (?) *(ngar ma?)*[7] = more orpiment yellow, less minium orange and a small quantity of white

yellowish green *(ljang ser)* = orpiment yellow + indigo

"sons of lac-dye maroon" *(skag gi bu):*

lung colour *(glo kha)*

pale mauve (?) *(zi hung)*

"sons of indigo" *(rams kyi bu):*

liver colour *(mchin kha)*

light indigo *(rams se)*.

In addition, there were two "older sisters" *(sring mo),* namely tea colour *(ja kha)* and smoke colour *(dud kha),* and also one "servant" – a mixture of vermilion and ink.

Yet another theory of colours appeared in a recently compiled textbook for Tibetan schoolchildren in India.[8] This system, like that of Bo-dong Paṇ-chen mentioned above, speaks of five basic colours *(rtsa ba'i mdog).* However, it substituted green *(ljang)* in the place of black *(nag).* Furthermore, within this system there are mentioned the following groupings of "intermediate branch colours" *(yan lag gi tshon 'bring po)*: orange *(li khri),* flesh colour *(sha kha),* and pink *(na ros)*; pale mauve (?) *(mon kha),* smoke colour *(dud kha),* and tea colour *(ja kha);*[9] dark maroon *(smug po),* bone colour *(rus kha),* and deep blue-green *(g.yu kha,* the colour of old Tibetan turquoise).

One of the best and most detailed accounts of colours and their combinations is to be found in the writings of Rong-tha Blo-bzang-dam-chos-rgya-mtsho.[10] As mentioned above, he was one of the scholars who adhered to a system of seven "father" colours and one "mother". His actual description of colour mixing, however, did not follow the system of Sum-pa and Mi-pham in every detail, and happily it was even more exhaustive. His account is particularly valuable because it helps to establish the values of some of the rarer terms for colours that occur in other texts on art.

Rong-tha listed the following combinations:

white + a little watery paint of azurite blue *(mthing chu)* = white milk colour *('o dkar)*

white + more of the above blue = bluish milk colour *('o sngon)*

white + a little thin light green paint from malachite *(spang chu)* = milk colour *('o kha)*

white + more of the same green = greenish milk colour *('o ljang)*

white + thin minium paint *(li chu)* = pale yellow *(ser skya)*

white + dilute vermilion *(mtshal chu)* = vermilion pink *(mtshal skya)*

white + vermilion pink = light flesh colour *(sha dkar)*

white + a larger proportion of vermilion pink = reddish flesh colour *(sha dmar)*

reddish flesh colour + indigo = the colour of an old person's flesh *(rgan sha'i mdog),* i.e. a purplish flesh colour.

reddish skin colour + orpiment = yellowish flesh colour *(sha ser)*

lac-dye (maroonish) pink *(na ros)* + indigo = pale mauve *(mon kha)*

lac-dye pink + a larger proportion of indigo = bluish mauve *(mon sngon)*

pale mauve *(mon kha)* + pale yellow *(ser skya:* white and dilute minium) = liver colour *(mchin kha)*

if white predominates in the above mixture = whitish liver colour *(mchin skya)*

liver colour + lac-dye = maroonish liver colour *(mchin smug)*

white + ink black *(snag)* = ash gray (literally "ash colour": *thal kha*)

white + gray = whitish gray *(thal dkar)*

whitish gray + light blue *(mthing skya)* = bluish gray *(thal sngon)*

white + orpiment = bone colour *(rus kha)*

white + vermilion pink + yellow *(ser po),* the latter two colours in equal proportions = ochre-y yellow *(ngang pa)*

ochre-y yellow + minium = golden colour *(gser 'dra)*

vermilion pink + orpiment + ink black added to white = tea colour *(ja kha)*

when vermilion predominates in the above mixture = reddish tea colour *(ja dmar)*

likewise the appropriate shade results when the other colours in the mixture predominate.

indigo + orpiment = compounded green *(sbyar ljang)*

tea colour + compounded green = greenish tea colour *(ja ljang)*

reddish tea colour + ink black = smoke colour *(dud kha)*

smoke colour + light blue *(sngo skya)* = bluish smoke colour *(dud sngon)*

vermilion + ink black + lac dye = a dark red *(dmar nag)* resembling sandalwood

white + lac dye = maroonish pink *(na ros),* an excellent pink *(dmar skya)*

green *(ljang* = compounded green?) + white *(dkar)* = yellowish green *(ser ljang)*

Colour Codes *(tshon yig)*

It was common in large projects for the master painter, when he had completed the sketch, to leave the filling in of the initial colours to his assistants or students. To indicate the correct colours to be applied to each place the artists used two systems of abbreviated notation. One common system used the numerals 1 through 5 and 7 through 9 to indicate the main colours. These numbers corresponded to the numbers and colours of nine-sectioned magic squares within the *sme ba dgu* of Tibetan astrology:

ༀ (1) = white *(dkar)*
ༀ (2) = black *(nag)*
ༀ (3) = blue *(mthing)*
ༀ (4) = green *(ljang)*
ༀ (5) = yellow *(ser)*
ༀ [6 = white, but omitted by artists as redundant]
ༀ (7) = orange *(li khri)*
ༀ (8) = gold *(gser)*
ༀ (9) = red *(dmar)*

For some artists, however, the numbers 8 and 9 indicated magenta pink *(zing skya)* and maroonish brown *(rgya smug)* respectively.

The second system used the main consonantal elements of the names of the colours. The names, so abbreviated, included the following:

ཀ་ *ka* = white *(dkar* or *ka rag)*
ན་ *na* = black *(nag)* — or for some artists, maroonish pink *(na ros)*
ཐ་ *tha* = blue *(mthing)*
མ་ *ma* = red *(dmar)*
ས་ *sa* = yellow *(ser)*
ལ་ *la* = minium orange *(li khri)*
ཇ་ *ja* = brown *(ja kha,* tea colour)
ཚོ་ *tso* = orange of realgar *(btso ma)*
ཡུ་ *yu* = deep blue-green *(g.yu kha,* turquoise colour)

Whitish *(skya bo)* tints of a few colours (made by the addition of a small amount of the colour to white) could be indicated by the addition of a subjoined *ya (ya btags)* to the appropriate letter. The most common example was pink *(dmar skya,* whitish red) which was written *mya,* a *ma* with subjoined *ya:* མ + ྱ = མྱ

In Wangdrak's system certain syllables indicated whitish shades even without a subjoined *ya:*

སྔོ་ *sngo* = pale blue *(sngo skya)*
ལི་ *li* = pale orange *(li skya)*

Another artist, Dorje Gyaltsen, used similar notations:

པ་ *spa* = pale green *(spang skya)*
(from སྔ་, *snga?)* = pale blue *(sngo skya)*
(from ལི་, *li?)* = pale orange *(li skya)*

The latter artist also wrote out the name for yellowish brown *(ser nag),* but in a slightly abbreviated form: *senag* སེནག་ . The systems of numbers and letters were often used in combination. For example, in the same painting numbers 1, 4 and 5 might be used for white, green and yellow, and the letters *tha, ma* and *la* could indicate blue, red and orange.

Notes

1. Sum-pa mkhan-po, p.398.6; Mi-pham-rgya-mtsho, *Bzo gnas,* p.86. Several painters corroborated the statement that orpiment and green should not be mixed. However, none said that vermilion and minium were incompatible.

2. Bo-dong, *Mkhas pa,* vol.2, p.255. Such colour theories were also one of the first subjects dealt with in introductory logic classes *(bsdus grwa).*

3. Rong-tha, p.183.

4. Sum-pa mkhan-po, p.389.4-5; Mi-pham-rgya-mtsho, *Bzo gnas,* p.88.

5. Mi-pham's text *(ibid.)* reads *ser,* but it should read *se* as confirmed by Sum-pa. Below, *ljang ser* itself is a "son of orpiment." But compare Rong-tha, p.184, where *ser ljang* is the product of the mixture of green (= "compound green"?) plus white.

6. Mi-pham-rgya-mtsho, *Bzo gnas,* p.88, erroneously reads *sla'i bu* instead of *bla'i bu.*

7. The text of Sum-pa available to us here (p.398.5) is very faint but appears to read *ngar pa.* Mi-pham has *ngar ma.* The only similarly spelled colour that we know of is *ngur* or *ngur smrig,* "saffron colour."

8. Council for Tibetan Education, *Reader 9* (Dharamsala, 1967), p.258.

9. The text, *ibid.,* reads *ljang kha* instead of *ja kha.*

10. Rong-tha, p.183f.

Sherpa artists at work on a mural. The painter at left is warming a bowl of paint over coals.

Eight
Techiques of Paint Preparation and Application

Once a pigment had been cleaned and ground, it had only to be mixed with the binder to become paint. For blending a pigment and binder most painters followed basically the same technique that they used for mixing "gesso". It may be useful to review that process, here following the method of the Ladakhi artist Wangchuk. This method can be employed profitably by any beginner.

The artist started by putting some ground pigment into a clean paint pot *(tshon kong)*. The paint pot was often a simple shallow glazed earthenware bowl, but for the preparation of more costly pigments a non-porous paint container such as a porcelain cup or a clam shell was often used instead. To the ground pigment the painter added a little warm size solution, enough to make it somewhat damp but not saturated. Then, using a blunt-ended wooden stirring stick or his fingers, he thoroughly kneaded the dampened pigment, crushing any lumps and bringing the mixture to the consistency of dough *(spag)* made from the flour of parched barley *(rtsam pa)*. Having rolled this dough-like mass into a ball, the painter next poured a little more warm size into the bowl and mixed it with the dough until it became a thick and homogeneous liquid. At this stage the paint was said to be like stirred yogurt *(zho)*. Finally, the artist added just enough size to bring the paint to the right thickness for painting, carefully stirring it until it was completely mixed. The ideal consistency was said to be like "buttermilk" *(dar ba)*.[1]

Remixing Paints

After a paint had been newly mixed in this way it could be tested and then immediately applied. Often, however, an artist had to remix his colours from paints that were left over from previous days. In such cases he was frequently faced with an old pot of paint that had either partially dried out, creating a crusty surface with a soft bottom layer, or completely solidified into a rock-hard mass. To prepare new paint from old the artist had to begin by crushing the dried paint into small pieces. Then he proceeded as above, gradually adding size as necessary, and grinding the mixture with a stirring stick until it became perfectly smooth. He could judge its suitability by watching for tracks left on the bottom of the paint bowl by the stirring stick. Paint that was too thin did not leave clear tracks. –

If the paint had dried rock-hard and the painter was in a hurry to reconstitute it, he could soak it under hot water, which quickly softened it. After soaking, the excess surface water had to be poured off before the paint was stirred again. If the hot water had blended with the paint to such an extent that it could not be poured off without losing a lot of paint, the artist had to pour out as much clear water as possible, and then evaporate the rest by heating the paint bowl over glowing coals. When the paint had become almost dry he could then reconstitute it by gradually adding dilute size solution and stirring.

Artist stirring paint.

Mixing and heating the paints was something that the artist or his assistants had to do from time to time during the day. At the beginning of work in the morning the size had to be heated up, and afterwards throughout the day it was kept warm over coals until it was needed, for if it was left to cool it would congeal. In the course of painting, too, the artist had to add a little warm size every now and then to keep the paint at its optimum consistency. Therefore not far from every working painter there was a pot of size solution, kept warm in a brazier over a low fire or bed of glowing coals. (The most common fuel for warming size was dried sheep or goat dung pellets. This fuel was valued because it burned slowly and produced a low, steady heat.)

95

Testing the Strength of the Paint

As the final step before applying the colours to the painting surface, it was a good idea to test the paint one last time to make sure that it contained the right amount of binder. For this purpose the artist generally applied a small amount of each paint with his brush to unused portions of the painting surface. In thangkas these testing spots were usually the strips of prepared canvas on each side of the rectangular painting area. Having applied a little paint, the artist could first judge its characteristics by noting how long it took to dry. At normal temperature and humidity, if the paint dried very quickly there was not enough size; if a very long time elapsed there was too much. After it had dried, the artist could judge its strength by rubbing it with his finger or scratching it with his fingernail. If it rubbed off or was easily chipped by the fingernail, more glue was necessary. A brittle, rough texture often indicated an excess of glue. Finally, the surface appearance of the dried paint could also tell the artist something: a slick or glossy surface meant that there was too much binder, while paint mixed to the right proportions was usually matte in appearance.

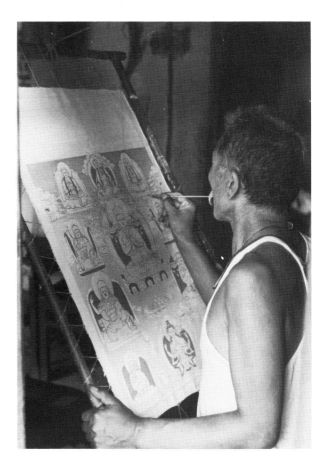

Principles Governing Paint Application

The application of the first coats of paint generally followed a fixed progression of colours. That progression itself can best be understood in terms of four main principles that governed the order of painting. To begin with, there was the principle that the distant planes of colour within the composition should be painted before those in front. Most thangkas had at least three planes in their composition. The most distant was the sky. Also distant, but less remote than the sky, was the landscape. The closest plane was that occupied by the deities. By proceeding from distant to near the painter could impart sharper edges to the foreward areas by slightly overlapping each underlying area with the edge of the subsequent colour. Painting in such a progression was not always crucial, since in many areas the painter would later sharply define the edges by dark outlining. However, when painting certain objects that traditionally received no outlining, such as clouds and some types of flowers, our main informants always applied the base coats to those areas after the surroundings had been painted.

   The second main principle could be called "economy of effort in paint mixing". Having mixed a certain colour, Tibetan artists tried to apply it to as many areas as possible, so that they would not have to mix the same colour several times in the course of one painting. The desire for efficiency was carried to an extreme by painters who sometimes adopted an assembly-line approach, when they would paint many copies of the same thangka at the same time. Such painters would begin by preparing several canvases (or a single large canvas) and establishing on them six or

Wangdrak applying paint at an earlier and later stage.

eight painting areas of the same size. The same number of sketches followed, often with the aid of a stencil. The painters then began their painting by colouring all the skies, then all the landscapes, and so on through the remaining steps of painting. Six or eight paintings at a time is indeed an extreme example, but it is very common to see two or three paintings (often different compositions) at the same stage of completion being painted in this way to achieve maximum efficiency.

The third main principle that governed the order of initial colouring concerned shading technique. Usually most shading or tinting was done by applying darker shading washes over a lighter base colour. This sequence was important to the painter during the application of the first coats of colour since the lightest colour of any area to be shaded had to be laid down first.

The fourth principle governing painting order was that important areas, especially those painted with light colours, should be applied last. The face and body of a white deity, for instance, were prone to be smudged by the artist's hand if they were applied at an early stage. Since most of the important areas were in the foreground this principle was in harmony with principle number one. However, some painters for the same reason painted all faces and bodies last — even those that were blue and green — and this ran counter to the principle of economy in paint mixing.

An Example of Painting Order

To see how these principles were actually applied, let us now describe the order in which the initial coats of colour were applied to a small, one-deity thangka with a very simple landscape. In this example there were four main planes: the sky, the landscape, the deity's nimbus and the divine figure itself. The first area to be painted was the distant sky, and this required the painter to prepare and apply a suitable blue paint. Next he applied this and other blue paints wherever else they were required in the landscape, for example on areas of water and on the blue parts of the traditional blue and green rocky crags. Last he painted the blue areas on and around the central figure, beginning with the body nimbus or backdrop since it was in the rear, and then moving to the body, if appropriate, and to any part of the clothing and accoutrements that were blue.

The colour green came next, being first applied to the green hillsides and meadows in the landscape, and afterward to large details in the landscape such as trees. Then, as with the blues, the artist continued to work forward in the composition, applying green as necessary to the nimbuses or back-curtains and then to the figure.

Immediately after the blues and greens, the artist mixed and applied white and bluish and greenish off whites to such distant objects in the painting as clouds and snow peaks. These colours completed most of the distant planes of the composition, and at this point it was also convenient to mix such off-white hues using the already prepared blues and greens. Areas of pure white

in the foreground, however, were not painted until last, to prevent them from becoming dirty.

The remaining colours were required for the most part in the forward plane of the composition. At this point the artist might apply the reds and oranges, followed by yellow. He continued to fill in as many areas as possible with each colour, painting such things as the flames, nimbuses or back curtain, robes and the deity's body, as appropriate. Next he applied such minor colours as ochre, brown, pink and finally white and gold.

Painting Techniques

Having briefly outlined the general order of paint application, we will now describe certain painting techniques in more detail, still following their usual progression.

Preliminary Colour Transitions

Since in general the most distant planes of the thangka had to be coloured before they were overlapped by the paint of the forward planes, the sky and the landscape had to be brought to a finished state much earlier than the other areas. If a background area required shading or gradual transitions of tone — and some regularly did — this would have to be done quickly, before some of the other areas received even their first coat of colour. Thus, even though shading was for the most part a secondary step, we cannot avoid describing here the basic techniques of shading that were employed during these first stages.

The colouring of a thangka began with painting the sky blue, and for this the artists were not content to lay down a uniform, flat coat of colour. Usually they strove to achieve an even gradation of hue, beginning with a deep-blue zenith at the top of the painting, and working down to a white or very light horizon. To accomplish this the painters used three main techniques. Of these, one employed washes of colour in varying degrees of transparency, another utilized only thick and opaque coats of paint, and the third was a combination of both methods.

One-Brush Dilution Shading

The first and simplest method for creating a colour transition in the sky consisted of the application of a mineral pigment in gradually diluted strengths. We have called this technique "one-brush dilution shading", and it is basically akin to the graded washes of a Western watercolour painter. To tint the sky in this method, the painter began by loading his brush with paint from the surface layer of the pot of blue colour. This paint had to be the deepest blue that he desired in the sky. Starting at one corner of the top he laid down a single sweeping stroke across the top of the sky (assuming that there were no clouds or figures to obstruct it). Then he returned to just beneath the starting point and applied another horizontal stroke just below and slightly overlapping the first. He continued with a series of such strokes — stopping at the edge of any obstruction and picking up again at the other side — all the while applying increasingly less pressure to the brush tip, thus achieving a thinner coat and therefore a lighter value of the blue. At some point, depending on the vertical depth of the sky, the painter had to reload his brush, but here instead of using the paint full strength as before, he slightly diluted it. If the sky was short or if the painting was small he had to begin diluting the paint after just a few strokes. He continued this process of applying steadily thinner and more dilute strokes of paint until he reached the horizon or just above the horizon, where the very dilute blue gave way completely to the underlying colour of the canvas.

Such gradations achieved through steady dilutions of the mineral paint were more common in thangka painting than in murals, and for the painting of the sky they seem to have been used on a wider scale by painters from eastern parts of Tibet. The technique was particularly effective when the sky transition was executed over a ground that was slightly tinged with yellow or ochre.

This one-brush technique demanded relatively quick work; the series of strokes had to be laid down fast enough so that the subsequent strokes would blend smoothly when overlapping the previous ones. Often a little unevenness in the gradation could not be avoided. When the painter had gone over the area once, he usually had to go back to touch up any streaky spots that appeared as the paint dried. A practiced painter could lay down a sky in this way very quickly. A beginner, on the other hand, would spend a great deal more time and still end up with a rather streaky and uneven gradation.

Two-Brush Wet Shading

The second main technique for shading the sky used uniformly opaque colours to affect the gradual transitions, and did not necessarily depend on the dilution of the paint to get more transparency, as in the method just described. This second technique was termed "wet shading" *(rlon mdangs)* since it entailed the gradual blending of two adjoining areas of wet paint. Because this technique usually required two brushes (one for the colour at either end of the gradation) it can also be called "two-brush shading".[2]

For painting the sky in this technique the painter began by preparing two values of blue paint, one deeper and one lighter. With azurite pigments the more finely ground powder would yield the lighter value, whereas with other blues it was necessary to mix the base blue with some white. The actual painting began with the painter laying down a full-length stroke of the darker sky colour across the top of the sky area. To avoid unwanted thickness and granularity he would use the surface layer of paint in the pot. He then followed with a quick succession of strokes, one beneath the other as described above. Here, however, the goal was not to

make each succeeding stroke lighter but to produce an unbroken, smooth field of colour. At some point — say at about half the way from zenith to horizon — the artist applied a few last thin paint strokes and, having put aside his first paint brush, began quickly laying down strokes of the lighter blue, beginning where the darker blue ended, or just above where it ended. He then continued to work down in a series of several brush strokes. Next, to make a smooth gradation where the two paints merged, he took up his dark blue brush again, and from above the juncture of dark and light he laid down another series of dark blue strokes to blend with the lighter wet paint beneath. Since the borders of both hues were still wet, the artist could continue to improve the gradation until he was satisfied, by brushing back and forth while moving up and down the area where they merged.

When this blending of the two values had been completed, the artist went back to his light blue brush and, continuing down from the bottom of the light blue area, he applied a smooth coat until he reached the horizon. Alternatively, he could continue a gradual transition using an even lighter blue. Or, as he neared the horizon, he could also gradually dilute the paint as in the first technqiue, causing it to become almost transparent and then finally to give way just above the horizon.

Dry Shading

The third and last major technique for tinting the sky consisted of the application of thin washes of blue dye over the ground or over some other base colour. Tibetan artists called this "dry shading" *(skam mdangs)* because the dye washes were applied to a dry surface. Most painters of Dbus and Gtsang used this technique when painting the skies of fine thangkas, and it was also used by a number of painters from other regions.

To shade the sky using the dry-shading method, the artist first prepared a blue tinting wash, usually from the dye of a light indigo *(rams, described in Chapter 10)*. The surface to which the dye was applied could be a plain white ground. But more commonly it was either a preliminary blue gradation applied by one-brush dilution shading, or a uniform light blue undercoat.

The actual dry-shading technique, as practiced by the artist Wangdrak, proceeded as follows. He began applying the indigo wash in a series of long thin strokes across the top of the sky. He gradually built up a deep blue through the successive accumulation of many thin washes, and never applied the dye in strong concentrations. As he proceeded down the sky he began to space his strokes further and further apart. In addition, he was careful not to overload his brush with dye, and when applying it he exerted gradually less pressure on the brush tip. In large thaṇgkas he used to apply the indigo shading to one side of the sky at a time if this was permitted by the composition. When one side of the sky appeared to be well shaded he went on to the other side. Later he went back to the first area and examined it for light patches that needed more shading. As long as the tinted area remained damp it was difficult to tell if the shading was right, and thus it was advantageous to work on a second area — or even the sky of a second thangka — while the first one dried.

Applying Blue to Other Areas

After painting the sky, the artist went on to fill in areas of uniform blues. First he filled in areas of deepest azure *(mthing)*, such as the blue parts of the blue-green rocky crags, the blue backgrounds of some body nimbuses, and the hair and begging bowls of Buddhas. To attain a uniform coat of the deepest blue, a painter sometimes had to apply the paint as many as three times, each time touching up the areas of insufficient coverage. The deepest of blues was also the coarsest of colours, and some painters said that it required more size in the binder.[3]

Next came the areas of medium blue, such as the water in the landscape. The lowest levels of the water areas were sometimes begun in a deeper blue if the whole area was to be wet shaded. Our main informants, however, normally applied a medium blue undercoat first, and later shaded these areas using the dry-shading method. The last of the blues to be applied were the lightest values, and these were applied to such places as certain jewels and textiles.

The Application of Greens

The simplest "landscape" consisted only of an empty green field in the foreground that faded into the horizon. For painting this the artist employed one of the above techniques for creating gradations, but here he began at the bottom and worked up. Painting his deeper green on the bottom edge of the painting area he effected a gradual lightening of the green as he worked upwards. In this simplest of backgrounds the lightest green would fade into an indistinct horizon where it met the similarly painted skyline. But if the landscape had clearly demarcated hills, crags, water and so forth, gradations of colour were applied to the green hills or meadows working from top to bottom as in the sky. Many painters coloured the tops of each hill a medium green, and gradually faded out this colour into a paler green as the bottom was reached. Following the completion of the large green areas in the landscape, the artist filled in the other green areas, first the deepest hues and finally the lightest green.

The Application of the Remaining Colours

After the greens there came the application of the reds, oranges, and so forth, as outlined above. When the artists had finished colouring all of the red areas within the composition, some of them also laid down a red border outside the outer edge of the whole painting. (Other painters applied this border after the initial base coats of all colours were complete.) Because in the completed and framed thangka a red silk brocade was used adjacent to the painting, this red-painted strip functioned later as a guideline (and a margin for error) for the tailor who sewed the brocade frame. This red paint around the border also immediately brought the painting to life by the contrast it created with the green landscape and blue sky. Areas to be painted later with gold now received, in their turn, an undercoating of ochre.

During the initial application of these colours some painters used wet shading here and there to create colour transitions. Our main informants, however, usually did not. A number of Central Tibetan painters seemed actually to disapprove of the wide use of wet shading in thangkas, even though in mural painting they considered it perfectly acceptable.

Except for the difficulties of shading the sky and landscape, the initial application of colour was among the easiest steps in the painting of a thangka. The painting in of flat areas of colour was one of the first tasks that a master might entrust to a novice; the master himself was thereby freed to devote his time to the more demanding tasks of shading and, especially, outlining. Even so the painter of the first coats of colour, whether master or novice, had to exercise a certain amount of care, particularly when painting the outside edges of each area. The paint had to cover the area completely, but of course it was also important not to let it spill over into adjoining colour areas. A simple method for applying paint accurately to a given area was first to apply a stroke to the middle of the area, and then to fill in around the edges using strokes that moved in general from the middle outward and from the top downward. By the time the edges were reached there was no danger of excess paint spilling over the borders and the edge of the brush tip could be used to execute sharp and exact borders. Darker colours were especially difficult to correct if they overlapped a lighter area. Some corrections could be made by immediately wetting the paint and blotting it with a brush, and as a last resort the artist could scrape off dry paint down to the white ground by using a very sharp blade.

In addition to basic accuracy in application, it was also desirable to apply the paints in coats as thin as would still give good coverage. In the usual Central Tibetan "full-colour" *(rdzogs tshon)* method this meant the thinnest opaque coat. For this purpose, and in general, the painter as he worked had to be sure to keep the paint at its optimum consistency.

Hand Supports

In order to increase their control while painting, the artists of Tibet traditionally used certain techniques for steadying both their "canvas" and their painting hands. To begin with, most painters worked with the stretcher propped upright in their laps or just in front of their crossed legs, the top of the stretcher being tilted slightly away from them. When working on the

Wangdu with canvas on his lap and resting his painting hand on the canvas.

top portion of the painting, the artists usually placed the bottom of the stretcher on the seat before them. But when working on the lower portion they commonly lifted the stretcher and placed its base on their legs or laps. Often the top of the stretcher was held up by a cord that was tied at its other end to a nail or rafter somewhere above. Alternatively, some painters worked with the bottom of the stretcher on their laps but with the top resting against a wall, pillar or any handy support. A few painters also found it comfortable to work for periods while supporting the back of the "canvas" with the free hand, for instance while sketching. But even then they commonly left a loose supporting cord tied to the top of the stretcher, so that if they let go it would be caught by the cord and would not fall to the floor.

To ensure maximum control the painters also supported their painting hands on or above the painting surface in special ways. A steady hand was of course important during many stages of painting, but it was crucial for any detailed work. For this purpose some painters — especially, we are told, the painters of the Shigatse school — traditionally worked while resting the painting hand on a small board that spanned the sides of the wooden stretcher. By using this "hand support" *(lag rten)* these artists could paint with great control without having to touch the painting surface with their hands, thus helping to avoid any accidental smearing of the wet paint.

Artists from Lhasa and other parts of Central Tibet (Dbus), however, were more apt to paint while resting their hands on the painting surface, allowing only a small area on the outer edge of the little finger to touch it. Legdrup Gyatsho used to place a small piece of clean cloth or paper under his little finger and then slide his hand on this over the painting while working. Such a procedure is especially helpful now for painters working in the hotter climates of South Asia, since it helps prevent smudging caused by a sweaty hand. For work on rougher surfaces, as during mural painting, a small leather covering was sometimes devised to protect the little finger and the edge of the painting hand. For many experienced artists, however, such protection was not necessary since they had long ago built up a heavy callous on the part of the little finger that was in constant contact with the painting.

Adjusting the Paint on the Brush Tip

When working, the painters commonly held the brush in the right hand and the dish of paint in the palm of the left. At the same time many of them also commonly employed the left hand as a sort of palette or testing surface. Just before applying the paint, some artists would stroke the loaded brush against the back of the left hand, between the thumb and index finger. This helped both to shape the brush tip and to distribute the paint load properly. It also allowed the artist to check for excess moisture in the paint. Some artists preferred to do the same thing by stroking the brush on the left thumbnail instead. For similar reasons others licked the tips of their loaded brushes or rolled them between their lips to point them. Painters who licked the brushes with their tongues not only shaped the loaded brush tips in this way, but also added a little saliva to the paint while doing so. As one painter pointed out, saliva was excellent for thinning paint during the painting of delicately shaded areas. Painters who licked their brushes, however, had to know which paints were poisonous and thus not to be ingested. This use of tongue and saliva by Tibetan painters was in fact quite widespread, judging from the funny stories circulating among Tibetans that allude to the technique.[4] These stories also reveal a somewhat disapproving attitude on the part of ordinary Tibetans towards this practice.[5]

Work Duration and Routines

It took the artist from a few hours to a few days or even weeks to complete the application of the first coats of colour. This depended on the size of the project (the number and size of the thangkas being painted together) and the complexity of the compositions. Painters normally worked only during daylight hours, and while painting they usually sat near a sunny window. Nowadays the older artists still typically prefer not to work at night under electric lights. Working in direct sunlight was also avoided for, as one painter pointed out, the hot sunshine made the paints dry too quickly.

A painter usually ended his day's work at the conclusion of a particular step, for instance when he had finished painting all of the areas of a certain colour. Then he washed his brushes and put aside his paints and stretchers for the night. To keep the paints fresh for the next day, some painters poured a spoonful of water over each colour. Excess water could be poured off the following morning, and the paints would then need only a little stirring to be ready again for application. Many artists also covered their paint bowls overnight to protect the paints from both excess drying and airborne dust and soot. Similarly, to protect the paintings the stretchers were commonly hung facing a wall, sometimes covered with a cloth. But even when such precautions had been taken, it was still usually best to begin work the next day by dusting off the painting surface, and this was essential if the stretcher had been set aside for more than a few days.

Final Scraping and Cleaning

At the completion of the initial application of colours, the artist had to scrape smooth *(gris 'brad)* the whole painted surface. When mixed with the size binder the mineral pigments became paints of somewhat differing consistencies, and these paints also dried into paint layers of different thicknesses and textures. To minimize the unevenness of the surface and to prepare the whole painting for the finishing work to come, many Central Tibetan painters at this stage would smooth the surface by gently scraping it with a razor-sharp knife.

Careful scraping, with the knife edge facing in the direction of the scraping motion, removed the top portions of the thickest paint layers. Wangdrak, for instance, first scraped from the bottom upward and then

Scraping smooth the initial coat of paint with a knife.

from the top down. An immediate result was that the painting took on a mottled appearance, with many shiny and a few matte areas visible when the canvas was held at an angle that reflected the outdoor light. These irregularities helped the painter make sure that his scraping was thorough, and anyway they did not remain long, because immediately after scraping the artist dusted off the painting with a feather duster or clean rag and then rubbed the whole surface with a small ball of parched grain flour *(rtsam pa)* dough.[6] The dough ball had to be almost dry so that it would not stick to the painting. The painter used it as if it were a large rubber eraser, rubbing it over the painting with large, sweeping strokes. When the sides of the ball became coated with colour he would knead the dough in his hand for a few seconds, thus exposing new clean surfaces. Rubbing with this dough restored the desired matte finish and picked up any paint dust that remained. It also left a thin coating of tiny dough particles and this had to be dusted off as the final step.

Not all Tibetan painters scraped and then cleaned their thangkas. It was not essential for example on paintings in which the colours had been applied in thin washes to begin with. Thus many Eastern Tibetan painters did not traditionally scrape their paintings. Once when the artist Wangdrak was working on a project with several painters from Amdo, the Eastern Tibetans expressed surprise when he took out his knife and began to scrape his partially completed thangka. They asked him if he was not damaging the painting, for indeed the scraping did seem to remove a lot of pigment. But, as Wangdrak showed them, there was no harm done. In fact if the paints were properly mixed they could actually be improved by scraping. Being thinner, they were less prone to cracking and peeling. Scraping off the surface layer also helped the appearance of some paints, such as poor grades of minium. But an equally important benefit was that this smoothing and cleaning made the subsequent steps of shading and outlining much easier. Nevertheless, scraping followed by rubbing with *rtsampa* dough did have one drawback: it could easily darken a pure white area. Therefore some painters waited until after the scraping and rubbing to fill in prominent areas of white such as the faces and limbs of white deities.

Cleaning off paint by rubbing with a ball of tsampa dough.

Jampa applying gold detail.

The Application of Gold

Gold was the last pigment to be laid down over large areas of the painting. Since gold needed a smooth undercoat when applied as a solid colour to a sizable area, its application was postponed until after the scraping of the initial coats of colour and the subsequent dusting and cleaning of the painting surface. Another reason was that no painter would ever scrape off and thus waste any of this precious pigment. The gold used in Tibetan painting was thought of as a pious offering; although the merit *(bsod nams)* of the painting project depended mainly on the attitude and motivation of those involved, the offering of more gold could make

the merit commensurately greater. Once the amount of gold had been determined by patron and painter, it was the duty of the painter to see to it that every bit of the gold was used as intended.

With the exception of a few recent paintings, nearly every thangka used at least a little real gold. One can discern at least four degrees of gold use in thangka painting. The ultimate application is the full-gold thangka *(gser thang)*, where the composition was rendered with a bare minimum of dyes and pigments over a solid field of unburnished gold. A middling use is found in paintings where the main figures, together with many details and outlines, have been rendered with gold paint. The minimum use is when only outlines and certain details were painted in gold, and the majority of thangkas incorporated this minimal application. Finally, a fourth and special type is found in black and vermilion thangkas, where the whole composition was usually executed with gold line drawings, sometimes combined with solid or shaded areas of gold.

When the painter applied gold in fine line drawings no undercoat was necessary; however, when painting larger areas a coat of yellow ochre or some similar colour had to be laid down as the gold undercoat (*gser rten*). Since yellow ochre itself had a subdued golden hue, an undercoat of it lessened the amount of real gold needed to achieve a rich, solid-looking coverage. For this reason painters nowadays continue to use such undercoats even when applying powdered-brass imitation gold *(rag rdul)*.

Other gold bases were also in use among Tibetan artisans, one of which was a mixture of orpiment yellow *(ba bla)* and calcium white *(ka rag)*. In addition, some artists when painting statues made of clay and papier-mâché preferred to use a flesh-tinted base coat on the areas designated for gold paint. The artist Tshoknyi Gyatsho, for instance, made such an undercoat by mixing yellow, white and red pigments. We also learned of some recently painted murals in Nepal where the artists had first applied imitation gold over an ochre base coat, and followed that by laying down a final layer of real gold. This spared much of the expense of using gold over large areas, and the effect was the same as if it had been done completely with real gold. Here the use of a modern acrylic medium reduced the danger of the brass undercoat darkening beneath the gold.

some blue areas at first had a rather coarse or rough appearance, so the painters polished them until they were smooth. First the areas had to be moistened with a little water. Then just before the paint became dry the artists rubbed them with a burnisher *(gzi)*, while holding a smooth and hard support beneath the canvas to prevent gouging. Azurite was burnished only on thangkas and not on mural paintings.

4. One irreverent anecdote goes to the effect: Said the young child of the painter to the shining new Buddha image just installed in the temple, "I recognize you! Inside you the lamas have poked a stick, and on your face my daddy rubbed his spit!" (The stick referred to is the central axis-pole inserted into the hollow center of the statue in preparation for consecration).

5. Some thangka painters, too, considered it sacrilegious to put a painting brush into one's mouth. See Hugh R. Downs, *Rhythms of a Himalayan Village* (New York, 1980), p.105.

6. The Tibetan term that Wangdrak used for this process of cleaning with dough was *spag phyi rgyab*.

Notes

1. Similes for paint consistencies that were derived from food and drink are also found in Bo-dong, *Mkhas pa*, vol.2, pp.255, 258: *ma zho tsam* "just the consistency of almost coagulated yogurt," *dar ba chu med tsam* "just the consistency of buttermilk without whey," *zan gron (dron) tsam* "just the consistency of warm porridge," and *skyo ma tsam* "just the consistency of pap or paste."

   Wangdrak mixed his dry pigment with strong size until it became the consistency of thick porridge and then stirred it very thoroughly. This initial stirring was called "pang nur" *(spag snur* or *sbang snur?)*, and he believed that it induced a good separation of the top and bottom layers when dilute size was stirred in and the preparation of the paint was complete.

2. Sometimes a third brush was also used, as described in Chapter 10.

3. The painter Wangdrak informed us that in the past some painters of the Central Tibetan Menri tradition used to apply the azurite paint quite thickly to achieve the deepest blues. As a result

The Sherpa artist Kaba Par Gyaltshen inspecting a finished brush.

Nine

Brushes

The brushes *(pir)* used by our main informants consisted of a brush tip of fine animal hairs attached to the pointed tip of a characteristic type of wooden handle. Brushes constructed in this manner contrast sharply with the Chinese style of paintbrush used throughout East Asia. The latter was usually made by bundling the brush hairs together and inserting them as a plug into a hollow-ended handle. Although many Tibetan artists were familiar with Chinese-style brushes, most applied their colours with brushes of the distinctively Tibetan "point-construction" type that they or their assistants made.

Brush Handles

The process of brush making began with the preparation of a suitable brush handle *(pir mda')*. Most handles were made from twigs of juniper *(shugs pa)* or coniferous trees such as pine *(thang shing)*. Occasionally an artist might also make a particularly fine brush using a rare wood such as sandalwood. In general for brush handles the artists preferred the woods of wholesome or medicinal trees *(sman shing)*.

The artist began by whittling a suitably sized stick of wood into a tapering shaft. When the basic handle shape had been achieved he concentrated on carving down the last half inch or so of the thicker end of the handle, to produce a sharp projection that jutted straight out from the end of the shaft. This projecting point would serve as the base around which the hairs were arranged and tied.

Brush Hairs *(pir spu)*

In Central Tibet the painting tips of thangka painting brushes were commonly made from cat and goat hair. Our main informants made their finest brushes from cat hair. Painters from Eastern Tibet similarly asserted that cats provided excellent hairs for brush making, but they preferred the hairs of wild cats *(ri'i zhim)*. Many painters also valued the hairs of the sable or weasel.

Hairs used for brush making had to be straight, glossy and resilient. For medium-sized brushes such as those used for applying the main coats of colour *(byug pir)*, some artists used to collect suitable hairs from kid goats. In Tibet the best goat hairs grew on the front hooves and muzzle of the animal, hairs from other parts of the goat were too long or curly. Tibetan artists living in non-mountainous parts of India or Nepal now have to look higher on the goat's flank for suitable hairs because in the warmer climate the hairs on the hooves and muzzle are too short.[1] Larger brushes were sometimes made from fine horse hairs, gathered from within the mane or from the chest or abdomen of the horse.

For the small outline brushes *(bcad pir)* a finer hair was required, and this was usually obtained from the pelts of cats, wild cats and sables. Good hairs could be chosen by blowing gently onto a piece of the animal's fur and selecting those hairs which remained erect. These upright hairs were more resilient, producing a brush tip that was very pliable and suitable for fine line work. These hairs occurred in the greatest numbers at the back of the neck, along the spine and at the base of the cat's back, just above the tail.

Brushes.

Brush Construction

After a suitable brush handle was prepared and a sufficient number of hairs had been gathered, the artist sorted the hairs according to length and coarseness, quickly rejecting any obviously defective ones. He then selected a number of good hairs – depending on how many were necessary for the brush he planned – and arranged them with all of their tips pointing one way. The artist had to distinguish the natural taper of the hair from the cut end or the bulb of the root, since only the natural tip was suitable for painting.

The next important step in the process began with the gathering of all of the selected hairs into a single tuft. For a good brush tip *(pir kha)* the ends of the hairs within the tuft had to be brought to about the same level, so the painters usually dropped the cluster tip-end first into a small cylindrical hole of an appropriate size, such as the hole in the end of a sawn and smoothly rounded bamboo section, and tapped the container to make all the hair ends fall to the bottom of the hole. For this purpose any other object with a suitable hole could also be used. Some painters, for instance, employed a fired slab of clay with a number of holes of different diameters and depths specially pressed into the clay before firing. The holes could not be too deep, because the root ends of the hairs had to project for easy removal. Furthermore, the sides of the hole had to be smooth so that the hairs could fall easily to the bottom without catching on the sides. Often the hairs would by themselves become tangled together or caught on the sides, and to prevent this the artists commonly added a pinch of fine ash dust before dropping them into the hole. Thus dusted they would usually fall to the bottom after just a few taps.[2]

At this stage the hairs were often sufficiently well arranged to permit the final shaping of the brush tip. Here, however, some artists rechecked them, and this was especially important if the artist had not previously examined them one at a time. To test the hairs he firmly grasped the projecting ends, pulled them from the hole, and then flicked the loose ends with the fingers of the other hand. This flicking knocked out any hairs that were too short to be held within the tip. The artist then closely examined the painting end of the bundle and removed any hairs with bent, split or broken ends. If not enough hair remained to make the desired brush, he added more and put the newly enlarged tuft back into the hole. He then repeated the above process until he obtained a cluster of hairs of the right size and quality.

When the artist was satisfied with his cluster of brush hairs and had them in the hole with their tips resting on the bottom, the next step was to give the brush tip its shape and to fix it in that position. First he grasped the projecting ends of the hairs and pulled them from the hole. Next, without letting the hairs move out of position, he dipped the painting end into some strong hide glue or size. Then, still grasping the unglued end of the cluster, he stroked the glued end against a smooth surface until the hairs came to a good tip. When the glue had set enough so that the hairs would not move he set the bundle aside and allowed it to dry completely.

After the glue had dried the painter began the final step, the attaching of the hairs to the brush handle. First he trimmed the loose, unglued hair ends to an equal length, cutting them straight across with a sharp knife. Then some artists dipped the same unglued ends into size solution and positioned the damp hairs around the projecting point of the brush shaft; others simply positioned the hairs while dry. When the hairs were evenly spaced and lying flat against the point, the artist tied them in place near their base with a fine thread. (This thread had to be strong as well as fine; one favorite type was silk thread salvaged from scraps of brocade.) The artist then passed several more loops of thread around the bottom third of the hairs and tied the thread again. After he had examined the hairs to make sure that they were lying in place and well distributed around the point of the shaft, he used more thread to wrap the base of the hairs in a series of tight, consecutive loops for the whole length of the projecting point beneath, and then knotted the thread. Finally he gave the thread a coating of size. At this point the construction of the brush was complete. The only thing still necessary to ready the brush for use was to soak the glued painting tip in warm water until the glue dissolved and the hairs came free.

The Care of Brushes

Because the brush hairs were usually attached to the handle only by thread and size and were not as a rule cemented in place with a waterproof glue, the artist had to treat his brushes with care. The brushes were not left soaking for long periods of time, nor were they used to stir colours. It was also best to clean them immediately after use. Some painters were noticeably gentle when handling and cleaning their brushes; we observed one painter carefully washing his brushes by pouring a little clear water into the palm of his hand and then slowly rotating the brush in this water to loosen the paint. Next he thoroughly rinsed the brush in some new water, and then formed the brush tip into a good point before putting it away into the container he used for storing his brushes.

After much use the brushes began to lose their original points. In some cases, however, a good tip could be restored; broken or bent hairs could be cut off individually, or, as one painter reported, bad hairs could be trimmed by careful singeing with a stick of burning incense. Larger brushes, such as those used for coating walls, could have their whole painting tip trimmed with a sharp knife.

a

b

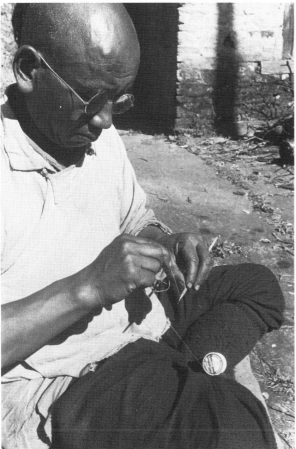

c

The Sherpa artist Kaba Par Gyaltshen: a) Straightening the newly glued brush hairs onto the pointed tip of the handle itself, b) Tying the brush hairs to the handle: the first knot c) Winding the thread around the hairs. Here the first loop was made near the tip of the shaft, and then the thread was wrapped around the hair moving away from the brush tip towards the wooden handle. When the thicker part of the handle was reached, the artist tied the two ends of the thread. (The shorter end had been held parallel to the point and wrapped under the successive loops).

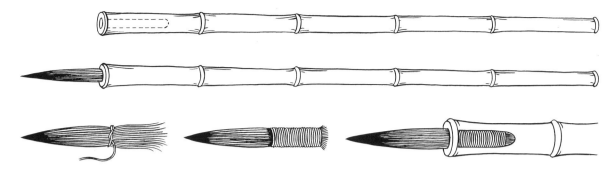

Bamboo brush with plug.

Another Variety of Thangka-Painting Brush

The above type of brush with the hairs attached to a projecting point on the end of the handle was by far the most common type used in thangka painting. In addition, we met a small number of painters who used brushes that resembled, at least superficially, the Chinese ink-painting type. For example, the painter Gömpo from Kyirong constructed his brushes by bunching a tuft of hairs into a plug, which he subsequently stuffed into a hollow brush handle. He had experimented unsuccessfully with quills for handles but ended up mainly using hollow bamboo sticks that had been cut near the joints to make a receptacle for the hairs.

Gömpo had studied under a painting master from Lhasa, and so it is possible that this kind of brush construction reflected the penetration of a Chinese brush type by way of the Tibetan capital where Chinese influence was felt more strongly. Indeed there is other evidence that in this century "plug-construction" brushes were used by certain influential artists of Lhasa. According to Rahula Sankrityayana, who observed the work of a court artist of the Thirteenth Dalai Lama in Lhasa in the 1930s:

> Brushes of various sizes are made from twigs of sandalwood or smooth pine, shaped narrow at one end and at the thicker end hollowed out to receive a bunch of goat or cat hairs, or any other variety capable of soaking up water. The hairs are tightly tied together, and one end dipped in glue made by boiling bits of hide . . . The glued end of the brush is then wrapped with cloth and again tied and inserted, with more glue, into the scooped-out part of the wood.[3]

Large Brushes

A special type of brush also deserving mention was a large horse-hair brush used by the painter Jampa from Lhasa. This brush was used for whitewashing or colouring walls and other large surfaces. The brush was large — about a foot long and one and one-half inches thick. A noteworthy feature of this brush was that its construction allowed the painter to trim its tip again and again. The brush was made from a sheaf of long hairs from the mane of a horse. The maker began by laying the hairs parallel and then arranging them in a cluster. Next he dipped the cluster in glue, and when the glue had partially dried he wound a string around most of the length of the hairs. When the bundle of hairs had completely dried the artist or brush-maker sewed a piece of sheepskin leather over the part of the sheaf of hairs that had been wrapped with string, leaving a few inches of hair extending beyond the leather to serve as the brush tip. After the leather had been moistened and dried, it would shrink and make a firm handle.

A brush such as this was subjected to a lot of wear and tear since it was used for the preparation and painting of rough surfaces such as walls. After a certain amount of use the painting end of the brush became considerably worn down. But since the brush hairs extended through the full length of the brush — even inside the "handle" — all the painter had to do to renew the brush was to expose more of the hairs. To do this he cut back an inch or so of the leather sheath, unwound the string, and then, if necessary for a good tip, trimmed the end with a sharp knife.

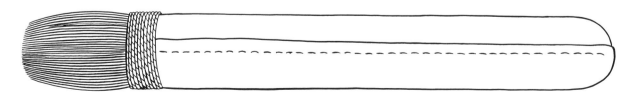

Large brush.

Brush container.

Notes

1. The painter Thargye informed us that painters in Nepal can now obtain suitable hairs from the ears of water buffaloes.

2. Compare Downs, p.104.

3. Sankrityayana, p.33.

A thangka of White Tārā in which a considerable amount of time has been spent shading the clouds, flowers and other parts.   Victoria and Albert Museum.

Ten
Shading and Colour Gradations

After the initial coats of colour had been laid down, the next step was to apply washes for shading and gradual transitions of tone. "Shading" *(mdangs)* in this context does not mean the treatment of light and shadow within the whole composition (chiaroscuro), for the distribution of light and dark was not systematically developed throughout a thangka painting. Nevertheless, Tibetan artists did practice shading in a different sense. Transitions of both tone and colour were regularly executed on single objects within the painting, and when used to create shadowing, the technique contributed a three-dimensional appearance to such things as clouds and the bodily forms of the divine beings. Especially when employed in the "modeling" of faces and bodies, shading lent a realism where it was needed most: on the sacred figures at the center of the icon.

Main Shading Techniques

The painters of Tibet used several techniques for shading and colour gradations, but most of them can be typed as either "wet" or "dry" techniques. "Wet shading" *(rlon mdangs)*, the blending of two wet colours on the painting surface, was employed for the most part only during the laying on of the initial coats of colour. "Dry shading" *(skam mdangs)*, on the other hand, was usually a secondary step. It consisted of the application of successive thin washes of colour over a dry preliminary coat. Both dry and wet techniques in their simplest forms have been described in Chapter 8 in connection with the painting of the sky.

Wet shading, as we have seen, usually required more than one brush. The colour at each end of the gradation needed its own brush, and often a third was used for the intermediate hue. Dry shading, conversely, was executed with only one brush, although this in no way prevented the artist from achieving a variety of shading effects by altering the size, shape, direction and frequency of the brush strokes. For the painting of skies alone the Bhutanese painter Kunsang Tobgye actually enumerated as many as four types of dry shading:

1) *byug mdangs* ("spread-on shading"): the usual evenly graduated dry-shading method. According to the artist this method was most appropriate for shading the skies in paintings that depicted peaceful *(zhi ba)* deities.

2) *'bru mdangs* ("granular shading"): shading with small dabs or dots of indigo, applied thickly and close together at the zenith, but less frequently

as the horizon was approached. A less time-consuming method, this was used for the skies of paintings of either peaceful or aggressive *(khro bo)* deities.

3) *sprin mdangs* ("cloud shading"): shading laid down in horizontal bands in imitation of cloud layers.

4) *char mdangs* ("rain shading"): indigo shading applied in vertical strokes, giving the appearance of a falling shower. This was to be used especially in paintings of aggressive, terrifying deities.

byug mdangs
("spread-on shading")

'bru mdangs
("granular shading")

sprin mdangs
("cloud shading")

char mdangs
("rain shading")

Four different types of dry shading.

Thus, even in the relatively simple matter of tinting the sky the artists had a considerable range of techniques available to them. It should be noted, however, that the last two of the above shading types were not commonly employed by Central Tibetan artists in the painting of thangkas. In modern thangka painting we have only seen the "spread-on" and "granular" shadings. Our main informants seldom used any but the first of these methods. Wangdrak for instance knew of both "smooth shading" (*leb mdangs*, his term for "spread-on shading") and "dotted shading" (*gtsag mdangs*, his term for "granular shading"), but by and large he used only the first of these. (He also had a term for the finest dry shading applied as a final step over the usual "flat shading." It was *khra 'drud*, literally "pulling out the glossiest," a term also used to denote the selection of the best hair or wool.) The painter Dorje Gyaltshen, by contrast, commonly used both the spread-on shading (calling it *gsed mdangs* "carded shading" or "smoothed shading") and the granular shading (calling it *gtsag mdangs*, "poked shading" or "dotted shading"). The latter technique he applied to green areas such as hills and meadows.

Diluting the Dye with Water

Another possibility open to the painter was to combine the application of dry-shading dyes with diluting strokes of water. Some painters preferred this technique particularly for the shading of small areas. As an example we may describe how the artist Legdrub Gyatsho shaded the small body nimbus behind a minor goddess.

He had begun the painting of the nimbus by applying a red undercoat. The object of the subsequent shading was to create a gradual transition of colour within a short space, darkening the outer edges of the nimbus but leaving the areas nearest to the goddess the original red.

To begin the shading the artist applied some dark tinting colour (here using a reddish-brown dye) in a solid band around the outer edge of the red nimbus. Then he applied a series of small brush strokes of dye parallel to the outer band, making them further apart as he proceeded inward. When he had applied sufficient colour he wetted the brush with water, and with this diluting brush *(chu pir)* he applied a series of thinning strokes to the area of the transition. Beginning in the middle of the gradation, he worked inward, and by diluting the innermost strokes of dye he caused the darker tint to disappear into the background colour in a smooth transition.

Further Varieties of Shading

The painters added yet another dimension to shading by combining the dry-shading and dilution-shading effects with the different types of undercoats. Such combina-

tions allow the classification of shading into at least three further types:

1) Shading using gradual transitions upon a base of uniform colour. This was the usual type, employed for example on meadows, back curtains and some clouds and flowers.

2) Shading upon a two-toned area. Some flowers and clouds, for instance, had middle sections receiving slightly darker undercoat colours.

3) Secondary dry shading on an area that had already been shaded by the wet-shading method. Some painters used this method for shading skies, as mentioned above.

Finally, we should also mention two further elaborations of shading technique. The first of these was the shading of an area where the application of the dye was preceded by the drawing of an intermediate sketch on the undercoat. Wangdrak, for instance, outlined many of the blue and green areas with indigo before shading them with the same dye. But for most of the areas to be shaded with lac dye he did not employ an intermediate sketch *(bar bris)*. In most cases such intermediate sketching was not essential because the artist could either see the preliminary drawing through the undercoat, or could mentally reconstruct the sketch by referring to the outer form of the object.

The second special shading technique was a variety of dry shading applied to bodily figures to give them the appearance of fullness. The technique consisted of the application of bands of dark dye to "model" the flesh. This could be called "contouring" because the artist mainly applied these bands around the borders of anatomical areas. The technique was especially important in the shading of dark-coloured deities.

The Dyes Used in Shading

For shading and outlining, few mineral pigments were used. Instead, the main shading colours were organic dyes and lakes, and of these the two most important were indigo and lac dye.

Indigo *(rams)*

Indigo is a dark blue dyestuff that until about 1900 was obtained entirely from plants (mainly of the genus *Indigofera*). At the turn of the century, however, a comparatively cheap synthetic indigo was developed. This caused severe economic disruption in India where huge tracts of land had been used for growing indigo plants, and nowadays very little of the dyestuff is naturally produced.

Tibetans used to import their indigo in slabs or chunks of prepared dye from India and Nepal.[1] Several qualities were available. Good qualities were light in weight and easy to break. The best grades could be identified by the fact that the new surfaces of freshly broken indigo would reflect light with a reddish tint. The authors of Tibetan *materia medica* similarly state that for medicine the inferior grades appeared light blue, while the best quality had a deep reddish tinge.

Other tests could be used to gauge the quality of indigo. If a little good quality indigo was moistened and rubbed between the fingers, it dyed them a dark blue-black that could not be washed off easily. Another test was to scratch a piece across the thumbnail. If the indigo left a black streak it was of good quality. A variety of light indigo that failed these tests was known as *he rams*. Although it was unsuitable for dark outlining it was good for making washes for the fine shading of such things as clouds and flowers.

For preparing indigo in a consistency suitable for painting the most important thing was to grind it well. Prolonged grinding not only produced a smooth, ink-like consistency, but was also said to improve the colour because the longer the dye was ground the darker its blue became. To grind indigo, the artist first crushed it into a powder and then added a little water and stirred it until it became dough-like in consistency. Then he ground it in a mortar until the once moist dyestuff became almost dry. He then moistened it again, and resumed grinding until it dried out again. He repeated this process of moistening and grinding many times, and sometimes a single batch of indigo would be ground for two days or longer.

Strictly speaking, indigo did not require any hide glue as a binder. The addition of a little glue, however, was said to facilitate the grinding process. Also, when it had been thoroughly ground its quality as a paint was improved by the presence of a little glue. This was because indigo in solution with water tended to coagulate in the paint pot as it dried out, but this drying process was slowed down and the indigo was held in aqueous suspension longer if mixed with a little glue.

Being a dye, indigo was well suited for both shading and outlining. In almost every instance where it appears that ink has been employed for either purpose in traditional thangkas, in fact it is indigo that has been used. Indigo was superior to Indian and China ink, according to one of our informants, because it was less prone to running and streaking if water was spilled on it. One painter also asserted that in an earlier period some artists used to employ indigo for reinforcing the initial charcoal sketches, instead of the usual ink.

Lac Dye *(rgya tshos)*

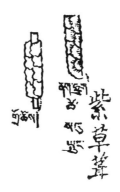

Lac dye or lac lake is a red dyestuff that is produced from resins secreted by the tiny lac insect *(Laccifer lacca)*, and which is still used in India and neighbouring countries. The lac insect is a species of scale insect, so named because the resinous products it excretes are deposited in tiny scales on the host trees. Tradition has it that the name lac derived from the Persian word *lak* or the Hindustani *lakh*, meaning "one hundred thousand", the insect being so named because such an immense number of insects was required to produce a small amount of shellac. Chemically, the dye is laccaic acid or its salts, and it is related to the carminic acid derived from cochineal. Lac dye may have been brought from India and introduced to Europe by the Arabs as early as the 7th century. It became commercially important in the 17th century when the East India Company exported it, even before shellac (the resinous by-product of lac) had been introduced into Europe.

Lac dye was sometimes imported into Tibet from India in the form of small dry cakes or pellets. Also it is said to have been received from China in the form of wafers of compacted cotton *(srin bal rgya tshos)* that had been saturated with the dye and dried.[2] However, most of the lac dye used in Tibet was probably produced from the raw materials by the Tibetans themselves.

Preparation

Tibetans extracted lac dye from crude forms of lac such as stick-lac (twigs encrusted with lac-insect scales) that they obtained from the warmer border regions of the Eastern Himalayas. Artists could also get the crude lac in the form of scales already separated from the twigs of the host tree. If stick-lac had been obtained, the artist first had to scrape off the scales from the sticks and remove any woody debris from the scales because heating the lac together with the sticks would yield an inferior dye.

Once he had removed, cleaned and crushed the lac scales, the dye maker next heated the scales in hot water to melt them and to extract the dye.[3] Care was taken not to overheat the lac, for this would blacken it and spoil the whole batch. Also, it was said that the pot used for heating the lac should not be made of copper because this metal tended to blacken the dye when the lac was heated. A large porcelain bowl was said by one painter to be the ideal container.

One important step in the preparation of lac dye mentioned by all artists was the addition of a leaf or two of the *zhu mkhan* tree to the water in which the lac was heated. These leaves, according to the artists, greatly facilitated the rendering of the dye into solution and they were also thought somehow to fix or make permanent the colour of the dye.

A number of different plant leaves were called *zhu mkhan* in Tibetan medicine,[4] but the *zhu mkhan* most commonly used in Central and Southern Tibet for preparing lac dye seems to have been the leaves of a tree in the genus *Symplocos*.[5] Trees of this genus were common, for instance, in the forests of the Eastern Himalayan foothills. The bark and leaves of the species *Symplocos racemosa* (the lodh tree), a species occurring at lower elevations, are said to yield a yellow dye,[6] and a concoction of the leaves of the same tree are also said to have been employed as a mordant.[7] Whatever the exact species, the leaves from this tree were best gathered in the autumn, when the concentration of dye in the leaves was at its peak.

Nowadays some Tibetan dyers in Nepal use the leaves of Indian Cassia *(Cinnamomum tamala)* in the preparation of lac dye, calling it *zhu mkhan*. Leaves of this plant are also effective in some kinds of dyeing, but the correct Tibetan nomenclature for the tree is *shing tsha*. In Hindi and Nepali its name is *tejpat*.

In addition to the *zhu mkhan* leaves, Tibetan painters sometimes also added native salts such as calcined borax *(tsha le)* to the lac dye solution to make the colour more permanent. The addition of these salts probably precipitated out some of the dye as lac lake. One painter described the calcined borax as acting as a sort of "binder" for the dye, since the dye became thicker and stronger when some borax was added.

Once the dye had been heated for a while and most of it had gone into solution, the red-coloured water was poured off, leaving the gummy lac *(la cha)* and any solid residues in the bottom of the pot. (This lac was used later for such things as sealing wax and by jewelers for cementing stones in silver bezels.) The dye or lake solution which was poured off was finally dried out by slow, careful warming over a low heat. What remained after drying was a solid dyestuff that could be reconstituted by putting some in a dish of warm water and stirring it until it dissolved. If, however,

the painter needed the colour immediately, he could produce some of it from crude lac as described above and then apply it directly, without having to wait for it first to dry completely.

The Preparation of Lac Lake as Described by Mi-pham-rgya-mtsho

To supplement the above account derived from interviews with living Tibetan painters, it is interesting to compare the following description of the preparation of lac lake from the pen of Mi-pham-rgya-mtsho:

> [Take some] yellow dye decoction of the leaf of *zhu mkhan* (a tree of the genus *Symplocos*) which has been made by warming [water and leaf] in the sun. And having poured some finely pulverized crude lac dye *(rgya tshos* or *rgya skyegs)* into it, grind the liquid mixture.
>
> If you boil it over a fire [the dye] will become dark brown in colour. If one grinds it in the shade the dye will not come into solution. Therefore, it is best to put it in the sunlight and [thus] warm it.
>
> In order to extract the dye, if one adds a little *rgya tsha* (sal ammoniac)[8] the dye will come out quickly and it will become red. If one adds *tsha la'i sbu ba* (a borax compound or solution?) [the colour] will be brilliant and permanent.
>
> If [when preparing lac dye] one does not have time to leave it in the sun for a long time, boil some tea leaves in clean water and into that, in a cup, pour some crude lac that has been finely pulverized in some *zhu mkhan* leaf solution. It is also possible to warm and grind the lac dye in boiled water.[9]

Painters who followed the above method would have produced the pigment lac lake since the addition of substances such as sal ammoniac *(rgya tshwa)* and alum *(tsha le)* precipitated out the redder lake.

Yellow Organic Dyes

In addition to indigo and lac dye a number of other dyes were used. Most of these were yellow, and they were used to brighten and highlight areas of green such as leaves and grassy hilltops. The three most common yellow dyes were made from petals of a wild rose, petals of the yellow *utpal* flower, and from the already-described *zhu mkhan*.

The wild rose used by Tibetan painters was the species *Rosa sericea* Lindl. which was called *se ba'i me tog* in Tibetan.[10] It grows in thorny bushes six or eight feet tall, and its petals, the source of the dye, are yellowish-white. The artists first gathered the petals and dried them in the shade, and then extracted the dye by soaking the petals in water with a little *zhu mkhan* leaf.

Rosa sericea Lindl. *(se ba'i me tog)*

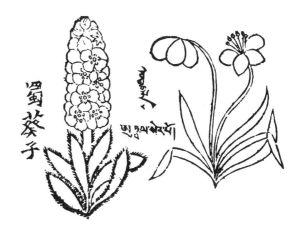

Two flowers called *utpal.*

Red sandalwood *(tsandan dmar po)*

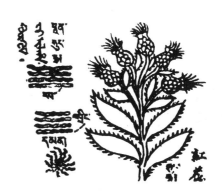

Safflower *(gur gum)*

The yellow *utpal (utpal ser po)* was a plant with yellow flowers that grew in high alpine meadows and in the grasslands of the Byang-thang.[11] Its fruiting body was light green and about three inches long. According to an old saying remembered by Legdrup Gyatsho, the fruit of the plant "resembled the musk gland of the musk deer" *(gla pho'i gla rtsi 'dra)*. To make the dye from this flower, the painters collected and dried the petals, and then soaked them in water just as with the wild rose petals.

Two other yellow dyes that were sometimes used in painting were those derived from barberry *(skyer pa)* bark and rhubarb roots *(chu'i rtsa)*.

Red or Orange Dyes

In addition to the above yellow colours there were also two red or orange dyes that some painters employed. The first of these was a reddish-brown shading dye made from red sandalwood *(tsandan dmar po)*.[12] One artist who used this dye for shading was Legdrup Gyatsho, who had learned its use from his father. The preparation of red-sandalwood dye posed no special problems. The artist began by crushing the wood into very small pieces and then he heated it in water (preferably with some *zhu mkhan*) until a dark solution was produced.

Next the pulpy residue of the wood had to be strained out. Then the dye was ready for immediate use, and it could also be dried and stored. Legdrup Gyatsho used this dye for shading certain red and brown objects and for special outlining effects around flames.

A yellowish-orange dye was made from either saffron *(Crocus sativus* Linn.*)* or safflower *(Carthamus tinctorius)*, both of which were called *gur gum* in Tibetan.[13] A painter from Khams who worked in the Karma-sgar-bris style told us of the use of this dye. He used to extract it by heating the dried flower parts in some water together with some home-brewed beer *(chang)*.

An Unusual Application of Dyes

Once in a great while the artists were asked to use these vegetable dyes for the creation of thangkas of exceptional sanctity. The Venerable Dezhung Rinpoche told us about one such thangka that his teacher Sga-ston Ngag-dbang-legs-pa had ordered to be made. It was a thangka of Mañjuśri that was to be used as the main icon during a special retreat for the propitiation of the great bodhisattva of wisdom. To maximize the holiness of the painting, Sga-ston instructed the artist to use only pure vegetable materials and to avoid glue and other products derived from animals.

Shading Washes Derived from Mineral Pigments

To achieve a particular tinting effect a painter would sometimes also employ thin washes of mineral colours. For example, where an artist wished to execute a gradation of orange to white on a jewel he could do so by applying some thin surface water *(kha chu)* of paint made from minium over the white background. Thin washes of vermilion and other pigments were similarly used; vermilion washes were used over base colours of yellow or orange in depictions of flames, and brown paints were used for shading the animal skins worn by wrathful and yi-dam deities, and the antelope, deer, leopard and tiger skin mats on which some figures were seated. Some painters on occasion even created transitions of value by applying light-coloured washes over dry darker base coats. Such artists employed this technique, for example, to lighten the tips of the small jewels commonly found as decorative details in the landscape. The painting of such small objects was thus an instance where the general dark-over-light progression for dry shading was not observed.

The Application of Shading Dyes

Which of the dyes and lakes the painter used and how and where he applied them depended little upon personal preference and mainly on the force of acquired habit. As with so much of Tibetan painting technique, most of the conventions of shading were established for the painter by the lineage of artistic practice he had inherited from his teacher.

The Relation of Dye Colour to Undercoat

Long ago artists had discovered that it was best to shade areas of blue and green with indigo, and this practice survived among modern Tibetan artists.[14] Lac dye or lake, by contrast, was best suited for painting over areas of red, maroon, orange, yellow or flesh colour. White areas could be shaded with either indigo or lac dye, but tradition decreed which objects should be shaded with one and which with the other. Yellows were mainly restricted to highlighting and intensifying greens. The artists who used red sandalwood for the most part employed it for dark shading over reds and browns. Laid down in thin washes, a few painters substituted it for lac dye in some applications.

Shading Order

No ironclad rules determined the order of dye application for the painter. But just as certain principles had influenced the order of pigment application, so here several practical considerations, such as the desire for maximum efficiency, guided the procedure.

As noted above, in laying down the main coats of pigment the artists generally worked from the rear planes of the composition forward. Accordingly the sky, which was the most distant plane, was also the first to be shaded. Later, during the main shading that followed the application of the flat pigments, the artists commonly began their shading by working on the other distant elements in the landscape, such as the clouds in the sky and the green meadows and hills below. For tinting the green, meadow-covered hills *(spang ri)* the painters usually shaded from the hilltops downward, using thin washes of green paints. A more varied effect was obtained by applying washes of alternating colours. The painter Wangdrak, for instance, used to tint his hilltops in some thangkas with alternating washes of brighter *(kha gsal ba)* and darker *(kha nag pa)* greens. The result was that some hills had yellowish hilltops, and others were a more bluish green. But as before, one of the main considerations was to use as much of one colour at one time as possible, to avoid having to waste time preparing the same colour many times. Therefore, if the artist began to shade with a bluish-green wash he would usually apply it to as many areas as he could before he went on to, say, the yellowish-green paint.

The Shading of Particular Objects

Beautifully shaded clouds, flowers and so forth were, like beautifully painted faces, a hallmark of a master painter. All artists knew various shortcuts in shading that speeded up the whole process, but a painstaking artist doing an important commission would usually linger over the shading for a long time. In old Tibet an artist often expended several months, and sometimes even up to a year, on one major painting. As one painter informed us, it was especially the detailed dry shading that used to take so long. Nowadays, of course, nobody can spare the time needed to create the exquisite "year-thangkas" *(lo thang)* as before, but dry shading continues to take up a large portion of an artist's time. In the following pages we will describe some of the techniques used for shading particular objects in the painting — objects that still receive careful treatment from the masters.

Clouds

There were two main types of clouds in thangka painting: (1) low mists that hugged the tops of low green hills, and (2) clouds floating high in the atmosphere or encircling lofty snow mountains.

Low Clouds

The low-lying mists were the simplest in terms of both design and shading. The artists usually drew them as repetitive series of lobed puffs that rose into the sky from behind a grassy hill. Often too, these clouds or mists were depicted as having two layers; there was a series of smaller, lower vapor puffs in front, backed by a repeating series of multi-lobed clouds behind each smaller one.

The technique for shading these clouds was often simple dry shading. The object of the shading was to

The shading of clouds.

create a contrast between the outer white edges of the clouds and both the shaded involutions of the clouds and the surrounding landscape. To produce this effect, the artists shaded from the bottom zone of each cloud area upward, leaving the top of each cloud lobe the pure white of the undercoat.

Some artists (e.g. Legdrup Gyatsho) used to apply two base colours to these clouds: greenish white to the small, inner nodes and white to the larger clouds just behind. Then they would shade both cloud layers with a greenish-yellow wash *(utpal ser po)*. Other artists (e.g. Wangdrak) left both layers of clouds the white base colour, and shaded over both with indigo for a monochromatic result. Whichever the artists did, shading was the final painting step for these clouds since they, like all clouds in these Central Tibetan painting styles, did not receive any final sharply defined outline *(bcad)*.

Atmospheric Clouds

The higher, atmospheric clouds were sometimes shaded by methods quite similar to the above, but many painters also employed other more involved methods. Like the low-lying mists, the higher clouds were usually drawn by our main informants in symmetrical, repetitive patterns.[15] However, each element repeated in the design was larger and more complicated than in the mists, and often each of the clouds in the overall design was set apart from those that adjoined it by means of different, alternating colours.

Technique 1: The painter Wangdrak used a relatively simple shading method for clouds, consisting of one-brush dry shading over undercoats of alternating colours. In particular, the artist would begin by giving base coats of white and greenish white to the clouds in an alternating sequence. Then, for the actual shading, he applied graduated tints of indigo over the white bases, and a greenish-yellow dye such as the traditional *zhu rams* (a mixture of light indigo and *zhu mkhan* yellow) to the pale-green undercoats. Because the maximum contrast was desired, the outer edges of the clouds were not darkly shaded, while most of the inner areas of the clouds were shaded to different degrees.

Variation of technique 1: For additional contrast and depth some painters applied two-tone base coats to each cloud during the application of the mineral colours. This technique required that the clouds as originally drawn possessed a central hole or deeply involuted recess, and it was this area that received a base coat that was a noticeably deeper (usually a greener or bluer) off-white shade than the surrounding cloud undercoat. During the actual shading this inner area received even darker shading washes to distinguish it further. For example, in a cloud of greenish white base colour the deep recess in the middle of the cloud was shaded using indigo, which made the area contrast even more sharply with areas tinted with greenish-yellow dye that surrounded it.

Technique 2: The painter Legdrup Gyatsho used a slightly more complex technique of cloud shading. As above, the clouds were drawn in balanced designs made up of repeating elements. However at the time of colouring, instead of applying uniform coats of the same hue, the artist used wet shading to lay down colour gradations in the base coat itself. Here too, the basic cloud hues were usually alternating blues and greens. Another favorite combination was alternating pale pinks and oranges. But in this technique the outsides of the clouds were left white, while only the interiors received shading with different colours.

For applying wet shading in the base colours of clouds, the artist used a two-brush technique. He first laid down a few strokes of the pale blue (or green) in the center of the cloud, and next applied strokes of white with his second brush above and below the first colour. Then, to effect a gradual transition, he used the brush bearing white paint to blend the borders of the darker colour into the white adjoining areas, leaving the central parts dark. For further contrast this artist often used undercoats of a darker hue. Whereas Wangdrak (in Technique 1) used to lay down a darker undercoat in just one central hole in each cloud, Legdrup Gyatsho often applied darker undercoats also to any other major recessed portion of the clouds, including the long trailing tails at the bottom of the cloud formations. Finally over the base coats he put down finishing washes of indigo or yellow-green dye, depending on the colour of the base. The finished clouds had centers of various shades, but the predominating edges, inside and out, were left white.

Although most Central Tibetan painters did not use outlining on ordinary clouds, some artists increased the contrast around the white outer edges of the clouds by applying a dilute hazy band of indigo there. This, however, was not considered to be real outlining *(bcad)*.

Technique 3: The last and most involved cloud-shading method was similar to Technique 2, except that it entailed a wet-shading undercoat applied with three brushes, and included the use of water dilution. We observed this method being employed by the Ladakhi artist Wangchuk, who had trained under a master painter from Shigatse.

The artist began to apply a wet-shaded undercoat by first loading the initial brush with white, wiping off the excess paint onto the edge of the paint bowl and further adjusting the load on the back of his hand. When the paintbrush was charged to his satisfaction, he applied the white to the tops and outsides of the clouds. Next, depending on the type of cloud, in the middle he applied a band of pale green, blue or gray, using a second brush, slightly merging the colour with the white where they met. Then he took a third brush from behind his ear, and moistened it with water. Using this diluting brush *(chu pir)* he further blended and smoothed the gradation of the two paints. No part of this wet-shaded undercoat could be very dark, so if it appeared as if too much dark paint had been used (keeping in mind that the colours became lighter when dry), more of the white could be pulled down into the central darker area from the overlying area of wet white paint.

In this technique the brush used for diluting with water needed to be only slightly moistened for the optimum result. Therefore, to avoid loading the brush with too much water, our painter used to dip just the brush handle into water, and then tap the handle end on the palm of his hand. Two or three droplets were in this way left on his palm, from which he could take exactly as much water as he wished.

Later, during the final dry shading of the clouds, he used to begin by drawing a light intermediate sketch to define the interior shapes of the cloud mass. Then, most often using indigo, he finished the shading using the dry-shading technique. In this style of painting the artist not only used alternating bluish and greenish clouds, but also sometimes painted series of clouds in identical colours. In some thangkas we saw him paint a series of green-tinted clouds over verdant hills, and a series of gray-shaded clouds clustered over a group of snow mountains. Incidentally, when he shaded these clouds above the snow peaks, the artist also shaded the white areas of the mountains.

Nimbuses, Back Curtains and Seats

Many head and body nimbuses did not require any shading. Especially if they were small, the base colour was enough. On the other hand some painters did apply shading tints to the body nimbuses and back curtains — even very small ones — by simply building up washes of dilute dye or by applying dye in a band around the inner or outer edge and diluting it with a water-brush.

The base colour of many body nimbuses and back curtain *(rgyab yol)* interiors was a deep or medium azurite blue. Shading the area just next to a figure with indigo served to darken that area and to set off the figure. Sometimes it was also desirable to shade in the reverse fashion, i.e. dark on the outside of the nimbus fading to light on the inside areas just next to the figure. The painter Wangdrak exemplified this second method when he shaded the blue body nimbus of a red ḍākinī. He applied the indigo darkly on the outer edges and then lightened the application so that by midway the dye was faint and near the ḍākinī's body only the medium-blue undercoat showed. The painters followed whichever method most heightened the appearance of depth in the nimbus by its greater contrast.

For some figures the blue-coloured nimbuses did not work at all. With dark blue deities not enough contrast was produced, and hence their backgrounds were painted red, pale reddish brown or pale maroon instead. In the case of tantric deities such backgrounds usually were meant to represent the center of a stylized mass of flames, and were later filled with emanating golden rays. Alternatively, such deities (particularly the fierce ones) were painted as standing in the midst of more realistic and less stylized masses of flames.

The head nimbuses *(dbu'i 'od 'khor)* could also

The shading of nimbuses.

be shaded either from the outside in or in the reverse direction, depending on which effect was desired. But the head nimbuses in general received less shading than the other areas surrounding the body such as the seat, back curtain or body nimbus. The blue and green portions of the back curtains *(rgyab yol)*, however, commonly received additional shading. Large fields in these back curtains were shaded from the top downward, while thinner strips along the edges were usually shaded from the inside out.

The most common type of seat used in thangka painting was the lotus seat *(padma'i gdan)*, and this was the usual seat placed below a figure if a standard body

nimbus was also depicted. The shading of such lotus seats is described below in the section on flowers since the seats are basically stylized flowers. Another common seat was the padded cushion *('bol gdan)*, which was often depicted beneath figures who had back curtains behind them instead of body nimbuses. The artists usually painted these padded cushions as thin rectangles. The rectangular bands representing the front of the mats were initially given base coats of blue and green. Later they were shaded with indigo from the bottom upward, fading out near the top.

One other type of seat that deserves at least a brief mention is the animal-skin mat. To paint one, the artists began by laying down a base coat of ochre and then shading the area from the center out. For the smooth shading of the interior of the skin they used either dry or wet shading methods, and then finished the skin with textured brush strokes that represented tufts of hair, spots or stripes. The painters also used white and black paint in a variety of ways for depicting such finishing touches as stripes and spots.

Lotuses and Flowers

For painting lotuses and flowers the artist could use either detailed or simplified shading techniques. Where a depiction of a lotus or peony flower was large, however, the drawing usually had greater detail and consequently its shading would be more intricate.

Lotuses

The lotus usually appeared in thangka paintings in the form of a lotus seat, the support for a sun or moon disc upon which the deity sat or stood. Small lotuses were also painted as the identifying hand-held attributes *(phyag mtshan)* of certain deities.

In terms of their colour there were two main types of lotus seats: those with varicoloured petals and those of basically monochromatic hues. Multi-coloured lotuses usually consisted of alternating pairs of inner and outer petals; the outer petals were blue and green while the inner petals were red and orange. The blue and green petals were almost always shaded with indigo, from the outer edges inward. The red and orange inner petals could also be shaded, but often they were not. After being shaded such lotuses were given a final outline of dye and gold.

Monochromatic lotuses were usually pink (or less frequently pale blue) and they most commonly consisted of a series of single petals all shaded with lac dye in the same way. The undercoat was white, and therefore the colour gradation of pink lotuses was from dark pink to white. The artists built up the darker tints on the inner parts of the petals, gradually fading out to the white petal edges. Painters used this technique regardless of whether the lotus was just a series of simple petals or whether it had compound and elaborate petals. Where specifically called for, monochromatic blue lotuses could be produced in the same way by substituting indigo for the usual lac dye. Lotuses shaded in this way (using either dye) did not require any final outlining of the petals, since the white outer edges gave enough contrast against the background colour.

Painters often employed a simplified method for shading the small lotus seats beneath minor figures

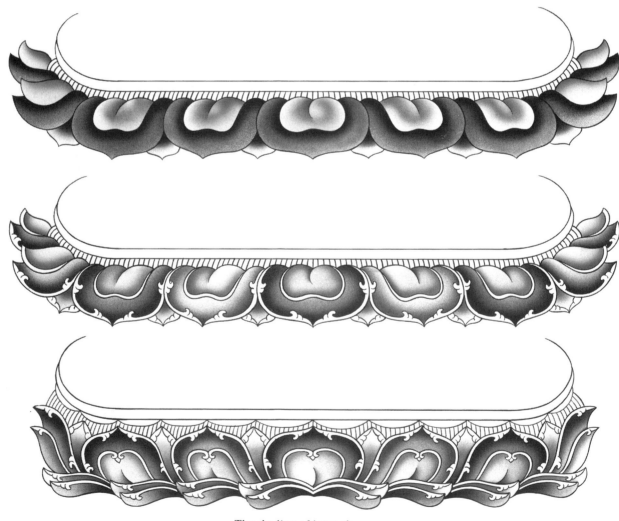

The shading of lotus thrones.

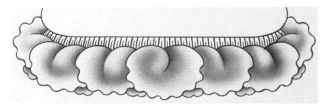

The shading of monochrome lotuses.

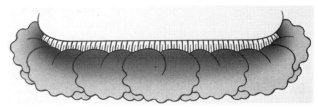

Flowers

where the detailed shading of each petal was difficult.

In this technique a simple lotus had to be painted in monochrome, and it was almost always pink, red lac dye being applied over a white background. As with the detailed monochromatic lotuses, the darker tints were applied to the inner parts of the petals, but here no petals were shaded individually, and instead the pink shading was applied in a single band along the base of the lotus. The petal tips of the lotus could face either upward or downward; hence the shading could be applied to either the top or bottom edge, whichever was the base. The white unshaded edge was where the outer edge of the petals would be drawn. All further details such as the shapes of individual petals were not indicated by detailed shading, but instead were rendered by means of lac-dye line drawings.

Apart from lotuses the main flowers of Tibetan painting were stylized peonies, which were also favorite floral motifs in Chinese decorative art. When peonies appeared in thangka painting, they were commonly painted in shades of pink or pale blue. The painters shaded a white or off-white pink or blue undercoat with red or blue washes, using techniques that were more or less identical to those used for tinting monochromatic lotuses. Each petal had to be shaded separately, working from the dark center toward the white outer edges.

A slightly more complex technique involved monochromatic shading on two-tone backgrounds. The purpose of this was to obtain greater contrast. Here the painter began painting the peony by leaving the area of the outer petals white, while applying an off-white hue (pink or bluish white) to the inner zone of flower petals. Later, both areas received the same shading tints. When completed the inner areas appeared to be darker immature petals while the outer petals with their lighter colour and white edges appeared mature and fully blossomed.

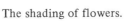

The shading of flowers.

Figure Shading *(sha mdangs)*

The application of shading to the bodies depicted was an especially important branch of shading technique, involving methods a little different from those already described. The object of figure shading was, of course, to create the illusion of a three-dimensional depth to the body of the figure. This body shading was most pronounced in the figures of dark blue and dark red forms of the wrathful and protective deities, as well as in the major yi-dams and other deities of dark colour, such as Green Tārā. The basic technique was to shade the major joints and recesses of the body, as well as to shade around all important anatomical features. The only parts left completely unshaded were some round and oval areas in the middle of the various parts of the body. These unshaded areas stood out to the eye like rounded bulges — the very effect that the painter desired to achieve.

To shade the bodies of deities whose base colours were fairly dark, such as green or blue deities, the artists had to apply the dye in more concentrated washes. The base coat for most wrathful *(khro bo)* deities was a medium to deep blue. To shade it the artist applied indigo in dark strokes in the natural folds and depressions of the body, and also around the edges of each anatomical region. Then lighter strokes might be used for lesser indentations and for softening the transition from the darker areas to the unshaded oval bulges of muscles. Sometimes, as on small figures, little or no transition between dark and light was attempted, so that the modeled effect resulted solely from the contrast of shaded against unshaded areas.

The shading of figures of lighter colours was the same as above, except that only dilute dyes were used, and hence the contrast between the shaded and unshaded was not so sharp.

Water

The procedure for painting water in a thangka consisted of a series of steps that the artist accomplished one by one as the painting progressed. The sequence of the main steps was preliminary sketch, undercoat, secondary sketch, shading, outlining and finishing.

Areas of water in the landscape, such as ponds and lakes, were commonly drawn in triangular shapes or as a series of triangles. One side of each triangle was positioned horizontally, with the other two sides meeting at a point below. During the application of the mineral colours, the artist gave the water areas a smooth undercoat of medium blue. Then, at the time of shading, he began with a secondary sketch in which he laid down some horizontal lines which divided the triangle into several parallel bands of more or less the same width. These lines established the borders for the shading that followed.

The placement of these dividing lines in the water was often connected with the lie of the land, and the artist commonly laid down a line opposite each major

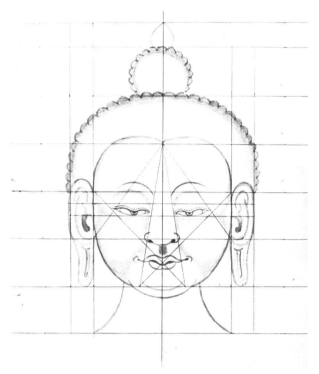

The shading of facial details on the Buddha by Tshedor, student of Pema Könchok.

The shading of facial details on Padmasambhava by Tshedor.

hill or craggy promontory abutting the water. But even in relatively simple landscapes where there was no corresponding division in the bordering land (for instance where the water was a simple blue triangle surrounded by an undifferentiated green meadow) the artists still subdivided the water into two or three levels.

The shading of water.

For the actual shading, the artist applied washes of indigo in the dry-shading technique to each layer or band of water. The shading began from the bottom edge, that is to say from the sketched-in horizontal lines or from the bottom point of the triangle. From that starting point the shading gradually faded out as the artist worked upwards, and it normally extended across about one-half the width of each zone. Although in other styles of thangka painting a more detailed secondary sketch led to a rather more intricate shading of the water, in this style the shading itself was simple. Here shading was but one of many elements contributing to the total effect, and the water did not attain a finished appearance until it had been completed by the drawing of waves on the surface with indigo, the outlining of the waves with white and the execution of some final touches with gold paint.

Flames

Of all the areas that required shading, the masses of flames were perhaps the most convoluted and complicated. The task of shading them had to be correspondingly more painstaking, since every convolution and tongue of flame in the blazing mass had to be dealt with individually. The painter Wangdrak was fairly typical in the way he painted detailed areas of flames. First of all he applied a uniform undercoat of minium to the whole area. He then applied washes of red to certain

areas; U-shaped troughs received full-strength vermilion with little or no gradation, while the tips of the flames were painted red and gradually faded into the orange undercoat. Along the inner edges of the flames (as indicated in the sketch), the painter laid down strokes of thin vermilion and gradually faded them out toward the outer edges. For the most effective contrast, this shading ended just before the outer border was reached, leaving a thin strip of pure orange along the outside edge.

Legdrup Gyatsho used a technique that was basically the same, except that he sometimes began with a yellow undercoat and painted the outer edges with minium. On top of this, he did some minor tinting with red. But both artists finished the flames with red (i.e. lac-dye) outlining.

Simplified Method

The painting of a convoluted mass of flames was more difficult to execute in a small area. Therefore simplified methods were devised for colouring the small flames surrounding the lesser deities; they became orange nimbuses with stylized flames in the outer areas. This type of flame was also used in its own right as the usual type of flaming nimbus around semi-wrathful tantric yi-dams and similar deities. For flames in this style the basic undercoat was minium orange. Just inside the outer edge the artist painted a strip of vermilion and toward the center made it gradually fade

The shading of flames.

into the orange background. Having obtained a smooth gradation, the shading *per se* was finished, and the actual drawing of the flames *(me ris)* was added later using red lac dye. In addition, as a final touch the artist Legdrup Gyatsho used red-sandalwood dye for creating a hazy outline of brown around the flames, both to indicate smoke and for more contrast with the background landscape.

Rocks and Crags

The depiction of rocks and crags in the landscape was one of the main means of adding more beauty — and even a certain realism — to the landscape. Many different techniques were practiced in the various schools of Tibetan painting, and some of the more sophisticated and realistic portrayals were no doubt adapted from Chinese examples. But whatever their ultimate stylistic origins, the painting of rocky crags as practiced by our main informants followed highly conventionalized and now typically Tibetan patterns.

Our two main thangka painting teachers for the most part depicted rocky crags in two ways: (1) with more naturalistic and irregular shapes, in which each crag possessed differently coloured strata, and (2) with repetitive designs which entailed shading over a continuous undercoat.

Irregular Rock Outcroppings

The first technique for painting rocks that we will describe began with irregular and non-repetitive designs. Such designs, however, still incorporated certain predictable features that were necessary for their successful execution.

Blue-Green Crags

Rocks or crags as painted by Legdrup Gyatsho generally had distinct inner and outer strips that portrayed projecting and receding layers. This structure permitted the artist to colour the adjoining strips alternately blue and green. In its simplest form such a crag consisted of a small irregular oval or irregular rectangle inside a larger form of approximately the same shape:

Usually the outer band was painted blue while the inner part was green. Such blue-green rocks sometimes appeared as solitary elements in the landscape, and they could also be combined or jumbled together to form larger crags. When a complicated cluster of crags was depicted, the artist assigned the colours to the different parts in whatever way would give the best alternation

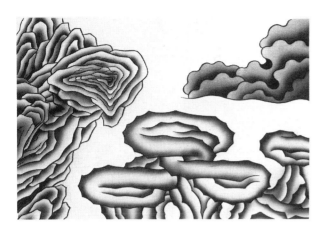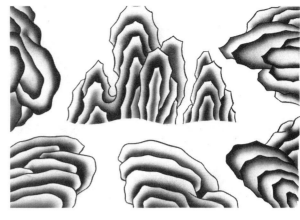

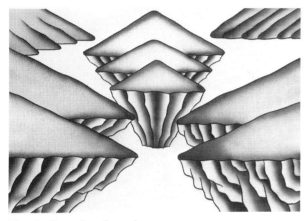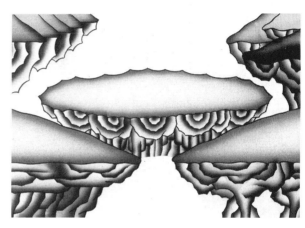

The shading of rocks and crags.

and contrast of the blue and green. The artist also sometimes painted blue-green crags in combination with brown stratified crags to create an even more intricate rocky outcropping.

Although the main base colours were blue and green, these colours did not fill the whole area of the rocks. The painter applied the blue and green paints only to the outer half of each band in the design, thickly near the edges and gradually thinner towards the middle. The shading of this type of rock consisted of filling in the unpainted parts of each band with a contrasting dye colour. Our artist in this case used the reddish-brown sandalwood dye for tinting the bands with blue, and the same dye or a yellow wash was used for the spaces opposite the green. Alternatively he sometimes used gold facing the green strips. These colours were applied in much the same way as the blue and green paints: darker near the edges of the bands and fading out gradually toward the middle. The opposing colours within one band did not actually touch, but faded into the base colour near their juncture.

Brown Crags

A second irregular rock design employed by Legdrup Gyatsho consisted of steep, vertically stratified cliffs or outcroppings. He coloured such crags brown, and commonly placed them in the landscape composition

at the base of snow mountains and grass-covered mountains, as well as in combination with the blue-green crags described above.

The artist prepared a pale brown base coat for this type of crag by combining orpiment, minium, ink and a little white. Then for shading this undercoat he used the reddish-brown dye of sandalwood. Since the designs for these crags were composed of a series of bands (representing rock layers or striations), the shading took place within each band. But instead of shading the outer edges of each band he left the outside the light undercoat hue, and it was the inner recesses of the design that received the dark shading.

Repetitive Designs

Wangdrak was one of the few of our informants who regularly depicted rocky crags using repetitive designs. He almost always drew these crags as outcroppings that adjoined a body of water, and one of the basic shapes he used was:

With slight irregularities from section to section, and by internal repetition of the same design elements, he achieved a much more craggy and irregular effect:

This painter also used other basic shapes for building rocks. The more intricate and irregular the basic shapes, the more random they would appear in combination, while with simple shapes the opposite was true. For instance:

Wangdrak always began his colouring of rocks by applying a single base colour, usually ochre brown, pale yellow or pale blue.

Monochromatic Shading

Shading followed the precise outlines of the layers of the crags, so it was useful to begin by sketching in the contours of the crags if they were not visible through the undercoat of paint. For the actual shading, Wangdrak employed single dyes or combinations of dyes, depending on the particular design and base colour. On rocks of pale blue backgrounds it was usual to see him employing indigo alone. Here, as for all rocks in this style, he shaded the outer edges and let the inner areas remain the lighter colour of the undercoat. For shading ochre-brown crags a thin wash of indigo worked well, for in combination with the ochre the indigo looked almost like a wash of ink.

Multicolour Shading

Over the pale yellow undercoats, however, Wangdrak usually applied a variety of shading dyes. One combination was to alternate blue and green in bands just inside the edges of the crags. Another method was to apply alternating green and blue as above, but to add a thin red wash to some of the exposed inner areas of the yellow undercoat and to the small niches in the crags. Because the undercoat was yellow, the red washes produced an orange result. This set up a contrast with the nearby green and blue areas.

Example of granular or dabbed-on shading from a thangka by Dorje Gyaltshen.

Notes

1. According to Hodgson (pp.101, 103, 108f., 113) in the early 19th century indigo was an important article of trade passing from India to Tibet via Nepal. In Nepal it had the highest customs duty of any commodity. Of an estimated 63,000 rupees worth imported into Nepal from India in 1830-1831, slightly less than one-fifth was believed to have been sent on to Tibet. As Hodgson then noted, p.109, "Nepal and Tibet are always very inadequately supplied with good indigo. There is a very great demand for it just now in the latter country."

2. A red dyestuff from the safflower plant *(Carthamus tinctorius)* was produced in this form by the Chinese. Some Tibetan artists may have confused this colour with lac lake. In Tibet safflower was classified as a type of saffron *(gur gum)*. See 'Jam-dpal-rdo-rje, p.77.5.

3. Tibetan doctors distinguished two types of lac dye by observing it when it dissolved in water. One that yielded a brighter colour was called *gro tshos*, while a second, called *nag hrug*, produced a darker, more maroon dye. See 'Jam-dpal-rdo-rje, p.127.

4. 'Jam-dpal-rdo-rje, p.108, distinguished two varieties of *zhu mkhan*. The first, called *spang zhun*, was the most desirable for medicinal use. It grew on a big tree, and the leaves were thick, shiny and yellowish. The inferior variety was called *nags zhun*. Its leaves were dark green, thin and soft. According to the same author, the Tibetan synonyms for the *zhu mkhan* leaf are *seng 'phro ma, skags grogs* ("friend of lac dye"), and *rgya skyegs dangs byed* ("clarifier of lac dye").

   In the Buriat region some three plants were called *zhu mkhan: Eriobotrya japonica* Lindl., *Rhododendron aurem* Georgi, and *Thelycrania (Cornus) alba* (L.) Pojark. See A. F. Gammerman and B. V. Semicov, *Slovar' tibetsko-latino-russkikh nazvaniĭ lekarstvennogo rastitel'nogo cyr'iâ, premeniâemogo v. tibetskoĭ meditsine* [Tibetan-Latin-Russian Glossary of Medicinal Plants] (Ulan-Ude, Akdemiia Nauk SSSR, Sibirskoe Otdelenie, 1963).

5. See the note of W. W. Rockhill in S. C. Das, *Journey to Lhasa and Central Tibet* (New Delhi, 1970), p.10. Concerning this dye, Rockhill there refers also to Hooker, *Himalayan Journals,* vol.2, p.41 (this should be p.63), and to Hooker's article in the 1891 volume of the *Journal of the Asiatic Society of Bengal*, p.218. Also, Vaidya Bhagwan Dash, *Tibetan Medicine with special reference to Yoga Śataka* (Dharamsala, 1976), p.341 identified *seng 'phrom* (a synonym of *zhu mkhan* mentioned above, note 4) as *Symplocos racemosa* Roxb.

6. R. N. Chopra, *Chopra's Indigenous Drugs of India* (Calcutta, 1958), p.413.

7. H. H. Haines, *A Forest Flora of Chota Nagpur* (Delhi, 1910), p.413.

8. According to Jäschke, *Tibetan-English Dictionary* (London, 1958), *rgya tsha* is the Tibetan name for sal ammoniac (ammonium chloride). See also B. Laufer, *Sino-Iranica* (Taipei, 1967), p.508. It should not be confused with the similarly spelled *rgyam tshwa*.

9. Mi-pham-rgya-mtsho, *Bzo gnas*, p.87.

10. *Bod ljongs rgyun spyod krung dbyi'i sman rigs,* p.620 and illustration no.404.

11. In India *utpala* denoted a blue lotus. However, the Tibetans used the term *utpala* or *utpal* for non-aquatic plants. Jäschke identified the *utpal* he had seen in the Western Himalayas as *Polemonium caeruleum*. Das, p.19, recorded seeing "an alpine shrub called *upala [sic]*, with large pink leaves at the top like those of the water-lily."

    In Tibetan medicine different varieties of *utpal* were distinguished, according to the colour of their flowers. One was blue *(utpal sngon po)* and one yellow *(utpal ser po)*. See 'Jam-dpal-rdo-rje, p.173. In *Bod ljongs rgyun spyod krung dbyi'i sman rigs,* illustration no.157, the blue *utpal* is identified as *Meconopsis sp.* Judging from the illustration in 'Jam-dpal-rdo-rje, p.173, the yellow *utpal* was a different species if not a different genus.

12. See 'Jam-dpal-rdo-rje, p.110. Mehra, p.208, also ascertained the presence of this dye in thangka paintings.

13. On a five-fold Tibetan classification of *gur gum* see 'Jam-dpal-rdo-rje, p.77. Saffron was also known as *kha che sha kha ma*.

14. See for instance the 15th-century account of Bodong, *Mkhas pa*, vol.2, p.260.

15. In the *Karma-sgar-bris* and certain *Sman-gsar* styles the clouds were commonly painted in unsymmetrical and more realistic forms.

Thangka of three religious masters, showing a wealth of outlining details. Victoria and
Albert Museum.

Eleven
Outlining

Almost every object depicted in a thangka required outlining or linear detail. Outlining proper *(bcad)* served to set off most objects from their surroundings, and it was used to demarcate the main subdivisions within them. Tibetan painters also used line drawings to develop the form or texture inside a given area, for instance within a swirling mass of flames or within the hair of a deity. Furthermore, fine linear drawings were the main way of indicating any other details within an object or field. Examples of this include the repeating designs on brocades, and the radiating golden light rays (*'od 'phro*) within a nimbus. Finally, artists also used line drawings to indicate any small or thin detail; on small deities, such details as eyebrows, eyelashes and ornaments of gold and bone could only be executed by thin line drawings.

Many linear details were final touches that completed the area being painted. Once the artist began outlining, he knew that the completion of the painting was drawing near.

Colours Used in Outlining

Of the various dyes used in shading only two were widely used during outlining: indigo and lac dye or lake. To create a satisfactory outline these colours had to be sufficiently dark to contrast sharply with the base colour and background, so the painters prepared them in solutions that were more concentrated than those used during shading. These dyes, however, could not be so thick that they would not flow freely from the brush. Outlining always required colours that could be applied in smooth, continuous strokes.

Indigo

Tibetan artists used indigo for outlining the areas that had already been shaded with indigo. These included many of the blue and green areas of the thangka. In addition, painters also employed indigo for outlining deep vermilion and maroon areas, such as robes, some

Detail of a partly completed thangka of Amitābha during the process of outlining by Dorje Gyaltshen.

The outlining of leaves.

nimbuses and jewels, and so forth. The reason for using indigo in the latter cases was that lac dye, being itself a deep reddish shade, could not provide enough contrast when applied over a vermilion or maroon area. Finally, we should note that the artists also outlined a few white objects with indigo, such as white robes, draperies and ornamental scarves.

Lac Dye

Lac dye was used as an outlining colour mainly around those areas that had been shaded with the same dye. This meant that most areas with base coats of warm colours were outlined with this colour, the main exceptions being the deeper vermilions and maroons as mentioned above. Also outlined with lac dye were many white areas and areas painted with gold. A particularly important application of lac-dye outlining was to the bodies, faces and limbs of all figures except those that had been painted blue, green or vermilion.

White

In addition to the two main dyes, several other colours were also used for painting linear details. These colours were applied after the ordinary outlining, and one of the most important of them was white.

Water

White was indispensable for putting the finishing touches on water, primarily to give waves their final outline. The artists applied lines of white next to the dark indigo outlines of waves that had already been painted. Often they applied the white lines *(dkar bcad)* just beneath the indigo, especially on surface waves. In the painting of minor waves lower down, however, the white lines often appeared above the indigo. Finally, the artists used white to paint in small ripples and bubbles on the surface of the water.

Bone Ornaments

The painting of the small bone ornaments of tantric deities was another important application of white line drawings. Here white was not used for outlining *per se*, but rather for the actual drawing of these details. The bone ornaments of large deities were sketched and painted in individual sections that then required final outlining with lac dye. But for small figures the bone ornaments were too fine to be depicted in this way, and therefore these ornaments were executed by means of simple white line drawings. For deities of medium sizes a middle course was also possible; the thicker bone ornaments such as the main elements of bone aprons were painted in full detail, complete with lac-dye outlining, while the smaller ornaments, such as bracelets, armlets and anklets, were painted freehand without a preliminary sketch. Expert artists experienced no particular difficulty when painting such complicated bone ornaments in this way. As in the

drawing of so many other designs in Tibetan art, here it was a matter of first establishing the main divisions of the pattern and then filling in the intermediate details.

For white outlines and finishing details the painters used their ordinary white paint, here made just thin enough for fine application. But when painting the bone ornaments of white tantric deities or ḍākinīs, a little yellow or ochre was mixed into the white so that the resulting yellowish-white details would stand out against the white base colour of the bodies.

Gold

In most paintings gold was used much more frequently than white. Like white, it was applied after the indigo and lac-dye outlining, because both white and gold were used for details that lay on top of the surrounding areas in the composition. Gold ornaments, for instance, had to be painted over the limbs or bodies of the deities, which by this point should have already been completed through outlining.

Gold had a wide variety of applications in outlining and linear details. For simple outlining, the artists commonly laid down one or more lines of gold inside and parallel to the outer dark outlines of such objects as nimbuses, seats, flower leaves, robes, multi-coloured lotuses and rocky crags. Sometimes the gold lines were applied in a thin line just inside and contiguous to the dark dye outline, but usually the artists

Wangdrak applying radiating gold lines to a figure's body nimbus. The cloth, held between his last two fingers, protects the painting.

placed them a little further inside the outline, leaving a thin strip of undercoat colour between each gold line and the outer border.

Another common use of gold was to finish the interiors of nimbuses with evenly spaced radiating lines that represented emanating light rays *('od 'phro)*. The artists drew these light rays either radiating out in all directions from the center of the nimbus (this was most common), or else as rays that spread out along flatter, mainly horizontal paths. In order to be able to place all the light rays at even intervals, the artist first drew in, say, every fourth ray, so as to subdivide the whole nimbus into larger sections of equal intervals. To draw these preliminary lines some artists now use chalk, and previously in Tibet they used sticks of *the la dkar* or *rdo rgyud* (soapstone). Then these sections could each be filled in with three evenly spaced light rays. For greater effect the artists commonly alternated the shape of the light rays, making every other one wavier.

Gold Brocade Designs

The most noteworthy use of gold in thangkas, however, was in the intricate repeating patterns used to complete depictions of brocades and other objects. In general, Tibetans were fond of decorative designs and minutely executed details, and here in the painting of golden brocade designs *(gos ris)* and similar details we find this tendency reaching its fullest expression. Some of the most obvious objects to receive such decoration were the brocaded robes of the Buddhas or saints. But the artists also applied gold brocade patterns to almost any area that could conceivably consist of cloth, including cushions and certain types of back curtains. Brocade motifs being among the most showy details in a thangka, they gave the artist with a flair for detailed work another chance to excel.

Tibetan artists possessed a wealth of decorative motifs that were perfect for repetitive application as brocade designs. Many of the motifs originated from the designs found on actual Chinese brocades. Some were extremely complicated, consisting of a series of stylized peonies, lotuses or auspicious symbols. On the other hand, many of the most commonly used patterns were very simple. For less important commissions, or for the smallest figures in any painting, the artists used a series of simple gold dots, circles or crosses to complete the areas of cloth or brocade. Here we will describe and illustrate just a few of the main designs used by our teachers, illustrating how the painters positioned them in relation to the underlying robes or cloth.

The two main types of brocade designs were (1) linear borders and (2) designs repeated in large fields. The master artist drew from large repertoires of patterns for both classes of design.

Border Designs

Linear border designs *(mtha' chag ri mo)* were used for representing strips of fine brocades occurring along the cuffs and edges of robes. These designs consisted of repeated motifs enclosed by gold outlines along the edges of the strips. The artists executed such designs not only on the edges of robes, but also at the borders of the patches making up a bhikṣu's upper robe *(chos gos)*, and on almost any strap or band, including the meditation bands *(sgom thag)* of siddhas.

An artist sometimes painted the borders of robes with base colours different from those of the main parts of the robes. Occasionally they also shaded the undercoat colours with dyes. (Similarly the undersides or inner linings of robes were also set apart from the outsides by being painted in contrasting colours such as yellow, pink or pale green.) Then as the final preparation for finishing with gold outlines and designs, the painter used indigo or lac dye to outline the edges, seams and folds of the robe.

When it was time to apply the gold, a painter first laid down one or two plain gold lines on either side of the garment's border. These lines were called "border outlines" *(mtha' bcad)*. Then having decided which design he would use, he divided the border into regular segments. Most designs alternated back and forth with symmetrical halves on either side of the strip. Thus, when using a common zigzag pattern as the basis for the design, he would first draw in the basic zigzag down the center of the strip. This established a series of triangular shapes on either side of the border, and the rest of the job was to fill in each of these triangles with the same design.

A similar brocade design for robe borders was built around an undulating, wavy line:

Having drawn such a line down the middle of the border, the artist then filled in the newly demarcated areas with semicircular elements such as half-flowers. Whether zigzag or undulating, the line had to be drawn with regular intervals so that the overall design was balanced and pleasing. On the upper robe of a bhikṣu, the gold designs of each square patch were commonly painted freehand. Here, for added realism, some artists slightly staggered the gold outlining of these patch designs *(dra bcad)* at folds in the robe.

Brocade Designs for Large Areas

A somewhat different set of designs was required for filling in the large areas of cloth within the borders of robes. For such large fields the painters used both simple and complex designs. Since the beauty of the design depended on a regular repetition of the elements (in imitation of the designs on Chinese brocades), it was important first of all to align the elements of the design at evenly spaced intervals. The artist often placed

Two thangkas belonging to different series of the sixteen *sthavira* with a rich variety of golden designs on the seats and brocades. Victoria and Albert Museum.

the brocade motifs in successions of parallel, more or less vertical lines. By spacing each element in the next line halfway between (and equidistant from) the elements of the previous series, the elements also became aligned along diagonal lines. The repeated motif could be as simple as a small dot or circle, or it could be as ornate as a detailed cloud or flower; but as long as the elements were placed in regular sequence they would produce the effect of a design woven with gold threads in silk brocade. It was more difficult to position the larger design elements at regular intervals when drawing them one at a time freehand; hence for such patterns the painter often began by laying down a series of simple dots to determine the centers of the repeated motif. Some beginners even sketched their brocade designs with charcoal before painting them. As with the border designs, so also here a slight staggering of the design at creases and folds in the fabric lent a greater realism to the painting.

Sometimes the artists combined simple and complex elements for their brocade designs. First a series of large, complex elements was painted at regular intervals as described above, and then the space in between the larger elements was filled in with repetitions of a simpler element, such as a dot or circle. For a more striking result the artists left a thin border of unpainted area between the large elements and the surrounding field of small elements.

Although brocade designs on areas representing

Thangka of Khri-srong-lde-btsan with fine brocade detail.

cloth were the most common application of gold finishing details, similar detailing was also applied to other objects. The various depictions of chain-mail armor, for instance, could be finished with gold outlining. In that case the design was already established by the dye outlines, and the gold was just a secondary outlining applied as a finishing touch.

Gold Details on Back Curtains

Nimbuses, it will be recalled, were usually completed with undulating gold lines that represented radiating light rays. However, for a backrest or "back curtain" *(rgyab yol)* — the other main type of background for a figure — the artists did not employ light rays. Instead, they completed it by means of various brocade motifs.

The painter Wangdrak depicted two main types of back curtains. Both were of similar shape, but while one type portrayed a smooth cloth curtain hung over a blue, disc-shaped background, the other type represented a blue or green field draped with a white cloth or ceremonial scarf on the top and sides. Since the first type mainly consisted of a cloth, the gold details were no different from those used for finishing brocade robes. The large field in the middle required one of the usual repeating brocade motifs, while the blue or green edges of the cloth curtain could be completed with one of the standard brocade border designs.

By contrast the second type of backrest — a blue or green disc-shaped field draped with a long white scarf — required some characteristically different gold designs. To execute these designs the artist began by dividing the blue or green background field into upper and lower parts. During the shading stage he would darken either the top or the bottom part of the backrest using indigo washes. Then during outlining he would produce a more pronounced division of the field by means of one or more horizontal gold lines near the middle of the field. Once the field was so divided, the artist would finish this middle horizontal band by developing it into a gold border design that incorporated the original lines. Then he would fill in the empty space in the upper half with large repeating brocade motifs. One characteristic feature of the gold brocade designs used in the top half of the backrest field was the employment of stylized crags, water and clouds along the bottom edge of the area, just above the central strip. This elaborate design was a well-known motif taken from Chinese brocades, but our main informants commonly used it in thangka paintings only on such back curtains.

Beneath the central border strip the artists used another characteristic design, one which originated from India. This was a depiction of hanging loops and strands of precious beads *(dra ba dang dra ba phyed)*. Such auspicious decorations were thought to be essential features of palaces, and Tibetan artists also commonly depicted them when painting the walls of temples, palaces and so on.

Gold Details on Seats

The paintings of thick, padded seats *('bol gdan)* were usually very simple affairs. Their frontal depiction consisted only of one or two flat rectangles, usually painted blue or green. The finishing of these seats with gold outline and detail, however, could be either simple or elaborate. The simplest finishing of such seats consisted of single gold outlines along the top and bottom of the form. The same rectangular areas could also be filled with gold brocade border designs, since the front covers of the seats were meant to be made of strips of cloth. If the painter was inclined to do something more elaborate, there were also some special brocade designs that he might employ here. The painter Wangdrak, for example, drew large and intricate brocade designs on the front of double seats in his thangkas of the Sixteen "Arhats". For this he first divided up the two rectangles that framed the front of the seats. On one strip he determined three segments of equal length, and then established three interior areas by drawing an oval in each area. On the second strip he divided up the space in a similar manner, but with the ovals staggered so that they were centered at the gaps between the ovals of the first strip. In the second strip, two full ovals were placed in the interior of the strip, while only half ovals would fit at either end. Finally, all the ovals were filled with large brocade motifs, usually ornate flowers or auspicious objects.

For the painting of the long straight lines at the top and bottom of the rectangular seats (as well as elsewhere in the painting) some artists guided their brushes with a wooden straightedge *(thig shing)*. Dorje Gyaltshen was one artist who used this method. He first placed the straightedge a fraction of an inch away from where the line was to be drawn. Then he put the brush in place at the starting point, leaning the side of the brush handle against the top edge of the straightedge. Finally he painted the desired line by moving the brush along the edge of the straight piece of wood. The brush hairs themselves were not to touch the straightedge, and for this reason the straightedge had to be fairly

Dorje Gyaltshen outlining with the aid of a straightedge.

thick. The one that Dorje Gyaltshen used was about three-quarters of an inch thick.

Gold Jewelry and Ornaments

Gold ornaments, like the bone ornaments described above, were rendered in both simple and detailed manners. In large paintings or depictions of large figures, the artists drew the ornaments as part of the original charcoal and ink sketch. Like all sizable areas painted with gold, large ornaments were first painted with ochre as an undercoat. Then, having coated each area with an application or two of gold, the artists gave each ornament an outlining with lac dye (or with a thin orange paint, in the case of Legdrup Gyatsho). Finally, as the finishing touch, the artists depicted the small jewels set in the gold ornaments, painting them as small circles of pink or pale blue with a dot of white in their centers.

In small paintings or for small figures, however, it was not practicable to sketch each tiny ornament or to give each an undercoat of ochre. Instead the artists merely painted freehand the various necklaces, bangles, anklets, and so forth, applying gold paint in thin line drawings over the already painted areas.

Minor Colours Used for Outlining and Linear Details

In addition to the above colours, a number of other paints were employed for minor finishing details. Many artists used, for example, black ink and pale blue paint for linear details of the eyes and face. Some (for instance Wangdrak) applied yellow linear details to the interior of flames while others (such as Legdrup Gyatsho) substituted a thin minium paint for lac dye when outlining gold ornaments. A few painters used vermilion for line drawing and outlining over gold. Special types of paintings such as black and vermilion thangkas sometimes also required line drawings done in yellow or vermilion. But among the colours most common in multicolour thangkas, just one more deserves special mention: the green dye used for depicting various details of grass and vegetation *(rtswa ris)*.

Many artists put a finishing trim of tufts of dark green grass or bush-like clumps along the top edges of the green hills in the landscape. To paint these they used a green dye called *zhu rams*, a mixture of indigo and yellow dye.[1] For painting linear details with this dye an ordinary outlining brush was used, whereas for a more clumpy effect the dye was dabbed on with the tip of a larger, nearly dry brush. When depicting a border of grass or brush on hillsides Wangdrak built up a clumpy effect by applying successive series of six or seven nearly overlapping dabs along the edges of each sloping hill.

He also painted triangular clumps of bushes using the same method. These he placed at even intervals in the middle of green hills, spacing them in the same way that large brocade motifs were placed in a field of cloth. He normally painted such triangular clumps larger in the areas of the distant hilltops, and made them smaller as he worked down the hill toward the foreground. Occasionally he did not paint any of these bushy clumps at all, while sometimes he applied them to alternating rows of hills in the landscape.

Wangdrak also painted vegetative details of a more linear sort, namely clumps of long-leaved grass. These he placed along the top edges of crags, positioning them in the main indentations at the top of the cliffs.

Other methods also existed for painting the strips of dark green vegetation along the edges of hills. Some artists combined the series of clumpy dry-brush "bushes" with linear detail. Thargye and Legdrup Gyatsho, for example, first applied a series of closely spaced curving horizontal lines along the edges of the green hills,

and then finished this strip with a series of dabs applied at about every second curved line:

in addition to clumpy rounded "bushes" similarly placed:

Just above this strip, Thargye also commonly painted a series of rounded clumps of vegetation made up of more linear elements:

Legdrup Gyatsho also painted a series of larger bushes along the upper edge of the vegetation strips on hillsides, but he used a combination of lines and dabs when painting these bushes. As a final touch he added a series of "flowers" to the strip, placing them in evenly spaced clusters of three. These flowers were just small dots of white arranged in a triangular grouping, and they themselves needed finishing by the application of a dot of red dye in the center and the addition of a few radiating pale red lines to indicate the edges of the petals. Other artists used similar series of simple flowers in their landscapes.

Linear Details Utilizing a Combination of Colours

Although not really considered to be types of outlining (bcad), several other finishing methods existed that entailed the application of colours in lines or thin strips. The areas so treated included rainbows, a particular variety of cloud lining, and a special type of scarf.

Rainbows

Rainbows were commonly used in thangkas, and they illustrate the celestial nature of the landscape. Frequently they were also painted as curved and radiating bands of colours, waving as they ascended and often crowned by the deities in the upper part of the thangka. All rainbows began with a thin band of maroon wash on the inside and proceeded outward in the colour sequence: blue, green, yellow, orange and red, each band of colour having the same width.

Cloud Linings

For finishing the edges of certain clouds, Tibetan artists also used a similar outer lining that consisted of a series of contiguous strips of medium blue, indigo and mauve. Called *phing bris* by Legdrup Gyatsho, this technique shows some similarities to a non-shaded colour gradation called *tsho sha dkar* that was used particularly in the painting of decorative motifs on woodwork and walls.

Cloud outlining.

The painter Wangdrak almost invariably used this style of outer lining for painting the clouds surrounding two of the four great guardians of the directions. The technique was a finishing step that he applied only after the interiors of the clouds had been painted and shaded. Wangdrak painted these clouds in a connected series that formed a nimbus-like strip surrounding the figure, and as usual he coloured the interiors of the clouds in an alternating sequence of blue and green.

The special outlining technique itself began with the artist's application of a continuous strip of medium blue paint all the way around the outer edge of the background clouds. Then on the inside of this blue strip the artist put down a continuous strip of deep pink or mauve, following the outer edges of the clouds. Finally, he completed the border by applying a dark indigo outline to the outer edge. This indigo outline, however, was painted as a series of rounded bumps, the bottom ends of which penetrated through the strips of blue and pink all the way to the edge of the cloud.

Multicoloured Designs on Scarves

One last type of linear detail was reserved for the decoration of the white centers of special scarves draped around figures such as Mahākāla, the great protector of Vajrayāna Buddhism. In terms of their designs, these decorations were basically the same as those used for the gold floral details in the border strips of brocades and robes. The only difference was that here the flower designs were executed in blue and red over a white background, while the leafy stems that wound back and forth in these designs were painted green.

Outlining Techniques

Excellence in outlining was something that every novice cultivated, and something that every master had to have achieved. In outlining, excellence meant not only fineness and accuracy, but also the ability to impart successfully a fluid tapering to the whole length of the outline. Such smooth gradations in the thickness of the outline gave a subtle illusion of depth or volume to an object that otherwise would have looked much flatter. The artist could also turn the tapering outlines to his advantage by using them to even out slight irregularities in the outer edges of the forms being outlined.

To achieve the optimum smoothness and taper in his lines, the first thing an artist needed was a good outlining brush (bcad pir). The brush had to be thin, its tip had to possess a perfect point, and the hairs had to be of sufficient length to hold enough dye for long, continuous strokes. Secondly the artist had to keep his outlining dye fluid and well stirred. Often we observed Wangdrak stop his work to stir the small pot of colour from which he was taking his outlining dye. Also, before applying each stroke, an artist rubbed the brush tip against his hand or against the edge of the colour pot or canvas to remove any excess dye. This helped prevent blots and irregularities. Finally, he had to apply the outlining brush strokes smoothly, while gradually altering the thickness of the line through increasing or decreasing the pressure on the brush tip. Usually the best procedure was to work with a smooth downwards sweep of the brush. However, on objects with sharp points or tips such as flames and leaves, it was best to begin the outlining stroke at the point of the object, whatever its orientation, and then work away from it. When outlining a leaf, for example, a painter could begin the outlining stroke at the tip of the leaf. Then, slowly increasing the thickness of the line, he would continue the same stroke all of the way down one side of the leaf to the stem. But to create a tiny curl at the tip of the leaf some artists used a deft brush movement in the opposite direction, towards the tip. Since such fine work required the maximum control and accuracy, the artist usually worked with his painting hand resting on the surface of the canvas or supported on a thin wooden board.

Artists used to notice and appreciate skillful tapering in the outlining of a thangka. Some lineages also passed down traditional sayings about the qualities of fine outlining. Wangyal of Dolpo, for example, remembered a saying of his teacher:

The waist [of an outlining stroke], since it
is the "wealth" [of the stroke], must be wide.

The point [of the outlining stroke], since it
is a "virtue", must be sharp.[2]

(Here there is a play on the word yon tan, "virtue", which also means wisdom, the mental quality that is cultivated through study. This, like intelligence, should be "sharp.") One of the older painters observed to us that many of the younger generation of Tibetan artists do not seem to cultivate much tapering in their outlining. As he pointed out, many artists now concentrate on producing very fine outlines, painting brush strokes that are too thin to allow much gradation in width.

Notes

1. The term zhu rams referred to a mixture of zhu mkhan dye and indigo (rams). Wangdrak said that for the best zhu rams, the light variety of indigo called he rams should be used.

2. The saying in Tibetan was:

   sked pa longs spyod yin pas sbom dgos/
   rtse mo yon tan yin pas sno dgos/

   Such sayings are a valuable part of the artistic heritage of Tibet. One hopes that older artists, as well as the younger ones who received traditional training, will record them and pass them on.

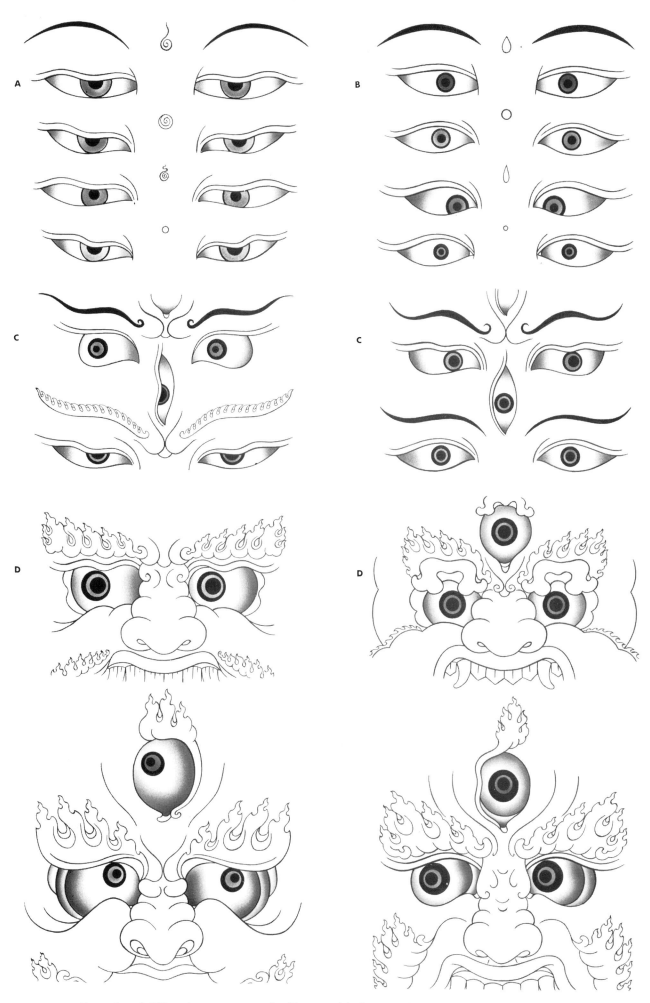

Examples of different eyes:

a) 'Bow eyes' (gzhu spyan)   c) Eyes of semi-wrathful deities.

b) 'Grain eyes' (nas spyan)   d) Eyes of extremely wrathful deities.

Twelve
Finishing Details

Facial Features

The last main step involving the application of colours was the rendering of the faces of the main figures. This was in effect the final stage of outlining, and sometimes a master painter would step in at this point and complete the painting of his student.

Of all the finishing details, the facial features demanded the most attention, and among these it was the eyes that received the greatest care. The painting of the eyes of a deity was one of the acts that brought it to life. "Eye opening" *(spyan dbye)* through painting in the eyes was one step in the elaborate consecration or vivification *(rab gnas)* ritual, and therefore for special paintings that required more than the usual abridged ritual the artist would wait until the consecration ceremony to complete the eyes. For major temple murals, as well as for the main statues and thangkas of a temple, the eye opening was performed on an auspicious day and it was often accompanied by a celebration.

As the first step in painting the eyes, Wangdrak redrew all the facial features with charcoal. He began by drawing the central axis of the face, and then drew in the outline of the head and face. These lines guaranteed that the facial features would be balanced and correctly aligned. Here and in other cases where sketching was done over areas of flesh, charcoal was superior to graphite pencil because charcoal lines were so easy to erase. Then he did the outlining of the face, a continuation of the flesh outlining *(sha bcad)* already begun.

Varieties of Eyes

Iconographic custom determined the shapes and dimensions of the various facial features. Buddhas and peaceful bodhisattvas, for instance, were always painted with "bow eyes" *(gzhu spyan)*, while goddesses, saints and ordinary humans had "grain eyes" *(nas spyan)*.[1] Distinct from these two types of eyes were the round and square eye shapes of wrathful deities. As with eyes, so too with mouths there existed several types, each appropriate only for certain classes of deities. Although the main features thus depended on iconography, certain characteristics depended on the skill of the artist. Well-executed eyes, for instance, might give the illusion of following the viewer *(gar gzigs)* even though that was not one of the compulsory features of the deity according to its iconography.

Facial proportions of a peaceful goddess by Wangdrak.

Facial proportions of an extremely wrathful deity by Wangdrak.

139

Eye-Painting Techniques

Although the techniques of our main informants for painting eyes were basically similar, they were different enough to prevent us from describing them in a single, unified account. Instead we can make the general technique clear by comparing the methods of two artists, Wangdrak and Legdrup Gyatsho. Here we will describe in particular the techniques they used for painting the eyes of peaceful deities and gurus.

For both artists the painting of an eye pre-supposed a finished sketch and a coat of white paint on the white of the eye (such white paint had the technical name *spyan dkar*). Wangdrak then began by applying a line of lac dye to the bottom eyelid. Then he painted the corners of the eye with a dilute orange, succeeded by a light shading with dilute lac dye. Next he painted in the eyelid base colour by applying a line of light blue to the upper lid. (In his painting style this light blue was also one of the main colours for other facial hairs such as eyebrows, mustaches and the goatees of peaceful figures). With the same light blue he also painted the iris. Next, he underlined the light blue eyelid edges with some dark blue indigo, thus indicating the eyelashes. Finally with the same colour he also outlined the outer edge of the iris and provided it with a small dot in the middle for the pupil.

The technique of Legdrup Gyatsho was similar. Starting with the drawing of the eye and painting the white, he then applied a line of light blue (or for some other figures, light brown) to the upper eyelid. With the same colour he also painted the iris. Next, he out-lined the upper eyelid and iris and painted the pupil as above, except that he used black ink instead of indigo. If the figure was sufficiently large, he liked to create a gradual transition from the black eyelash into the light blue eyelid by means of shading. Then he filled in the corners of the eye with faint orange. Finally, he com-pleted the eye by shading the corners with dilute lac dye, and outlined the bottom lid of the eye with the same colour.

Some other artists did not apply an undercoat of light blue or light brown to the eyelid, and some preferred a brown or yellow colour for the irises of the eyes of both peaceful and fierce figures. For wrathful deities a number of artists painted the whole iris black, and then indicated a pupil with a thin circle of yellow or gold.

When painting smaller figures the artists could not follow in every detail the techniques described above. Instead, they depicted rudimentary eyes by laying down a line of lac dye for the bottom edge or eyelash, a dark blue or black line for the top eyelash, and a black dot in the middle of the white for the iris and pupil. Once again, the artists here speeded up their work by painting at one time all areas requiring the same colour.

Outlining the eyes and other facial features required the greatest care and control. Dorje Gyaltshen stated that to steady their hands the artists of his tradition used to hold their breath for the duration of each stroke. He was taught by his teacher that detailed outlining should be done on an empty stomach if possible, and never immediately after a full meal. A full stomach was thought to impede one's ability to hold one's breath. Similarly outlining should not be under-taken after strenuous physical work, for at such times one's hand tended to become shaky.

Sequence of painting eyes according to Wangdrak.

Sequence of painting eyes according to Legdrup Gyatsho.

ORANGE SHADING

LAC DYE

LIGHT BLUE or BROWN

INDIGO or BLACK

Burnishing the Gold

The final step for many areas painted with gold was burnishing. In an ordinary - full-colour *(rdzogs tshon)* painting the artist did not burnish every area of gold. One master painter from Central Tibet stated that in general the main places needing burnishing were depictions of objects that were made of shiny gold in real life. Gold jewelry, for instance, needed burnishing, while faces and bodies painted with gold were to be left with an unburnished, matte finish. However, in actual practice this artist also burnished the gold line drawings executed in a few other places such as on the rocks in the landscape and in the flames. Most artists were freer than this in their use of the burnisher, some even burnishing gold faces and bodies. Nevertheless, few of the Tibetan painters we worked with burnished every bit of gold in the painting.

There were two principal types of burnishing. The first, called "flat burnishing" *(leb gzi)*, consisted of the uniform polishing of a whole line or an entire area of gold. The second type consisted of selective burnishing, whether by drawing designs onto an area of gold using the point of the burnisher, or by partial flat burnishing of a large area of gold. In thangkas where gold was used only for minimal outlining and gold ornaments, most or all of the gold received a full burnishing of the first type. The more gold the painting contained, however, the more important the matte areas and etched designs *(gzi ris)* became. In gold thangkas, for instance, selective burnishing came to perform some of the functions that would have been fulfilled by shading and outlining in an ordinary thangka. On large areas of gold the painter could both draw in detailed designs with the burnisher and also create an illusion of volume through gradually burnishing some areas while leaving other parts unburnished and thus of a darker, matte appearance.

Burnishing Tools

The burnishing of gold required two main tools. To begin with there was of course the burnisher *(gzi)* itself. This was a polishing instrument with a hard, generally conical end. Some artists actually used two burnishers, one for each type of burnishing. The one employed in flat burnishing had a point that was smooth and slightly rounded. The one used for executing drawings on gold needed a sharper point. Often these burnishers were made by mounting on a handle a *gzi* stone, a small cylinder of banded onyx with one end ground to a tip. Some painters had burnishers that consisted of *gzi*-stone tips mounted on elaborately chased silver handles; and among all the tools possessed by a Tibetan painter, his burnisher was often the one that he prized most highly.

The fact that in Tibetan the word for "*gzi* stone" is synonymous with "burnisher" possibly indicates that the use of *gzi* stones in this capacity goes back a long way. In general, Tibetans traditionally believed that *gzi* stones worn on the body were effective in driving away harmful influences. This esteem for the stone may have helped them become established as the burnishing stone *par excellence*. Most Tibetan artists would choose a *gzi* stone over an ordinary agate that was equally suitable.

It is likewise possible that the use of *gzi*-stone burnishers derived from the practice of early Chinese

Wangdrak burnishing gold outlines on a robe.

Rear view of above.

Writing the sacred syllables on the back of the painting.   Cutting out the completed painting.

artisans. Such burnishers continued to be used in China down to the present century, for instance by the silver gilders of Kansu Province. Daniel V. Thompson, an authority on European medieval painting methods and materials, visited Western China in the first decades of this century, and there he discovered how highly the Chinese artisans valued their *gzi*-stone burnishers:

> One of the industries of Lanchow is the manu-facture of silver-gilt ornaments, a sort of monopoly of that city. There is one street which is occupied by silver-gilders, and they were all supplied with exquisitely made and finished burnishers which they used in their profession. These burnishers were not of hematite, but of some sort of agate, beautifully veined and striped, and mounted in delicate ivory handles, with ferrules of silver. Offers even of fantastic prices met with blank refusal from every worker.[2]

Nowadays, Tibetan artists use various types of burnishers besides the *gzi* stone, including animal teeth, other siliceous stones, and suitably shaped pieces of metal.

The second necessary tool was a burnishing support *(gzi rten)*. When burnishing gold one had to bear down on the gold paint with some force, and since the thangka was painted on a cloth support, any pressure sufficient to burnish the gold involved the danger of gouging the painting surface. Therefore, while burnishing the canvas with one hand, the artist used his other hand to press a support against the back of the canvas. Objects nowadays used as burnisher supports include smooth flat pieces of glass, small mirrors, and small smooth pieces of wood.

Burnishing was executed only when the painting was finished in other respects. The painter proceeded from one deity and its surroundings to the next, and in that way systematically covered the entire painting surface. As he burnished he held the canvas at an angle that reflected light so that he could easily gauge his progress. Where gold had been used only for outlining and detailed line drawings, most or all the gold — such things as the light rays in the nimbuses, outlines of leaves and rocks, and details on fabrics — received burnishing. Similarly in black thangkas the painters burnished all the gold line drawings. For burnishing such lines accuracy was not essential and the work proceeded very quickly. The artist simply rubbed along the gold lines (and inevitably over ˙some of the surrounding painted area too) with the burnisher until the gold began to shine. By contrast, the drawing of designs on larger areas of gold was done slowly and deliberately, as when painting similar details.

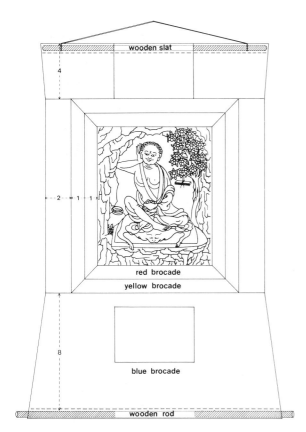

Common proportions of the brocade thangka frame.

Other Finishing Steps

With the completion of the faces and the burnishing of the gold, the production of the painting came to an end. Some fine thangkas, such as those belonging to a large set, at this point received gold inscriptions beneath each major figure. It was important to do this with correct spellings and in a fine hand. Therefore, if this was beyond the capabilities of the artist, some other person such as a learned lama or a scribe would be called upon to help.

Next some artists gave the completed painting a final dry-polishing on its back. Wangdrak was one who did so, and it made his finished paintings soft and resistant to cracking. First he laid a flat sheet of wood on a smooth surface and covered it with a clean cloth. Then he placed the stretcher face down on the cloth and rubbed the canvas all over with his dry-polishing stone.

Finally, to function as a sacred object of worship the painting had to be mounted in a cloth frame, and then consecrated through the ceremony of vivification *(rab gnas)*. As a preparation for this consecration, while the painting was still in the stretcher many artists wrote in the sacred syllables OṂ ĀḤ HŪṂ on the back of the canvas behind the forehead, throat and heart of each main figure. These syllables represented the essence of the enlightened body, speech and mind with which the figures were to be imbued during the consecration ritual. In special instances, other syllables also had to be written on the back of the painting in their appropriate places. To position each syllable correctly, some painters first held the canvas up to a light source and put dots of vermilion at each of the spots needing a syllable. The

dot was later incorporated into the head of the syllable.

When the syllables had been written in with red letters, nothing remained for the painter to do but to clean the painting once more (with tsampa dough or a clean rag) and to remove it from the stretcher. For the latter task he took a sharp knife and carefully cut all four sides leaving only the corners uncut. Then, holding the painting in place with one hand, he severed the four corners, first the bottom two and then the top ones. The artist had to take care to leave enough of a border (approximately half an inch on each side of the painting) so that a brocade frame could later be sewn on without damaging the painting itself. This was not difficult, for the red border strip around the edges of the painting gave him a guideline for the width of the required edge.

Once the painting was removed from the stretcher, the artist rolled it up, tied it with a strip of cloth or a piece of twine, and kept it carefully until the patron called for it. The painter then needed only remove the remaining edges of unused canvas to free the stretcher for his next painting.

Notes

1. An exception was White Tārā, who was often depicted with "bow eyes" *(gzhu spyan).*

2. Thompson, p.214.

143

Appendix A:
Iconometric Controversies and Sources

In the brief description of iconometric classes and proportions given above in Chapter 4 we pointed out a few differences among the textual sources we used. Some of these variations were minor and may have originated from the innovation of a single influential artist. Somewhere in the Indian or Tibetan traditions, for instance, a painter may have decided for aesthetic reasons to draw the necks of humans four *sor* long instead of the two *sor* prescribed by some texts. Other more important differences also existed among the iconometric sources, differences which indicate the presence of sharply diverging traditions. This we saw in the case of the proportions of humans, where one text prescribed a height of seven spans and the other called for a height of eight. And even more significant was a difference that we did not mention above, a disagreement concerning the proportions of the Buddha image itself.

Throughout the history of Tibetan art (even down to the present) there has been no single universally accepted system of proportions for the Buddha image. The techniques for painting Buddhas entered Tibet at different periods and from different regions, and they were never forced into complete agreement. Systems of iconometry, like painting styles, led lives of their own. With the passing of the centuries some systems gradually flourished, some maintained only a very small following, and still others fell into complete oblivion.

The iconometry of the Buddha described in detail above was one of the predominant systems, and in recent times it was widely reputed to be the most orthodox. It did not reach Tibet until the second or later spread of Buddhism there; the system was derived from the *Kālacakra* cycle, which itself was not translated and propagated in Tibet until the early 11th century. By the 14th and 15th centuries this system of Buddha proportions had gained influential adherents such as Bu-ston and Sman-thang-pa Sman-bla-don-grub, but it was by no means the only living iconometric tradition. Alongside it there existed other systems, and Bo-dong Pan-chen took pains to include some of these when compiling his *De nyid 'dus pa* compendium in the first half of the 15th century. These early iconometric systems have yet to be thoroughly studied.[1]

The development of iconometry continued in the 16th and 17th centuries with what seems to have been a general trend toward standardization of art in the main monasteries of Central Tibet. This movement was linked to the growth of the Gelugpa Order, and two names associated with it were the Second Dalai Lama Dge-'dun-rgya-mtsho (1476–1542) and the artist 'Phreng-kha-ba. In 1642 the Fifth Dalai Lama gained political control, and in the subsequent decades the religious life of Tibet became somewhat more constricted. Not that there was any suppression of art styles in favor of just one (both the Sman-ris and Mkhyen-ris styles received official patronage), but in the second half of the 17th century the Dga'-ldan pho-brang government made efforts to legitimize itself and to standardize various aspects of religious and cultural life. It was in this general context that the question of the Buddha's bodily proportions came up for review.

We know that in the late 17th and early 18th century at least two distinct iconometric traditions continued to be followed, because notable scholars are known to have championed each system. The protagonist of one system was Sde-srid Sangs-rgyas-rgya-mtsho, the man who succeeded the Fifth Dalai Lama as the ruler of Tibet. He took what is nowadays a controversial position in asserting that paintings of the Buddha should measure only 120 *sor*, or ten spans of twelve *sor* each. One generation later these opinions were critically answered by the artist and redactor Zhu-chen Tshul-krims-rin-chen (1700–1769). The latter held that a painting of the Buddha must have a total height (and arm span) of 125 *sor*, i.e. ten spans of twelve and one-half *sor* each. Zhu-chen, like the Sde-srid, believed that the establishment of an authoritative iconometry was a desirable thing; the only question was what the standard proportions should be.

The Sde-srid was not ignorant of the statements in the *Kālacakra Tantra* to the effect that a Buddha image should measure 125 *sor*, or ten spans of twelve and one-half *sor*. This measure, according to him, did indeed apply to some Buddha images, but only to three-dimensional representations such as statues, and not to paintings. Painted Buddhas, he said, were separately taught as measuring 120 *sor* in another text, the *Samvarodaya Tantra*.[2] Thus, according to the Sde-srid, paintings of both Buddhas and bodhisattvas should have the same proportions. The differences being talked about here can scarcely be detected in a finished piece, but in the theory of iconometry a difference of one-half *sor* per span was a crucial matter.

Sde-srid Sangs-rgyas-rgya-mtsho presented his argument for the 120-*sor* Buddha in his *Bstan bcos baidūrya dkar po las dris lan 'khrul snang g.ya' sel*.[3] Many artists were presumably following this tradition when the Sde-srid wrote about it, and in the first half of the 18th century such painters were numerous in all parts of Tibet (in fact, the tradition continues even today).[4] However, the position set forth by the Sde-srid could not escape criticism indefinitely. Zhu-chen, who helped proof-read the *G.ya' sel* during its printing in Derge after the Sde-srid's death, questioned the 120-*sor* proportion in a text that he later wrote, making an appeal to both the Indian canonical tradition and the early Tibetan authorities. It is worth summarizing Zhu-chen's role in this exchange because it nicely exemplifies the approach a great scholar of Tibet would take to solve controversial points of this nature.

The Iconometric Studies of Zhu-chen

Zhu-chen was born in 1697 into an old family of artists in Khams. He was the great-great-(great?)-nephew of the outstanding 16th-century painter Sangs-rgyas-lha-dbang.[5] Zhu-chen's parents dedicated him to the monk-hood as a boy, but before his advanced studies he learned painting from his father. Thus he first learned the system of proportions that had been handed down within the family (a system perhaps influenced by the iconometric writings of the Eighth Karma-pa Mi-bskyod-rdo-rje). Later on in his studies he became keenly interested in establishing the textual basis of the sacred artistic proportions. He sought out a learned teacher, Sangs-rgyas-chos-'phel, and studied with him the artistic treatises of five great Tibetan authorities:[6]

1) Sman-thang-pa Sman-bla-don-grub (fl. mid-to-late 15th century).[7]
2) 'Phreng-kha-ba Dpal-dlan-blo-gros-bzang-po (fl. mid-16th century).[8]
3) Bu-ston Rin-chen-grub (1290–1364)[9]
4) Stag-tshang lo-tsā-ba Shes-rab-rin-chen (fl. 15th century)[10]
5) Bla-ma Sangs-rgyas-lha-dbang (fl. mid-16th century)[11]

Afterwards Zhu-chen also studied a sixth treatise, the above-mentioned *G.ya' sel* of Sde-srid Sangs-rgyas-rgya-mtsho, a polemic that grew out of the Sde-srid's monumental treatise on astrology and related topics, the *Baidūrya dkar po*.

Following a careful study of those texts with his teacher, Zhu-chen concluded that one had to accept as the fundamental treatise the work of Sman-thang-pa, since it was in perfect accord with the Indian sources accessible to him in Tibetan translation. He also found the treatise of 'Phreng-kha-ba to be basically sound, as it did not conflict with that of Sman-thang-pa. However, in the work of 'Phreng-kna-ba there occurred an interlinear note *(mchan bu)* that he took to be the careless insertion of a later scribe or editor. The note stated that while sculpted images of the Buddha should measure 125 *sor,* painted images were to measure 120 *sor.*[12] According to Zhu-chen, it was precisely this dubious note that gave scholars of subsequent generations their basis for perpetuating this opinion. Some of the later scholars,

such as the Sde-srid, attempted to reinforce their position by citing the *Samvarodaya Tantra,* thus lending apparent textual support to what had become a wide-spread artistic practice.[13]

In Zhu-chen's opinion, however, a painted image of the Buddha could only measure 125 *sor.* To paint one with proportions of 120 *sor* was foolish and erroneous, he said, and to prove his point he turned to the basic Sanskrit commentary on the *Samvarodaya Tantra* in its Tibetan translation.

The primary means for a Tibetan scholar to interpret a tantra was the South Asian commentarial tradition as preserved in the *Tanjur.* In this case the commentary on the *Samvarodaya* explicitly stated that the large unit of measure of a Buddha should measure twelve and one-half *sor,* whereas in all other figures it should measure only twelve.[14] Hence a ten-span Buddha image must measure 125 *sor.* To make the basis for this conclusion clear, Zhu-chen quoted at length the very words of the commentary.[15]

Thus the position of the Sde-srid, although widely followed in Zhu-chen's time, could not be justified as being a continuation of South Asian Buddhist tantric scholarship. Indeed, a century before the Sde-srid lived, other great Tibetan scholars were already aware that the somewhat misleading statements of the *Samvarodaya* could not be taken at their face value. As 'Brug-chen Padma-dkar-po (1526–1592), an earlier authority unavailable to Zhu-chen, wrote, "The failure [of the *Samvarodaya*] to mention the half *sor* [to be added to each span of the Buddha] should be understood as being merely a lack of clarity of expression on the part of the tantra. In fact that [extra one-half *sor*] is required."[16]

120-*sor* Buddha by Tshedor.

An even earlier scholar, Bo-dong Paṇ-chen (1375–1451), took the same position regarding the presence of an extra one-half *sor* in the *Samvarodaya* tradition.[17]

Zhu-chen was thus not alone in rejecting that the *Samvarodaya* taught a 120-*sor* Buddha image. Furthermore he found nothing to substantiate the practice of assigning different proportions to paintings and statues. To make this last point he cited the great Tibetan authorities of the past such as Sman-thang-pa. Although those early Tibetan authorities explained the proportions of a Buddha many times as being 125 *sor*, Zhu-chen never found any place where Sman-thang-pa or the other early masters had differentiated between proportions on the basis of media.[18]

The Indian Sources of Tibetan Iconometry

Zhu-chen thus considered Sman-thang-pa to be one of the greatest Tibetan authorities on iconometry. One finds, not surprisingly, that even the Sde-srid described his position as representing the opinion of Sman-thang-pa.[19] But for the Tibetans even more important than Sman-thang-pa were the Indian textual sources on art that were translated from Sanskrit and preserved in the canonical collections of Tibet. These were the very texts upon which Sman-thang-pa had based his own work. Indeed the Sde-srid himself also claimed the basic tantric scriptures of the canon as his sources, though he did not directly quote from any of them.

Actually, a variety of iconometric sources were preserved in the *Kanjur* and *Tanjur* canons. Of these only some were followed by the living artistic traditions or cited by writers on iconometry. Here, to conclude our brief discussion of these aspects of iconometry, it might be useful to list the basic Indian sources and to describe their relative importance in Tibetan painting.

To begin with, the most important textual sources for Tibetan iconometry were passages from certain Buddhist tantras and their commentaries.[20] Zhu-chen, for instance, in one of his works mentioned the following texts as the main sources of iconometry.[21]

> *Kālacakra Tantra* and its commentary, the *Vimalaprabhā*
> *Samvarodaya Tantra* and its commentary
> *Kṛṣṇayamāri Tantra* and commentary
> *Mañjuśrimūlakalpa Tantra*

None of these texts contained descriptions of all of the iconometric classes, and therefore one had to refer to several texts to get all the proportions. The following correspondence of texts to iconometric classes is presented in another work by Zhu-chen:[22]

> Class 1: *Kālacakra Tantra*, and the commentary on the *Samvarodaya*
> Class 2: *Samvarodaya* and also the *Kriyāsamuccaya* (read *bya ba kun btus* instead of *bslab btus*)[23]

Class 3: *Samvarodaya*
Class 4: *Samvarodaya* and *Kṛṣṇayamāri Tantra*
Class 5: *Kriyāsamuccaya* and a work by Kṛṣṇapāda
Class 6: The *Kālacakra* commentary *Vimalaprabhā*

In addition, other Tibetan authors such as Rong-tha also mentioned the *Catuḥpiṭha Tantra* as a source for the proportions of figures measuring nine and twelve spans, including multi-headed *yi-dam* deities.[24] Rong-tha also attributed the 7-*mtho* proportional class ultimately to the *Kālacakra*.[25]

Besides these tantric sources, there also existed in the canon a group of independent treatises on the subjects of art and iconometry. The *bzo-rig* section of the Peking *Tanjur* contained four such full-length treatises on art:[26]

1. *Daśatalanyagrodhaparimaṇḍala-buddhapratimālakṣaṇa*
2. *Sambuddhabhāṣita-pratimālakṣaṇa-vivaraṇa*
3. *Citralakṣaṇa*
4. *Pratimāmānalakṣaṇa*

Most Tibetan writers on iconometry did not use these four texts as primary sources. In fact only one was commonly mentioned in the later Tibetan treatises: the first text in the above list, also known as the *Sha ri'i bus zhus pa'i mdo*. The latter title could be translated as "The Discourse (sūtra) Delivered at the Request of Śāriputra," which would seem to mark it as belonging to the sūtra class of scriptures within the *Kanjur*. Tucci, in his monumental *Tibetan Painted Scrolls*, mentioned that four different versions of that text were known to the 15th-century authority Sman-thang-pa, including one that was said to have been delivered by the Buddha in Tuṣita and another that he gave in Jetāvana (the places of the other two Tucci did not specify).[27] According to Mi-pham-rgya-mtsho, however, the basis for this text on iconometry was a discourse given by the Buddha in a third place. Mi-pham described the *Sha ri'i bus zhus pa'i mdo* as follows: "It was a treatise (śāstra) summarizing the import of the discourse (sūtra) given by the Buddha when he was dwelling in the deva-realm of the Thirty-three (trāyāstriṃśāḥ) that sets forth the proportions of figures, delivered at the request of Śāriputra."[28] As a treatise and not a true discourse of the Buddha it thus rightfully belonged in the *Tanjur* and not together with the true sūtras of the *Kanjur*.

Mi-pham pointed out that the proportions set forth in the above text differ from those found in the tantras and their commentaries, but he also followed previous masters in asserting that there was no basic incompatibility between the two systems. (How the blatant differences could be glossed over is not clear). Mi-pham, however, did not list the proportions of the Buddha in this system (which prescribed a measure of 120 *sor*!) but contented himself with a description of the widespread 125-*sor* tantric system described above.[29] The main iconometric system of Tibetan authors thus agreed with the tantras and their commentaries, and not with the four iconometric treatises in the *Tanjur*.

Non-Scriptural Sources on Iconometry

Finally, it is worth noting that some later Tibetan writers on iconometry stressed that a number of proportional classes had no demonstrable origins in the tantras themselves. The more recent Khams-pa scholar Rong-tha Blo-bzang-dam-chos-rgya-mtsho (1863–1917), for instance, asserted in his text on iconometry that the classes of wrathful deities whose proportions measured three and six spans had actually originated from the explanations of previous learned and spiritually accomplished Tibetan masters who had themselves arrived at these proportions based on the measures of old, correctly proportioned images from India.[30] Rong-tha also stated that the five-span proportional class derived from the artistic tradition of such learned Newar masters as Ratnarakṣita.[31] As we have seen, Zhu-chen did cite certain texts as the basis for at least the fifth class, the five-span proportion. But he could not cite any tantra, and instead mentioned only secondary texts, whereas for class I he did cite a work by Ratnarakṣita, the commentary on the *Samvarodaya Tantra*.[32]

Notes

1. The most valuable scholarly work on Tibetan iconometry to date has been done by K. M. Gerasimova. Unfortunately only a fraction of her writings are available in English. From among these see for example her "Compositional Structure" and "The Anthropometric Foundation of the Tibetan Canon of Proportions," *VIIIth Congress of Anthropological and Ethnological Sciences,* pp.325-327. For a list of the related studies by scholars who preceded her, see her "Compositional Structure," p.40 and p.50 n.5.

   For a brief review of studies on Buddhist iconometry by Gerasimova and other recent Soviet scholars see S. Frye (transl.), "Study and Publication of Indian and Tibetan Monuments on the Theory of Art," *The Tibet Journal*, vol.6 (1981), pp.3-5.

   Recently K. W. Peterson has also discussed some aspects of the problem of the different Buddha proportions in her "Sources of Variation in Tibetan Canons of Iconometry," *Tibetan Studies in Honour of Hugh Richardson* (Warminster, 1980), pp. 239-248.

2. Sde-srid, vol.1, p.621. In the reprint based on the Lhasa Zhol prints (New Delhi, 1971) the relevant passage is found in vol.2, pp.645-677. However, one should also compare the detailed proportions that the Sde-srid proposed. See Peterson, pp.247.

3. Sde-srid, vol.1, p.621. An earlier Tibetan to describe a Buddha proportion of other than 125 *sor* was Bo-dong Paṇ-chen. See below, note 17. For Bo-dong the other proportion was not prescribed, but only a possible alternative to the systems of the *Kālacakra* and *Samvarodaya*.

4. For an 18th-century example of a 120-*sor* Buddha see the illustration in the iconometric treatise of Mgon-po-skyabs, *Chinese Tripiṭaka*, Taisho no.1419, p.939. More recent examples of 120-*sor* Buddhas are found in Pallis, following p.334, and B. C. Olschak, *Mystic Art of Ancient Tibet* (New York, 1973), p.13.

5. Zhu-chen, *Chos smra [Autobiography]*, p.347.4.

6. Zhu-chen, *Chos smra,* p.348.

7. Sman-thang-pa's classic has recently been published. See above, Chapter 4, notes 7 and 8.

8. 'Phreng-kha-ba's famous text was carved onto blocks at Lhasa Zhol, and this became the basis for the new edition printed in Dharamsala in 1978.

9. We have not been able to locate in the *Collected Works* of Bu-ston any separate work on the subject of proportions. Such a work would be the earliest surviving text on this topic, and it would be of great importance for students of this subject. Rong-tha, p.134, presents a synopsis of Bu-ston's system.

10. Stag-tshang lo-tsā-ba's text, *Rten gsum bzhengs tshul dpal 'byor rgya mtsho,* is known to survive in the library of Otani University, Kyoto.

11. This author was a distant ancestor of Zhu-chen Tshul-khrims-rin-chen. His work, entitled *Skor thig gi 'grel pa*, does not survive and was probably rare in Tibet.

12. 'Phreng-kha-ba, p.11f: *sgril bas mtho bcu sor brgya ('bur sku'i dbang du byas/ bris sku la brgya nyi shu) nyer lngar 'gyur/*. A similar insertion is found on p.10, to the effect that the height of the cranium *(thod pa'i dpangs)* should be only four *sor* for a painted Buddha, but four and one-half for a sculpted Buddha.
    Curiously, the same notes *('bur sku'i dbang du byas,* etc.) are found in the recently published manuscript of Sman-thang-pa's work. See p.10f. But on p.68 Sman-thang-pa specifically states that the image of the Buddha should measure 125 *sor* whether it is drawn (or painted), cast, carved or modelled, i.e., no matter what medium is used.

13. Sde-srid, vol.1, p.621.1.

14. Ratnarakṣita, *Śrī samvarodaya mahātantrarāja padmini nāma pañjikā*. Tib.: *Dpal sdom pa 'byung ba'i rgyud kyi rgyal po chen po'i dka' 'grel padma can* (Peking no.2173; Derge no.1420). Peking Tibetan Tripiṭaka, vol.51, p.113.2.1.

15. Zhu-chen, *Gtsug lag,* p.152.5.

16. 'Brug-chen Padma-dkar-po, *Bris sku'i rnam bshad mthong ba don ldan, Collected Works* (Darjeeling, 1973), vol.7, p.310: *'dir sor phyed pa ma gsungs pa ni rgyud zhal gsal mi gsal gyi khyad tsam du rig par bya ste/ don la de dgos pa yin no/*

17. Bo-dong Paṇ-chen, *Sdom 'byung nas gsungs pa'i sku gzugs sogs kyi cha tshad bshad pa, Collected Works,* vol.2, p.356. Here the body length of the Buddha in the *Samvarodaya* tradition is said to measure ten *thal mo* of twelve and one-half *sor.* See also p.373.2, where for the bodhisattvas he specifies that the extra one-half *sor* must be omitted from each *thal mo* measure. However, in another work on religious art by Bo-dong Paṇ-chen, *Rten gsum bzhengs tshul bstan bcos lugs bshad pa, Collected Works,* vol.2, p.313.5, the class of peaceful deities (including, apparently, Buddhas) are given a measure of nine *zhal tshad.* See p.314.4. In the same text (p.324.6) Bo-dong says that peaceful proportions are mainly in accord with the *Samvarodaya* and the *Sha ri bu yis zhus pa'i mdo.* In this system, he adds, the 125-*sor* measure of the *Kālacakra* is not to be employed. See p.325.1.

18. Bo-dong in his *Rten gsum,* vol.2, p.317, stated that sources such as the *Samvarodaya* mainly set forth the proportions of pictorial representations: *sdom pa 'byung ba'i rgyud sogs las/ ri mo'i phyag tshad gtso bor gsungs/.* But he does not seem to be contrasting the *Samvarodaya* with the *Kālacakra* system. He merely explains how the surface measures of a three-dimensional figure must be appropriately expanded.

19. Sde-srid, vol.1, p.621.2: *sman thang pa'i cha tshad kyi dgongs par gnas pa 'dra.* See also vol.1, p.586.2.

20. One of Gerasimova's main contributions to our understanding of Tibetan iconometry was her insistence on this point, quite in agreement with the Tibetan sources. See her "Compositional Structure," p.41, and also her "Anthropometric Foundation," p.325.

21. Zhu-chen, *Chos smra,* p.348.4.

22. Zhu-chen, *Gtsug lag,* pp.150-156.

23. *Kriyāsamuccaya,* Peking *Tanjur,* vol.86 *(Rgyud 'grel, 'u),* p.312.4.1 (f.351a.1).

24. Rong-tha, p.133; Dagyab, p.29.

25. Rong-tha, p.135.

26. Peking Tibetan Tripiṭaka, vol.143, numbers 5804-5807. But in the Derge *Tanjur* (according to the Ui catalogue) only two of these texts are found in the *bzo-rig* section: no.4315, *Sambuddha-bhāṣita-pratibimbalakṣaṇavivaraṇa* and no.4316, *Pratibimbamānalakṣaṇa.*

The *Citralakṣaṇa* was originally translated by B. Laufer into German. See his *Das Citralakshana* (Leipzig, 1913). That translation has recently been rendered into English and published under the title *An Early Document of Indian Art* (New Delhi, 1976).

27. Tucci, vol.1, p.292.

28. Mi-pham-rgya-mtsho, *Sku gzugs,* p.50.5.

29. No Tibetan writer known to us attributed the origin of the 120-*sor* Buddha to the *bzo-rig* treatises in the *Tanjur.*

30. Rong-tha, p.133: *yang thal mo drug pa dang/ zhal tshad gsum pa gnyis ni/ sngon rgya gar nas byung ba'i sku gzugs tshad ldan la dpag nas/ bod kyi mkhas grub snga ma dag gis bshad la/.* These two proportional classes, which Rong-tha termed "Tibetan traditions" *(bod kyi lugs)* went back to at least the 14th century, since Rong-tha includes them within Bu-ston's eighth class. See *ibid.,* p.134, lines 11-13.

There are a number of other traditional and historical accounts which refer to the basing of the proportions of painted images on old Indian statues. The *chu len ma* image, which in some traditions was held to be the basis for an early style of painted Buddha images, was said by Stag-tshang lo-tsā-ba to have originated from an impression of the Mahā-bodhi statue at Bodhgaya, made on a cloth using saffron dye. See Kong-sprul, *Theg pa'i sgo kun las btus pa shes bya kun khyab,* (New Delhi, 1970), vol.1, p.571.2. For a similar story see also Kaḥ-thog Si-tu, *Gangs ljongs dbus gtsang gnas skor lam yig* (Tashijong, 1972), p.30.5. Nam-mkha'-bkra-shis, the founder of the Karma-sgar-bris painting style, as well as the Tenth Karma-pa Chos-dbyings-rdo-rje were two later painters who are recorded to have modeled some of their painted images on Indian metal figures.

31. Rong-tha, p.133: *yang zhal tshad lnga pa ni/ ratna rakṣita sogs bal po'i mkhas pa'i lugs yin la/.* Ratna-rakṣita was the author of the *Samvarodaya* commentary. Dagyab, p.30, attributes to Ratna-rakṣita the dimensions of the various postures of figures, the eighth main section *(thig chen* or *thig khang)* of the Sman-thang-pa system.

It is interesting to compare the Tibetan (or as Rong-tha calls it, the "Newar") five-span proportion with the similar five-"face" proportion for Gaṇeśa as described by W. S. Hadaway, "Some Hindu 'Silpa' Shastras in Their Relation to South Indian Sculpture," *Ostasiatische Zeitschrift,* vol.1 (1914), p.41f.

32. Another *Tanjur* text, the *Kriyāsaṃgraha,* actually gives proportions for all of the iconometric classes called into question by Rong-tha. To our knowledge no Tibetan writer on iconometry has cited this source. See Rigs-kyis-byin, *Kriyāsaṃgraha* (Tib.: *Bya ba btus ba),* Derge *Tanjur,* Ui catalogue no. 2531. See also Peking *Tanjur,* vol.74, p.156.

Appendix B:
Resources

Painting Materials

Although many of the younger generation of Tibetan painters no longer prepare their paints from mineral pigments, we believe that the use of the old colours should be maintained – even if this entails extra expense and work. Much of the charm of old thangkas derives no doubt from the intrinsic beauty of the pigments and dyes themselves. Moreover, the mixing of paints from raw pigments has a special appeal for students of thangka painting coming from countries where pre-mixed colours are the rule. But whether in South Asia or abroad, the basic problem for those wanting to use the traditional colours is how and where to obtain them. Therefore it may be helpful to say a few words about the present sources of the old pigments.

South Asia

Students in India or Nepal who are studying under Tibetan painters should have little trouble in locating most of the pigments and dyes. The majority of them are readily available in the bazaars. But since they are not sold in any single shop, it is best if one's teacher directs one to the various shops and stalls the first time one goes shopping for them. Synthetic cinnabar, minium and indigo are widely available, and one can even find orpiment and realgar, though modern substitutes are advisable for the latter two.

The major difficulty is finding the mineral blues and greens. For these, many artists are now substituting high quality artist's colours, while others are using poster colours or even commercial cement colours. The latter may sound particularly dreadful, but certain brands give muted colours combined with a slight granularity reminiscent of the traditional pigments. A serious problem with many cement colours is that they contain a large proportion of soluble dye.

Real azurite and malachite are relatively hard to come by. If the artists have any, they jealously reserve it for only the most important commissions. This is a sad state of affairs, for copper minerals – including malachite – are mined in parts of India. Forgers of old Indian miniatures have been obtaining these colours for years. But it is also understandable that the pigment sources of such secretive and illicit entrepreneurs would remain unknown to the thangka painters from Tibet.

For the time being the best way to obtain azurite and malachite is from firms that sell semi-precious stones to jewellers or that sell mineral specimens to schools. High-quality malachite can be bought in quantity from such dealers, and sometimes they also have azurite in limited amounts. One established mineral dealer in New Delhi is Starke & Co., 138 Kamala Market.

Europe and North America

Most major cities in Europe and North America have stores that specialize in artist's supplies, and they are the first place one should go when searching for pigments. Even if they do not stock all of the required pigments, such shops can often order them specially or will advise one about possible sources.

In London one of the oldest and best pigment shops is L. Cornelissen & Son, 22 Great Queen Street. They are agents mainly for Sennelier pigments of Paris, and they sell all the major pigments except azurite and malachite. They also have a long list of pigment dealers in all parts of the world. Other reputable dealers in London include E. Ploton Ltd., Atlantis Paper Co., Windsor & Newton, C. Robertson & Co., Rowney & Co., and Brodie & Middleton. E. Ploton Ltd. is an agent for the colours of Le Franc & Borgeois of Paris. In Italy a colour supplier of note is G. Maimeri Fratelli in Milan.

Again, azurite and malachite are the least readily available of the pigments. Though excellent in tempera and distemper, these two are unsuitable for oil painting and watercolour, and thus have almost completely dropped out of use in the West. In the Southwest United States, however, these minerals are plentiful, and with a little effort one can obtain all that one needs. Though small amounts of azurite and malachite can be bought or ordered from local rock and mineral stores, it is best to purchase larger quantities by mail from dealers specializing in minerals and geological specimens. A good way to find out the names of several such mineral suppliers is to ask the geology department of the nearest college or university. Some of these dealers can be very cooperative. One should explain that these minerals are to be ground for pigments because they will then supply small pieces of good pigment quality – pieces that otherwise are of little use to rock collectors or geologists.

Conservation of Old or Damaged Thangkas

In Tibet it was not uncommon for ordinary artists to retouch or repaint old works, sometimes with the result of piously and unwittingly defacing ancient master-pieces. Nowadays if one needs to restore an important painting the preferable course is to entrust the work to a trained conservator. Such professionals can be located through local museums or knowledgeable dealers in Asian art. One conservator in North America who has worked extensively with thangkas is Ms Ann Shaftel Heisler, P.O. Box 18, Maitland, Nova Scotia, Canada.

Appendix C:
Motifs and Symbols and Deities
drawn by Robert Beer

The eight auspicious signs (Tashi Thargye), combined.

The eight auspicious signs, separate.

Offerings to peaceful deities

Offerings to wrathful deities

Landscape elements

Flowers

Flowers and buds

Trees

157

158   Rocks

Flames

Clouds

Clouds and cloud thrones

Lotus thrones

Lotus thrones

Lines in body nimbuses

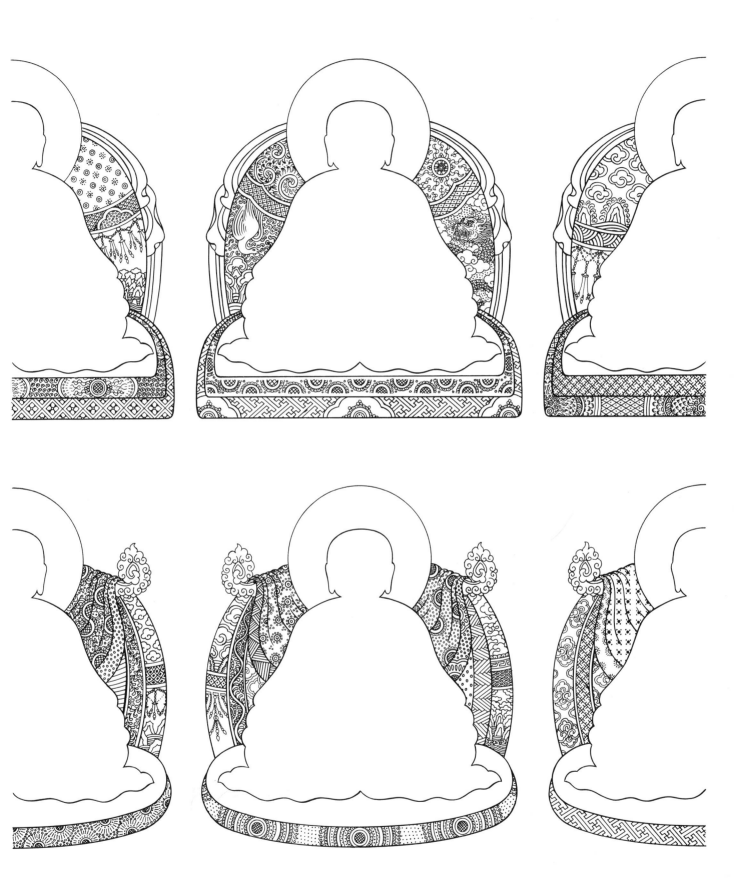

Thrones and throne-backs

165

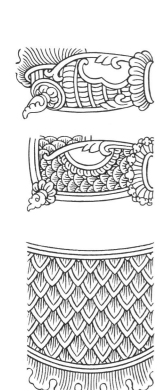

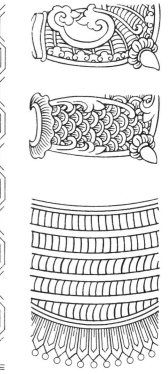

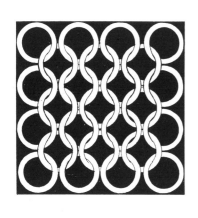

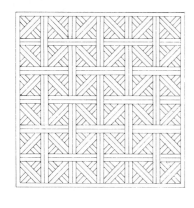

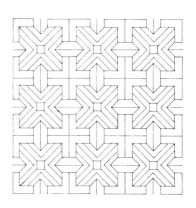

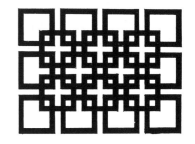

Armour designs

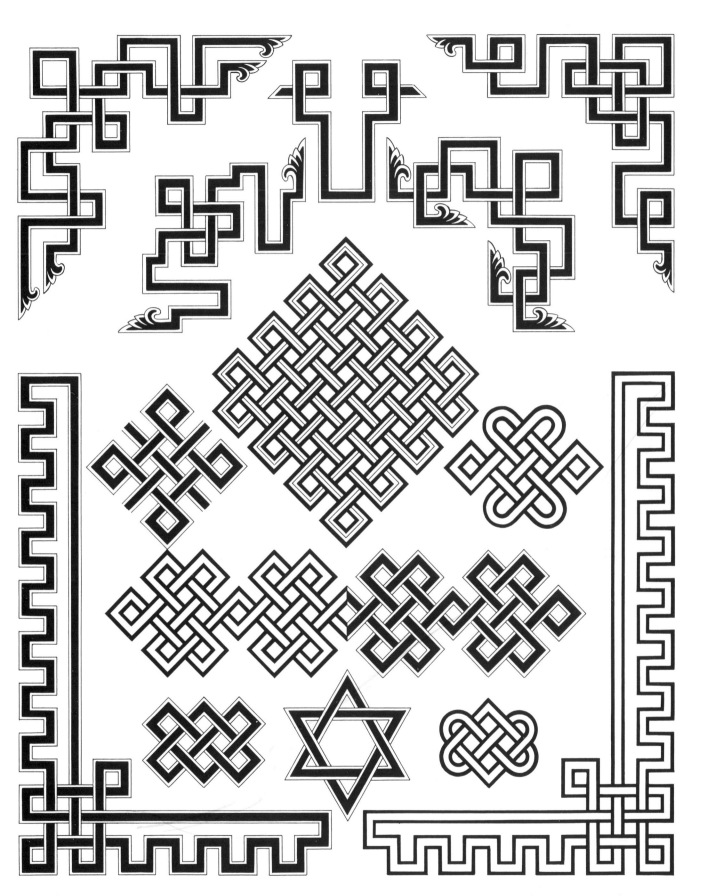

Knots and borders

167

Geometric border designs

Geometric and curved border designs

169

Brocade designs

Drapery swirls

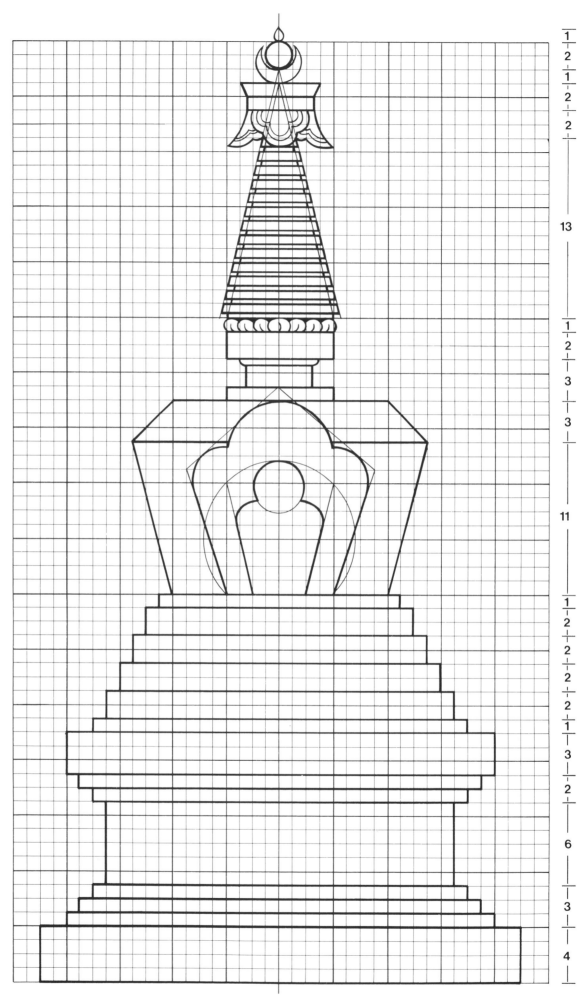

The proportions of the stupa

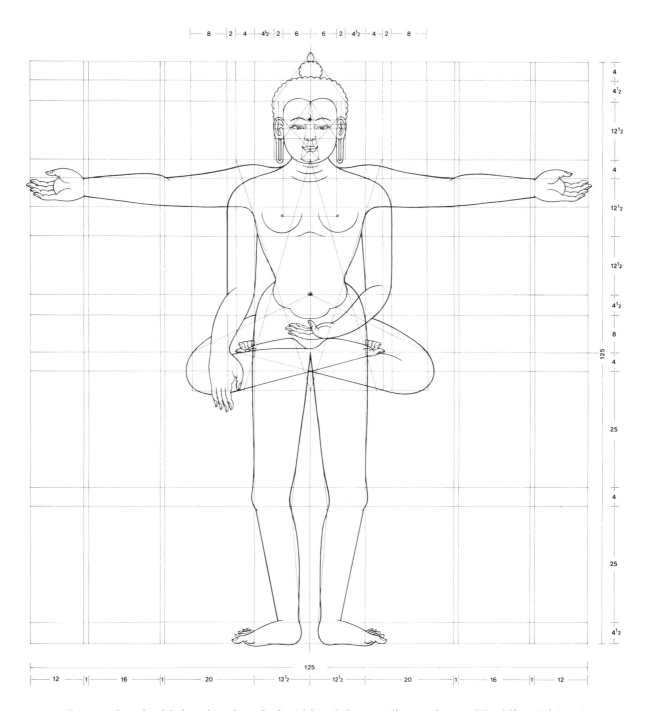

Proportional grid showing the relationship of the standing and seated Buddha. (125 *sor*)

173

The Medicine Buddha, Baiṣajyaguru. An example of a seated and throned Buddha.
(125 *sor*)

The seated Buddha Maitreya. (125 *sor*)

175

The standing form of the Bodhisattva Mañjuśri. (125 *sor*)

Marpa the translator. (120 *sor*)

The Yidam deity Guhyasamāja. (120 *sor*)

The Goddess Uṣṇīśavijāya. (108 *sor*)

Vajra Yoginī. (108 *sor*)

Kurukulla. (108 *sor*)

The six-armed standing form of Black Mahakālā. (96 *sor*)

Vairocanabhisaṃbodhi. (84 *sor*)

The twelve-armed Yidam deity Cakrasaṃvara. (120 *sor*)

Kālacakra, drawn to the same proportional grid as Cakrasaṃvara. (120 *sor*)

Appendix D:
Guidelines for Thangka Painting Using Modern Techniques and Commercially Available Materials

by Robert Beer

Drawing

It is best to begin to practise drawing with the least complex deities such as the form of the Buddha or of peaceful bodhisattvas such as Manjushri, Chenrezig or Tara. One should first become familiar with the proportional measurements of the face and body, and begin by lightly drawing in the outline of the unclothed figure and the lotus throne. Next, one should proceed to add the robes and drapery paying particular attention to the folds in the clothing which are never angular but always drawn with a subtle curving line. It is also important to note that when, for example, a scarf passes behind an arm, it always emerges in the continuous flowing lines with which it entered. The hands, feet and facial features of the deity are difficult to draw, and it is useful to practise drawing these elements repeatedly.

The line proportion should be drawn either with a very hard pencil such as a 3H or 4H, or with a rapidograph pen using a fine point such as 0.1mm or 0.15mm: this is because initially you may do so much erasing that the construction lines will soon disappear. The figure should be lightly drawn with a softer pencil such as H, HB or F; a putty rubber is the best eraser to use as it is clean and soft and neither leaves particles nor damages the paper. For symmetrical details such as the faces of deities, moon discs, lotus thrones or the forms of certain symmetrical deities such as four-armed Chenrezig, one can use the technique of reverse tracing. One first draws one half of the composition and over this is placed a sheet of medium weight tracing paper (90gsm) on which a vertical axis is drawn. When this is aligned with the axis of your drawing, you hold the tracing paper down firmly and trace the drawing with a 2H pencil. The tracing paper is then turned over and the mirror image of your composition can be traced onto the paper. It is usually easier for a right-handed person to draw the left half of a symmetrical composition first, especially with details such as eyes, eyebrows and ears.

The finest paper to use for drawing or painting is a German-made paper known as Schoellershammer or 'hammer' paper. This is available in both smooth and textured sheets in a variety of weights. Because this paper is pressed from particles rather than from rag fibres one can erase on it repeatedly. It has an exceptionally fine and hard surface and a line does not 'bleed' with inks or water-colours. Its chemical composition also prevents yellowing or brittleness with age. It is available either in sheets measuring $21\frac{1}{2}'' \times 28\frac{1}{2}''$ or in standard A5, A4, A3 and A2 sketch pads. For drawing, one should use the smooth form of 'hammer' paper which is designated by the letter G. 3G or 4G are the best weights for drawing, 5G or 6G for painting. If one cannot obtain this make of paper, then ask at your local art store for the best quality 'hot pressed' paper which has a much smoother and harder surface than 'not pressed' paper.

When somewhat proficient in pencil drawing, one should begin to use brush and ink, progressing from the pencil sketch to the finished ink drawing. The finest sable brushes are made by Windsor and Newton and should be selected individually by licking the hairs and testing the point against the back of the thumbnail. The smallest brush is used for drawing and painting details and the best available are Windsor and Newton, Series 7, size 000. There is also a Japanese company, Inscribe, which makes size 00000 brushes, but these are made from nylon bristles and are not as good as pure sable brushes. One often hears stories of painters who used 'one hair' brushes, but this is a modern myth, as a one-haired brush cannot hold any colour.

For finished drawings, I prefer to use Chinese ink which is denser than Indian ink and flows better. One must, however, use waterproof Indian ink for the preliminary ink drawing for a painting, as Chinese ink is not waterproof and would bleed into the water-colour. The ink should be kept in a small porcelain pot or egg-cup and tilted at an angle to prevent it drying too quickly. A small quantity is used at a time and should be changed every few hours, the brush must be rinsed in a jar of water every few minutes and cleaned in hot water every hour or so. It is useful to rest your hand on a separate sheet of paper and brush off the excess ink before each brushstroke; this also keeps the drawing clean.

When choosing a scale for your drawings, it seems easier to use millimetres rather than divisions of the inch. A good proportion to use is 3mm to 1 unit of measurement (*sor*), or 2mm to a *sor* if you are able to work on a smaller scale. Tibetan artists normally use measuring sticks for drawing their grids and these can easily be made by drawing the vertical and horizontal units of measurement on a flat piece of wood or cardboard. When drawing circles for the halo and body aura it is a useful tip to cut a small square of cardboard and position it on the drawing with masking tape at the circle's centre; this prevents the compass point from piercing the surface of the paper. The circles for the halo are centred on the

186

hair-line and the circles for the body aura are centred slightly to the right and left of the heart-line. For drawing very small circles such as for earrings and jewellery a 'pump-action' compass may be used, either with a lead point or rapidograph fitting.

Painting on Paper and Cloth

Although traditionally thangkas are painted on cotton cloth with a brocade mount, this process is both difficult and time-consuming for the beginner. It is easier to paint on paper and the finished painting can then be protected behind glass in a frame. There are a variety of art-boards available such as Daler board, Frisk board, CS.10 and CS.2 boards which have a perfect surface needing no preparation. To work on paper one needs to stretch the paper first. This is accomplished by wetting the back of the paper several times with a damp sponge, the paper is then turned over and the edges are taped to a board using gummed sealing or postal tape in strips about an inch wide. The paper is ready for use after a few hours drying. Taping to hardboard is suitable for smaller paintings up to 12″, but plywood is better for larger sizes, as hardboard will warp too much under the tension of the paper.

For those who are more ambitious and would like to work on a traditional cotton support, a wooden stretcher and canvas can quite easily be made. Having established the size of the painting, the wooden stretcher (see pp. 16–17) is measured about 6″ to 8″ larger than the canvas. 2 × 1″ planed softwood can be used, the corners can be jointed or screwed, with a flat right-angled bracket on each corner to provide additional rigidity. The inner frame can be made of split lengths of bamboo or plant-sticks available from garden centres. The cotton, calico or linen ground should be of fine woven material a little heavier than a linen tablecloth. It should be unbleached, unwaxed and free from any seams, faults or knots.

When the cotton support has been sewn to the inner frame and tied and stretched in the outer frame, it is ready for priming. The canvas can first of all be sized with a solution of rabbit-skin glue, which prevents the cotton support from rotting and provides a firmer surface for the gesso. The solution is prepared by dissolving one part of the rabbit-skin glue in twenty parts of warm water and left to dissolve overnight. The size should be applied to both sides of the canvas in a single coat. Prepared gesso is readily available in any art store; it goes under the name of 'white primer' or the brand name of Liquitex. There are two kinds of gesso which can be purchased. One is an acrylic or cryla base which is suitable only for acrylic and oil colours, the other is an emulsion base and is known as 'universal primer', and is suitable for water-colour and gouache—it is this kind that you need to use. The gesso can be thinned with about 20% water for the first few coats on the canvas. Apply the gesso to both sides with a large 1″ or 2″ brush and allow the coats to dry for an

hour or so. After two or three coats of gesso it can be thinned further with water, gradually applying thinner coats until the required surface is built up. The coats of paint should be applied with alternate brushstrokes, the first coat vertical, the second horizontal, etc. When the canvas looks smooth and reveals no 'pin-holes' when held up to the light, it is ready for polishing. The surface can be sanded with very fine emery paper which can be bought in stores specializing in car spraying equipment. Finally it can be polished using a smooth object such as a glass jar —it must be polished both horizontally and vertically while using a board or wooden support behind. Personally I like to apply a few more coats of very dilute gesso after the ink drawing has been completed. This has the effect of lightening the black outline of the drawing making it easier to paint over the lighter areas for clouds and flowers, etc.

Materials and Colour Pigments

You will need a good selection of brushes such as Windsor and Newton Series 7, Nos. 000, 00, 0, 1, 2, 3, 4, 6, 8. In the larger sizes, Series 16 are cheaper. You will also need some brushes for mixing colours (size 3 or 4) but these can be of a cheaper make. Palettes can be white china plates; ice-cube holders and sea shells are useful for holding larger amounts of colour which tend to dry out on the larger surface of a plate.

Masking film and fluid are materials which make life very much easier for the modern painter. One can use a low-tack masking film or 'frisket' over large areas and the borders of the painting. The film can be applied over areas already painted, and individual elements can be masked by cutting around the outline with a swivel scalpel. This technique is particularly useful when painting large areas such as the sky. When the clouds, central figure and borders are masked one can quickly paint in the whole of the sky with bold brushstrokes and wet shading. When the masking is removed it leaves a clean edge to the unpainted areas. Water-colour masking fluid can be used in a similar way for smaller and more detailed areas, but it cannot be applied over a painted surface as it leaves a stain. Masking fluid dries in a few minutes and can be peeled off as a rubber mask after painting. Masking fluid dries on the brush very rapidly and the brush must be regularly cleaned in brush-cleaning solvent and then in soapy warm water. These techniques of masking are extensively used in airbrush painting.

The mineral pigments used in Tibetan thangka painting have a certain esoteric mystique surrounding them, but essentially they are similar to the pigments used today, with the exception of the blues and greens made from malachite, azurite and lapis. In fact an ultramarine made of pure lapis lazuli was available a few years ago in tube form, but I believe it is no longer on the market due to its very high price.

When considering the colour stability of old thangkas and frescoes one has to remember that murals were often painted in dark monasteries or cave temples where they were not exposed to the ultra-violet fading effects of direct sunlight. Thangkas were frequently veiled and often only unrolled and displayed on certain religious occasions.

Gouache or designers' colours are the nearest equivalent to Tibetan pigments. Gouache is a water-based pigment ground with white and with a gum arabic binder. It produces a very dense and matt surface with a brilliance of colour. Unfortunately it is very fragile and scratches easily, it cannot be over-painted and the slightest spillage of water will ruin the surface. However, it can be diluted with acrylic medium to give it a more permanent and waterproof surface, which also allows for a certain degree of overpainting. There is a wide range of colours available in gouache or designers' colours, but one should be careful to use only those colours that are marked permanent and non-staining. With certain colours, especially reds, I find it preferable to use poster colour, and use vermilion, vermilion hue, carmine and Indian red (brown) in poster form. The greens are also a difficulty, and I find it easier to mix greens from blue, yellow and white. Listed below are the main colours of my palette and their employment.

Permanent White (gouache): the most opaque white, used for all white elements, for skin colour, as a base for clouds and flowers, for small white details such as bone ornaments.

Zinc White (gouache): used for all tinting, especially on clouds and flowers.

Naples Yellow (gouache): can be used for shading skies through green to Prussian blue. It is also used for belts on monastic robes and can be used on vermilion robes as a substitute for gold brocade decoration.

Spectrum Yellow (gouache): a good general yellow and for mixing with Prussian blue and ultra-marine to produce greens.

Vermilion (poster): extensively used for robes and clothing; for flames around wrathful deities; for shading flowers; for mixing with Naples yellow or yellow ochre as a gold substitute; for outlining real gold.

Carmine (poster): mixed with vermilion for robes and clothing; for flower shading; for lotus thrones and altar cloths.

Indian Red (poster): used for dark robes and as an outline colour; for shading rocks.

Burnt Umber (gouache): for shading rocks along with indigo on a yellow ochre ground; for the hair and eyes of deities; for trees and branches.

Yellow Ochre (gouache): as a ground colour for rocks and crags.

Flesh Tint (poster): for the flesh colour of many human representations, often mixed with a little white and vermilion; the flesh is shaded either with a little Indian red or burnt umber.

Prussian Blue (gouache or poster): used for painting skies, clouds and water. It is used extensively as the body colour for deities such as Cakrasamvara, Vajradhara and Vajrapani. Also used for jewels, the hair of Buddhas and all ritual objects representing iron. When mixed with yellow and white it is used as a viridian green for leaves, clouds, scarves, lotus thrones, etc.

Ultramarine (gouache or poster): a more brilliant blue than Prussian blue. It is used for skies, flowers, lotus thrones, scarves, etc. When mixed with yellow and white it produces a grass green for hills.

Turquoise Blue (gouache): used for bluish leaves and water; also on rock and ground shading.

Indigo (gouache): used for rock shading and outlining leaves and green robes.

Black (gouache): rarely used except for the background colour of wrathful deity paintings and for the lines in hair.

Gold: there is no substitute for real powder gold obtained from Kathmandu. Gold harmonizes with all colours especially deep hues, and is used to a great extent in thangka painting. Gold leaf may be employed with some success if one is skilful in its application, but gold leaf tends to be very reflective and small details are hard to apply. Synthetic golds should be avoided as they tarnish to a dark brown very rapidly. If real gold cannot be obtained it is better to mix a gold hue from vermilion, Naples yellow and white.

For outlining figures and objects I mix an outline colour of vermilion and Prussian blue, adding white to the mixture depending on the tonality of the object being outlined. For outlining reddish objects one adds more vermilion, for bluish objects one adds more blue. For white and flesh outline the mixture is almost a neutral grey with a slightly reddish tinge. If deities are to be painted with a white body colour one should add a minute amount of Naples yellow or vermilion to produce a warm white, as a pure white is a very cold colour.

Mistakes made in painting with gouache are hard to rectify and it is a medium which demands a lot of control. Small mistakes can be scraped from the surface using a curved scalpel blade. As the colours actually dry to a lighter tone than they appear to be when wet, it is useful to test a new colour on a scrap of paper before applying it.

Some people may prefer to use acrylic colours which employ a different technique to gouache. Acrylic colours are completely waterproof, enabling one to overpaint and the shading of areas can be rendered with a series of glazes. At Samye Ling Monastery in Scotland a group of Western artists under the guidance of Sherab Palden Beru are using acrylic colours to create a series of large Gadri style compositions with very subtle colour gradations and spacious perspective effects.

Tibetan art has gone through various stylistic movements over the centuries, absorbing influences from many countries such as Persia, Central Asia, India, Nepal and China. Now for the first time we have a situation where the indigenous art of Tibet is transposed to a Western culture. That there will be new developments in the Western practice of Tibetan art is certain; how far reaching these developments may be, remains to be seen.

Glossary

This glossary was compiled for the benefit of those who wish to study thangka painting with an artist from Tibet, but who have never learned any Tibetan. In the text of the book all the terms have been cited in their literary Tibetan forms, and these are listed alphabetically in the first column below. To the uninitiated these literary spellings appear to be veritable tongue-twisters. But fortunately their modern colloquial pronunciations are much easier.

In the middle column below we have given an approximate pronunciation for each of these terms. The phonetic system we have used is non-technical and in some ways oversimplified. It should, however, be enough for most students since they will in any case have to ascertain how each word is pronounced in the dialect of their own teacher. (The pronunciations vary considerably from dialect to dialect).

The first important thing to note about our phonetic system is that the vowels indicate approximately the following sound values:

a —	as in father
i —	as in machine, but short
u —	as in tube
e —	as in bed
o —	as in go
ay —	as in say, but short
ee —	as in see
ö —	as in the French *peu*
ü —	as in the French *duc*

Regarding the consonants, the letter *g* is always "hard" as in gate. Combined with other consonants, *h* indicates aspiration except in the combination *sh*, which is pronounced as in *sh*ell. Thus the combinations *ph* and *th* are pronounced as in *p*ot and *t*op. Aspirated *tsh* has here been written as *ts* (as in Pa*ts*y) to avoid confusion with *sh*. As an initial, *r* is pronounced with some friction.

One source of trouble for beginners is that Tibetan has a series of unvoiced, unaspirated consonants that appear in an initial position, something unknown in English. Here the unvoiced and unaspirated Tibetan syllables *ka, ca, ta, pa,* and *tsa* have been indicated by the voiced unaspirated equivalents: *ga, ja, da, ba* and *dza*. Also *ng* as an initial (the same sound as in si*ng*ing), and *lh* do not occur in English. Another major omission in our system is the absence of any indication of tones. Once again, we encourage the student to follow his or her own ear in learning the pronunciation of the teacher. Those who invest a little extra time at the beginning studying Tibetan will be amply repaid later.

Literary Spelling	Approximate pronunciation	Definition
ba bla	pha bla	orpiment yellow
bar bris	phar tree	intermediate sketch
bcad pir	jay bir	outlining brush
bod ljang	phö jang	Tibetan green (malachite)
bod mthing	phö thing	Tibetan blue (azurite)
'bol gdan	böö den	padded cushion
bris thang	tree thang	painted thangka
'bru mdangs	dru dang	granular shading
btsag	dza(k)	red ochre
btso ma	dzo ma	realgar orange
btsod	dzö	madder
byug mdangs	chu(k) dang	"spread-on shading", shading applied through a smooth transition
byug pir	chu(k) bir	brush used for applying main coats of colour
cha chen	cha chen	the larger main unit of measure, made up of twelve smaller units *(cha chung* or *sor)*
cha chung	cha chung	the smaller main unit of measure, also called *sor*
chang	chang	home-brewed beer
char mdangs	char dang	"rain shading", an unusual type of sky shading applied with vertical strokes
chos gos	chö khö	upper robe of a fully ordained monk
chu pir	chu bir	"water brush", a brush loaded with water used for diluting
chu'i rtsa	chüü dza	rhubarb roots
chu ris	chu ree	drawings of water, especially of waves
cog la ma	jo(k) la ma	cinnabar
da chu	tha chu	synthetic cinnabar
'dam	dam	"gesso"
'dam khri	dam tri	gesso knife
dar ba	da ra	buttermilk
dar mtshur	thar tsur	alum

Literary Spelling	Approximate pronunciation	Definition
dbang lag	wang lak	plant root used as an adhesive
dbang po'i lag pa	wang bö lak ba	same as above
dbu'i 'od 'khor	üü ö khor	head nimbus
dbur rdo	ur do	stone for polishing or burnishing the ground
dkar bcad	gar jay	white outlining
dkar po	gar bo	white
dkar rtsi	gar dzi	whitewash
dmar nag	mar na(k)	dark red
dmar po	mar bo	red
dmar rdzas	mar dzay	depiction of sacrifices
dmar skya	mar gya	pink
dngul rdul	ngüü düü	powdered silver
'dod lha	dö hla	deity chosen by the patron
dpag bsam gyi shing	ba(k) sam gi shing	wish-granting tree
dpar ma	bar ma	thangka made by block printing
dra bcad	tra jay	outlining on patched monk's robes
dras drub ma	tray drup ma	appliqué thangka
dud kha	thü kha	smoke colour
dud sngon	thü ngön	bluish smoke colour
gar gzigs	khar zi(k)	the appearance of the eyes of a painted figure seeming to follow the observer
gdong	dong	"face", a synonym of *cha chen*
glo kha	lo kha	lung colour
gos ris	khö ree	(gold) brocade designs
grang gser	trang ser	"cold gilt", powdered gold applied in a medium such as size or flax-seed binder
gris 'brad	tree dray	scraping smooth with a knife
gru mo	tru mo	a cubit, the distance from the elbow to the knuckles of a closed fist, equal to two *cha chen*
gsed mdangs	se dang	smooth dry shading
gser	ser	gold
gser 'dra	ser dra	"like gold", of a golden colour
gser gyi thigs po	ser gi thik bo	gold in drop form
gser rdul	ser düü	powdered gold
gser rten	ser den	undercoat for gold paint
gser shog	ser sho(k)	gold leaf
gser thang	ser thang	a thangka in which the colour gold predominates
gsung rten	sung den	"speech support", a technical term for scriptures
gter bdag	der da(k)	a guardian deity of a treasure *(gter)*
gtsag mdangs	dzak dang	granular dry shading
gtsag par	dzak bar	stencil; tracing
gtso bo	dzo wo	main or chief figure
gtun	dün	pestle
gtun khung	dün khung	mortar
gur gum	khur kum	saffron (or safflower)
'gying	gying	contrapposto
g.yu kha	yu kha	"turquoise colour", the deep blue-green colour intermediate between azurite and malachite
gzhu spyan	shu jen	"bow eye"
gzi	zi/si	burnisher, a banded onyx commonly used for burnishing
gzi ris	zi ree	designs drawn with the tip of the burnisher on gold
gzi rten	zi den	"burnisher support", an object held beneath the canvas during burnishing
hal tshon	?	same as hang tshon?
hang tshon	hang tsön	painting done with thin washes of colour over a line drawing
he rams	he ram	an inferior quality of indigo
ja dmar	cha mar	reddish tea colour
ja kha	cha kha	tea colour
ja ljang	cha jang	greenish tea-colour
ka rag	ga ra(k)	a white earth colour
kha che sha kha ma	kha che sha kha ma	saffron
kha chu	kha chu	the thin surface layer of paint in a pot
kha gsal ba	kha sa la	brighter, as of colours
kha nag pa	kha nak ka	darker, as of colours
'khor	khor	the retinue or group of lesser figures placed around the main figure
khra 'drud	tra drü	"pulling out of the glossiest (hairs)", a term for fine dry shading

Literary Spelling	Approximate pronunciation	Definition
khro bo	tro wo	wrathful or agressive, a wrathful deity
ko spyin	go jin	hide glue or size derived from animal hides
la cha	la cha	lac
la chu	la chu	shellac
lag rten	lag den	hand-support, a board upon which the painting hand was rested during painting
lcang ma	jang ma	willow
ldong ros	dong rö	realgar
leb gzi	leb zi	flat burnishing (of gold details)
leb mdangs	leb dang	flat shading, ordinary dry shading
lha spyin	hla jin/lha bing	the best quality size adhesive, used for religious paintings
lhan drub ma	hlen drub ma	appliqué thangka
lhan thabs ma	hlen thab ma	glued-appliqué thangka
li chu	li chu	"minium water", thin minium paint
li khri	li tri	minium orange
li ser	li ser	yellowish orange
li skya	li gya	whitish orange
ljang ku	jang gu	green
ljang se	jang se	light green
ljang ser	jang ser	yellowish green
lo thang	lo thang	a thangka which took a year to paint
mchin kha	chin kha	liver colour
mchin skya	chin gya	whitish liver colour
mchin smug	chin mu(k)	maroonish liver colour
mda' tshad	da tsay	an arrow's length
mdo mthing	do thing	mineral blue, azurite
mdo spang	do bang	mineral green, malachite
me ris	me ree	drawing of flames
mgon khang	gön khang	chapel housing images of the fierce protectors
mi sha	mi sha	human skin (colour), flesh (colour)
mi tshad	mi tsay	the height of a man
mo dkar	mo gar	softer variety of *ka rag*
mo rag	mo rak	same as above
mon kha	mön kha	pale mauve
mon sngon	mön ngön	bluish mauve
mtha' bcad	ta jay	outlining along an outer edge
mtha' chags ri mo	ta chak ri mo	brocade designs for robe linings, borders of cloth, etc.
mthil	thil/thee	"palm", the measure of the length of the palm and fingers of the hand, a synonym for *cha chen*
mthing	thing	azurite; deep blue colour
mthing 'bru	thing dru	deepest azure-coloured paint
mthing chu	thing chu	a light watery paint made from azurite
mthing shog	thing shog	black paper
mthing shul	thing shüü	medium blue azurite pigment
mthing skya	thing gya	light blue
mthing zhun	thing shün	synonym for azurite
mtho	tho	"span", the distance from the extended thumb to the tip of the middle finger, a synonym for *cha chen*
mtshal	tsal/tsay	vermilion
mtshal chu	tsal chu/tsay chu	dilute vermilion
mtshal dkar	tsal gar/tsay gar	bright vermilion; also a synonym for synthetic vermilion
mtshal nag	tsal nak/tsay nak	darker vermilion
mtshal rgod	tsal gö/tsay gö	native vermilion, cinnabar
mtshal skya	tsal gya/tsay gya	vermilion pink
mtshal thang	tsal thang/tsay thang	a thangka in which the colour vermilion predominates
mu men	mu men	lapis lazuli
na ros	na rö	pink with a maroon-ish tinge
nag po	nak bo	black
nag thang	nak thang	a thangka in which the colour black pre-dominates
nas	nay	"grain", a measure equalling one-eighth of a *cha chen*
nas spyan	nay jen	"grain eyes"
ngang pa	ngang ba	yellow ochre
ngang sang	ngang sang	same as above
ngar ma	ngar ma	creamy saffron colour?
ngur (-smrig)	ngur (-mik)	saffron colour
nor lha	nor hla	god of wealth

Literary Spelling	Approximate pronunciation	Definition
'o dkar	o gar	white milk colour (with a slight bluish tinge)
'o kha	o kha	milky white (with a slight tinge of green)
'o ljang	o jang	greenish milk colour
'o sngon	o ngön	bluish milk colour
'od 'phro	wö tro	radiating light rays
padma'i gdan	baymay den	lotus seat
phing bris	phing tree	a special outlining technique for clouds
pho dkar	pho gar	a harder variety of *ka rag* white
pho rag	pho rag	same as above
phyag mtshan	chag tsen	identifying hand-held emblem or implement of a deity
phyag rgya	chag gya	formalized hand gesture, mūdra
pir	bir	brush
pir dong	bir dong	brush container
pir kha	bir kha	brush point
pir spu	bir bu	brush hair
pra rtsi	drak dzi	varnish
rab gnas	ram nay	ritual consecration of a sacred image
rag rdul	rag düü	powdered-brass imitation gold
rams	ram	indigo
rams se	ram se	light indigo colour
ras gzhi	ray shi	cotton support of the thangka
rdo thal	do thal/do thay	lime
rdo tshon	do tsön	mineral colour
rdo zho	do sho	slaked lime
rdzogs tshon	dzo(k) tsön	"complete colour", the painting method using opaque colours applied in distemper
rgan sha'i mdog	gen shay dok	the colour of an old person's flesh
rgya ljang	gya jang	"Chinese green", verdigris?
rgya mthing	gya thing	"Chinese blue"
rgya mtshal	gya tsal/gya tsay	Chinese or Indian vermilion
rgya skyegs	gya gyek	lac dye
rgya smug	gya muk	maroonish brown; deep maroon
rgya snag	gya nag	Chinese ink
rgya tsha	gya tsa	sal ammoniac (ammonium chloride)
rgya tshos	gya tsö	lac dye
rgyab yol	gyap yö	back curtain
rigs bdag	rig dak	lord of a particular tathāgatha lineage
rkang pa	gang ba	"leg", one-fourth of a *cha chung* or *sor*
rkyang shing	gyang shing	stretcher
rlon dbur	lön ur	damp polishing
rlon mdangs	lön dang	wet shading
rlon rdul	lön düü	wet grinding
rlon thig	lön thig	"wet line", a line marked with a wet marking string
rten	den	"support", a technical term for physical embodiments of enlightened body, speech or mind
rtsa ba'i mdog	dza way dok	basic colour
rtsam pa	dzam ba	parched barley flour
rtswa ris	dza ree	depictions of grass
rus kha	rü kha	bone colour
sa dkar	sa gar	white earth
sa tshon	sa tsön	earth pigment
sbyar ljang	jar jang	"compounded green", a mixture of indigo and orpiment
sdom tshad	dom tsay	abbreviated method of drawing proportional lines
se ba'i me tog	se way me tok	a wild rose, the petals of which yield a yellow dye
ser ljang	ser jang	yellowish green
ser nag	ser nag	yellowish brown
ser po	ser bo	yellow
ser skya	ser gya	pale yellow
sgom thag	gom thak	band wrapped around the legs by yogis in meditation
sha bcad	shab jay	outlining of flesh
sha dkar	sha gar	light flesh colour
sha dmar	sha mar	reddish flesh colour
sha kha	sha kha	flesh colour
sha mdangs	sham dang	the shading of flesh
sha ser	sha ser	yellowish flesh colour
shing bu	shing bu	stirring stick
shing tsha	shing tsa	Indian cassia, *Cinnamomum tamala*
shugs pa	shug ba	juniper

Literary Spelling	Approximate pronunciation	Definition
skag	gak	lac dye; maroon colour
skam dbur	gam ur	dry polishing
skam mdangs	gam dang	dry shading
skam thig	gam thig	line laid down with dry chalk line
skor pang	gor bang	compass board
skor thig	gor thig	compass
sku rten	gu den	"body support"
skya bo	gya wo	whitish or pale
skya ris	gya ree	sketch
skya tshon	gya tsön	paints applied in thin washes, giving a pale result
skyer pa	gyer pa	barberry
smug po	muk bo	dark maroon; dark brown
snag tsha	nak tsa	black ink
sngo sang	ngo sang	sky-blue; also the shade derived from azurite
sngo se	ngo se	light blue; the lightest shade of azurite blue
sngo si	ngo si	same as above
sngo skya	ngo gya	light blue
sngon po	ngön bo	blue
snum tshon	num tsön	paint applied in opaque coats, yielding rich colours
snur skyogs	nur gyok	stirring stick for mixing paints
sol ba	so la	charcoal
sol dong	sol dong/söö dong	charcoal container
sol ris	sol ree/söö ree	charcoal sketch
sor	sor	"finger-width", a synonym for *cha chung*
sor mo	sor mo	same as above
spag	bak	dough
spag phyi rgyab	bak chi gyap	cleaning by rubbing with dough
spang	bang	malachite; the medium green derived from malachite
spang chu	bang chu	thin, light green paint made from malachite
spang ma	bang ma	malachite
spang ri	bang ri	hills covered with green meadows
spang skya	bang gya	second to lightest shade of malachite green
spang si	bang si	lightest shade of malachite green
spang smug	bang muk	deep green; the darkest shade of malachite green
spang tshon	bang tsön	malachite green; malachite
sprin mdangs	drin dang	"cloud shading", shading applied in horizontal cloud-like bands
sprul pa'i lha bzo	drül bay hlab so	divinely emanated artisan
spyan dbye	jen ye	eye opening, the painting of the eyes of a deity
spyan dkar	jen gar	white paint applied to the eyes of deities
spyin	bing/jin	glue or size
spyin chu	bing chu/jin chu	dilute size solution
srid pa'i 'khor lo	see bay khor lo	the wheel of existence
'thag drub ma	thak drup ma	woven thangka
thal dkar	thal gar/thay gar	whitish gray
thal kha	thal kha/thay kha	ash colour; gray
thal mo	thal mo/thay mo	"palm", the length of the palm and fingers, a synonym of *cha chen*
thal sngon	thal ngön/thay ngön	bluish gray
thang ka	thang ka	Tibetan scroll painting
thang ma sgron shing	thang ma drön shing	larch tree
thang nag	thang nak	black thangka
thang tshad	thang tsay	a standard thangka size
thig chen	thig chen	major proportional class
thig khang	thig khang	proportional grid of exactly positioned lines
thig rkud	thig gü	chalk line
thig rkyal	thig gyal/thig gyay	powder bag for chalk line
thig shing	thig shing	ruler, wooden straightedge
thig tshad	thig tsay	proportions of a figure laid out with the aid of lines
thog tshad	thok tsay	the height of one storey

Literary Spelling	Approximate pronunciation	Definition
thugs rten	thug den	"mind support", usually a stūpa
tsandan dmar po	dzenden mar bo	red sandalwood
tsha gser	tsa ser	"hot gilt", gold applied with mercury amalgam
tsha la	tsa la	borax
tsha le	tsa le	same as above
tshangs thig	tsang thig	vertical central axis of a figure
tshem drub ma	tsem drup ma	embroidered thangka
tsho sha dkar	tso sha gar	a non-shaded colour gradation commonly used in the painting of woodwork, etc.
tshogs zhing	tsok shing	"assembly field"
tshon	tsön	colour; paint
tshon chen	tsön chen	synonym of *rdzogs tshon*
tshon kong	tsön gong	paint pot
tshon ljang	tsön jang	"green colour", a synonym for malachite
tshon mdog	tsön dok	colour
tshon yig	tsön yig	colour notation or code
tshos	tsö	dye or lake
tshos gzhi	tsö shï	colour
utpal ser po	üpay ser po	a yellow derived from the petals of an alpine flower
yan lag gi tshon 'bring po	yen lak gi tsön dring bo	intermediate branch colours
zar khu'i snum rtsi	sar khüü num dzi	linseed oil
zar ma'i 'bru	sar may dru	flax seeds
zhal	shal/shay	"face", a synonym of *cha chen*
zhal mtshal	shal tsal/shay tsay	red colour applied to the lips of deities
zhal tshad	shal tsay/shay tsay	"face measure", a synonym of *cha chen*
zhi ba	shi wa	peaceful, as of deities
zhing	shing	field
zho	sho	curds, yogurt
zhu mkhan	shung khen	leaf of a tree of the genus *Symplocos*, the source of a yellow dye and mordant
zhu rams	shung ram	a green dye made by mixing *zhu mkhan* and indigo
zhwa lu ngang pa	sha lu ngang ba	yellow ochre from Zhwa-lu
zi hung	si hung	pale mauve
zing skya	sing gya	pink made from magenta

Bibliography

I. Tibetan Sources

a. Non-canonical Works

Bo-dong Paṇ-chen Phyogs-las-rnam-rgyal (1375-1451). *Mkhas pa 'jug pa'i [sgo] bzo rig sku gsung thugs kyi rten bzhengs tshul bshad pa, Collected Works*, New Delhi, Tibet House, 1969, vol.2, pp.215-265. See also vol.9, pp.461-501.

Rten gsum bzhengs tshul bstan bcos lugs bshad pa, Collected Works, vol.2, pp.265-342; vol.9, pp.501-559.

Sdom 'byung nas gsungs pa'i sku gzugs sogs kyi cha tshad bshad pa, Collected Works, vol.2, pp.355-376.

Bod ljongs rgyun spyod krung dbyi'i sman rigs, Peking, Bod ljongs mi dmangs dpe skrun khang, 1973.

'Brug-chen Padma-dkar-po (1526-1592), *Bris sku'i rnam bshad mthong ba don ldan, Collected Works*, Darjeeling, Kargyud Sungrab Nyamsokhang, 1973, vol.7.

Chos-dpal-dar-dpyan (13th century). *The Biography of Chag lo-tsā-ba Chos rje dpal* (Dharmasvāmin), edited by Champa Thubten Zongtse, *Śata-piṭaka Series*, vol.266, New Delhi, 1981.

Council for Tibetan Education. *Reader 9*, Dharamsala, 1967.

Dil-dmar dge-bshes Bstan-'dzin-phun-tshogs. *Bdud rtsi sman gyi rnam dbye ngo bo nus ming rgyas par bshad pa dri med shel phreng*, Leh, 1970.

'Jam-dpal-rdo-rje. *Gso byed bdud rtsi'i 'khrul med ngos 'dzin gso rig me long du rnam par shar pa mdzes mtshar mig rgyan, Śata-piṭaka Series*, vol.82, New Delhi, 1971.

Kaḥ-thog Si-tu Chos-kyi-rgya-mtsho (1880-1925). *Gangs ljongs dbus gtsang gnas bskor lam yig nor bu zla shel gyi se mo do*, Tashijong, Tibetan Craft Community, 1972.

Khetsun Sangpo. *Biographical Dictionary of Tibet*, Dharamsala, 1973–. To be completed in 12 volumes?

Klong-rdol-bla-ma Ngag-dbang-blo-bzang (b.1719). *Gsung 'bum*, Mussoorie, Dalama, 1963.

Kong-sprul Blo-gros-mtha'-yas (1813-1899). *Theg pa'i sgo kun las btus pa gsung rab rin po che'i mdzod bslab pa gsum legs par ston pa'i bstan bcos shes bya kun khyab, Śata-piṭaka Series*, vol.80, New Delhi, 1970.

Lo-chen 'Gyur-med-bde-chen (b. 1540). *Dpal grub pa'i dbang phyug brtson 'grus bzang po'i rnam par thar pa kun gsal nor bu'i me long*, Bir, 1976.

Mgon-po-skyabs. *Sman sna tshog gi per chad* [sic!], trilingual xylograph, British Museum, no.19999, 28(2)ff.

Mi-pham-rgya-mtsho (1846-1912). *Bzo gnas nyer mkho za ma tog, Collected Writings*, Gangtok, Sonam Topgay Kazi, 1975, vol.9, pp.71-138.

Sku gzugs kyi thig rtsa rab gsal nyi ma, Collected Writings, vol.9, pp.1-70.

'Phags pa 'jig rten dbang phyug gi rnam sprul rim byon gyi 'khrungs rabs deb ther nor bu'i 'phreng ba, Dharamsala?, n.d.

'Phreng-kha-ba Dpal-ldan-blo-gros-bzang-po (16th century). *Bzo rig pa'i bstan bcos mdo rgyud gsal ba'i me long*, Dharamsala, Tibetan Cultural Printing Press, 1978.

Rong-tha Blo-bzang-dam-chos-rgya-mtsho (1863-1917). *Thig gi lag len du ma gsal bar bshad pa bzo rig mdzes pa'i kha rgyan*, New Delhi, Byams-pa-chos-rgyal, n.d.

Sa-skya Paṇḍita Kun-dga'-rgyal-mtshan (1182-1251/2). *Bu slob rnams la spring ba, Sa skya bka' 'bum*, Tokyo, Toyo Bunko, 1968, vol.5, p.401f.

Sde-srid Sangs-rgyas-rgya-mtsho (b. 1653). *Bstan bcos baidūrya dkar po las dris lan 'khrul snang g.ya' sel don gyi bzhin ras ston byed*, Dehra Dun, Tau Pon & Sakya Centre, 1976, 2 vols. See also reprint by T. Tsepal Taikhang, New Delhi, 1971.

Sman-thang-pa Sman-blo-don-grub. *Bde bar gshegs pa'i sku gzugs kyi tshad kyi rab tu byed pa yid bzhin nor bu*, Gangtok, Bla-ma Zla-ba and Sherab Gyaltsen, 1983. Reproduction of a manuscript from the Library of Bla-ma Sengge of Yol-mo.

Sum-pa mkhan-po Ye-shes-dpal-'byor (1704-1788). *Sku gsung thugs rten gyi thig rtsa mchan 'grel can me tog 'phreng mdzes, Collected Works, Śata-piṭaka Series*, vol.217, New Delhi, 1975. Vol.4, pp.353-402.

Zhu-chen Tshul-krims-rin-chen (1700-1769). *Chos smra ba'i bande tshul khrims rin chen du bod pa'i skye ba phal pa'i rkang 'thung dge sdig 'dres ma'i las kyi yal ga phan tshun du 'dzings par bde sdug gi lo 'dab dus kyi rgyal mos re mos su bsgyur ba, The Autobiography of Tshul-khrims-rin-chen of Sde-dge and Other of His Selected Writings*, New Delhi, 1971.

Gtsug lag khang chos 'byung bkra shis sgo mangs rten dang brten pa ji ltar bskrun pa las brtsams pa'i gleng ba bdud rtsi'i rlabs phreng, Collected Writings, New Delhi, N. Lungtok & N. Gyaltsan, 1973, vol.7, pp.127-195.

b. Canonical Works

1. Tantras

Caturpiṭha Tantra. (Śrī-caturpiṭhamahāyoginītantrarāja). Tib.: *Rnal 'byor ma'i rgyud kyi rgyal po chen po dpal gdan bzhi pa.* (Peking no.67; Derge no.428). Tr. and Rev.: Gāyadhara, 'Gos Khug-pa-lhas-btsas.

Kālacakra Tantra. (Paramādibuddhoddhrita-śrī-kālacakranāmatantrarāja). Tib.: *Mchog gi dang po'i sangs rgyas las phyung ba rgyud kyi rgyal po dpal dus kyi 'khor lo.* (Peking no.4; Derge no.362). Tr.: Somanātha, Shes-rab-grags-pa. Rev.: Shang-ston Mdo-sde-pa, Khrims-dar; Blo-gros-rgyal-mtshan, Blo-gros-dpal-bzang-po, Shong-ston.

Kṛṣṇayamāri Tantra. (Sarvatathāgatakāyavākcitta-kṛṣṇayamārināmatantra). Tib.: *De bzhin gshegs pa thams cad kyi sku gsung thugs gshin rje gshed nag po zhes bya ba'i rgyud.* (Peking no.103; Derge no.467). Tr.: Dīpaṃkaraśrijñāna, Tshul-khrims-rgyal-ba. Rev.: Dar-ma-grags, Rdo-rje-grags.

Mañjuśrīmūlakalpa Tantra. (Śrī-mañjuśrīmūlakalpatantra). Tib.: *'Phags pa 'jam dpal gyi rtsa ba'i rgyud.* (Peking no.162; Derge no.543). Tr.: Kumārakalaśa, Śākya-blo-gros.

Saṃvarodaya Tantra. (Śrī-mahāsaṃbarodayatantrarāja). Tib.: *Dpal bde mchog 'byung ba zhes bya ba'i rgyud kyi rgyal po chen po.* (Peking no.20; Derge no.373). Tr.: Gzhan-la-phan-pa-mtha'-yas, Smon-lam-grags. Rev.: Gzhon-nu-dpal.

2. Tantric Commentaries and Related Texts

Kriyāsaṃgraha. Tib.: *Bya ba bsdus pa.* (Peking no.3354; Derge no.2531). A.: Rigs-kyis-byin. Tr.: Kīrticandra, Yar-klungs-pa Grags-pa-rgyal-mtshan.

Kriyāsamuccaya. (Vajrācāryakryāsamuccaya). Tib.: *Rdo rje slob dpon gyi bya ba kun las btus pa.* (Peking no.5012; Derge no.3305). A.: 'Gro-ba'i-me-long (Jagaddarpaṇa). Tr.: Mañjuśrī, Blo-gros-rgyal-mtshan. Rev.: Vajraśrī.

Kṛṣṇayamāritantrarāja-prekṣaṇapathapradīpa-nāma-ṭīka. Tib.: *Gshin rje gshed nag po'i rgyud kyi rgyal po mngon par mthong ba lam gyi sgron ma zhes bya ba'i rgya cher bshad pa.* (Peking no.2783; Derge no.1920). A.: Kṛṣṇa-pa chen-po. Tr.: Prajñāśrijñānakīrti. See especially the commentary on the 14th chapter, Peking, vol.66, pp.295.5.3.-296.1.7.

Śrī-saṃvarodayamahātantrarāja-padminī-nāma-pañjikā. Tib.: *Dpal sdom pa 'byung ba'i rgyud kyi rgyal po chen po'i dka' 'grel padma can.* (Peking no.2173; Derge no.1420). A.: Ratnarakṣita. Tr.: Thams-cad-mkhyen-pa'i-dpal. Rev.: Shong Blo-gros-brtan-pa. See especially the commentary on the 30th chapter, Peking, vol.51, pp.112.5.6-116.4.7.

Vimalaprabhā-nāma-mūlatantrānusāriṇa-dvādasasahasrikā-laghukālacakratantrarājaṭika. Tib.: *Bsdus pa'i rgyud kyi rgyal po dus kyi 'khor lo 'i 'grel bshad/ rtsa ba'i rgyud kyi rjes su 'jug pa stong phrag bcu gnyis pa dri ma med pa'i 'od.* (Peking no.2064; Derge nos.845, 1347). Derge no.1347: A.: Spyan-ras-gzigs-dbang-phyug. Tr.: Tshul-khrims-dar,

Shang-ston Mdo-sde-dpal, Shong-ston Rdo-rje-rgyal-mtshan, Blo-gros-rgyal-mtshan. Rev.: Blo-gros-dpal-bzang-po. See especially the commentary on the *Ye shes kyi le'u*, Peking, vol.46, pp. 282-321. Derge no.845 preserves an earlier translation by Somanātha and Shes-rab-grags-pa.

3. Non-tantric Treatises in the Bzo-rig Section of The Tanjur

Citralakṣaṇa. Tib.: *Ri mo'i mtshan nyid.* (Peking no. 5806). A German translation of this text was produced by Berthold Laufer: *Das Citralakshana,* Leipzig, 1913. This was recently translated into English and published under the title *An Early Document of Indian Art,* New Delhi, 1976.

Dasatalanyagrodha-parimaṇḍala-buddhapratimālakṣaṇa. Tib.: *Sangs rgyas kyi sku'i gzugs brnyan gyi mtshan nyid mtho bcu pa shing nya gro dha ltar chu sheng gab pa.* (Peking no.5804). Also known in Tibetan as *Shā ri bus zhus pa'i mdo.*

Pratimāmānalakṣaṇa. Tib.: *Sku gzugs kyi mtshan nyid.* (Peking no.5807; Derge no.4316). A.: Ātreya. Tr.: Dharmadhara, Grags-pa-rgyal-mtshan.

Sambuddhabhāṣita-pratimālakṣaṇa-vivaraṇa. Tib: *Rdzogs pa'i sangs rgyas kyi gsungs pa'i sku gzugs kyi tshad kyi rnam 'grel.* (Peking no.5805; Derge no. 4315). Tr.: Dharmadhara, Grags-pa-rgyal-mtshan.

II Sources in English and Other Languages

Agrawal, O.P. "Conservation of Asian Cultural Objects: Asian Materials and Techniques; Tibetan Tankas", *Museum* (UNESCO), vol.27 (1975), pp.181-197.

Ardussi, John A. "'Brug-pa Kun-legs, the Saintly Tibetan Madman," M.A. Thesis, University of Washington, 1972.

Bhagwan Dash, Vaidya. *Tibetan Medicine with special reference to Yoga Śataka,* Dharamsala, 1976.

Chieh Tzŭ Yüan Chuan (1679-1701), *The Mustard Seed Garden Manual of Painting,* translated and edited by Mai-Mai Sze, Princeton, Princeton University Press, 1977.

Chogay Trichen, Thubten Legshay Gyatsho. *Gateway to the Temple, Bibliotheca Himalayica,* series III, vol.12, Kathmandu, 1979.

Chopra, R. N. *Chopra's Indigenous Drugs of India,* Calcutta, 1958.

Dagyab, L.S. *Tibetan Religious Art,* Weisbaden, 1977.

Das, S.C. *Journey to Lhasa and Central Tibet,* New Delhi, 1970.

Downs, Hugh R. *Rhythms of a Himalayan Village,* New York, 1980.

Duka, Theodore. *Life and Works of Alexander Csoma de Körös,* New Delhi, 1972.

Frye, S. (transl.), "Study and Publication of Indian and Tibetan Monuments on the Theory of Art," *The Tibet Journal,* vol.6 (1981), pp.3-5.

Gammerman, A. F. and Semicov, B. V., *Slovar'tibetsko-Latino-russkikh nazvaniĭ Lekarstvennogo rastitel'nogo cyr'iâ, primeniâemogo v. tibetskoĭ meditsine.* [Tibetan-Latin-Russian Glossary of Medicinal Plants]. Ulan-Ude: Akdemĭa Nauk SSSR, Sibirskoe Otdelenie: 1963.

Gerasimova, K. M. "Compositional Structure in Tibetan Iconography," *The Tibet Journal,* vol.3 (1978), pp.39-51.

"The Anthropometric Foundation of the Tibetan Canon of Proportions," *VIIIth Congress of Anthropological and Ethnological Sciences,* pp. 325-327.

Gettens, R. J. and Stout, G. L. *Painting Materials, A Short Encyclopaedia,* New York, Dover, 1966.

Godwin-Austen, M. H. "On the System Employed in Outlining the Figures of Deities and other Religious Drawings as Practiced in Ladak, Zaskar, etc," *Journal of the Asiatic Society of Bengal,* vol.33 (1864), pp.151-154.

Hadaway, W. S. "Some Hindu 'Silpa' Shastras in Their Relation to South Indian Sculpture," *Ostasiatische Zeitschrift,* vol.1 (1914).

Haines, H. H. *A Forest Flora of Chota Nagpur,* Delhi, 1910.

Hodgson, B. H. *Essays on the Languages, Literature and Religion of Nepal and Tibet, Together with Further Papers on the Geography, Ethnology and Commerce of Those Countries,* New Delhi, 1972.

Huntington, John C. "The Technique of Tibetan Paintings," *Studies in Conservation,* vol.15 (1970), pp.122-133.

Jäschke, H. A. *Tibetan-English Dictionary,* London, 1958.

Khosla, Romi. *Buddhist Monasteries in the Western Himalaya,* Kathmandu, 1979.

Laufer, Berthold, *Sino-Iranica,* Taipei, Ch'en-wen Publ. Co., 1967.

Li Ch'iao-p'ing. *The Chemical Arts of Old China,* Easton, Pa., 1948.

McGraw-Hill Dictionary of Art, 1969.

Mehra, V. R. "Notes on the Technique and Conservation of Some Thang-ka Paintings," *Studies in Conservation,* vol.15 (1970), pp.190-214.

Morita, Tsuneyuki. "Technique and materials of the Tibetan *thangka* in the Aoki's Tibet Collection [in Japanese], in Y. Nagao ed., *The Bunkyo Aoki's Tibet Collection at the National Museum of Ethnology,* Bulletin of the National Museum of Ethnology [Suita, Osaka], Special Issue no.1 (1983), pp. 205-249.

Moti Chandra, *The Technique of Mughal Painting,* Lucknow, 1949.

Needham, Joseph. *Science and Civilisation in China,* Cambridge, 1954-1959, 5 vols.

Olschak, B. S. *Mystic Art of Ancient Tibet,* New York, 1973.

Pallis, Marco. *Peaks and Lamas,* New York, Alfred A. Knopf, 1940.

Peterson, K. W. "Sources of Variation in Tibetan Canons of Iconometry," *Tibetan Studies in Honour of Hugh Richardson,* Warminster, 1980, pp.239-248.

Roerich, G. N. *Tibetan Paintings,* Paris, Librarie Orientaliste Paul Geuthner, 1925.

Roerich, G. N. (transl.) *Biography of Dharmasvāmin (Chag lo-tsa-ba Chos-rje-dpal),* Patna, 1959.

Sankrityayana, Rahula. "Technique in Tibetan Painting," *Asia,* vol.37 (1937), pp.711-715. See also *Marg,* vol.26 (1963), pp.30-33.

Snellgrove, D. L. *Four Lamas of Dolpo,* Oxford, 1967/8, 2 vols.

Thompson, Daniel V. *The Materials of Medieval Painting,* London, 1936.

Trungpa, Chogyam. *Visual Dharma,* Berkeley, 1975.

Tucci, G. *Tibetan Painted Scrolls,* Rome, 1949, 3 vols.

Indexes

Living Artists — Individuals Cited — Deities and Other Figures Depicted in Paintings — Places — Subjects

Figures in Italics are page-references to illustrations.